Dan Toma
Esther Gons

T0382242

Innovation Accounting

A practical guide for measuring your
innovation ecosystem's performance

BIS Publishers
Borneostraat 80-A
1094 CP Amsterdam
The Netherlands
T +31 (0)20 515 02 30
bis@bispublishers.com
www.bispublishers.com

Cover design, book design and illustrations: Esther Gons, NEXT.amsterdam
Graphic execution: Jorine Zegwaard, jorinezegwaard.nl
Editor: Alison Griffiths

www.danto.ma
www.estheremmelygons.nl
www.innovationaccountingbook.com

ISBN 978 90 636 9620 7

Copyright © 2021 Dan Toma, Esther Gons and BIS Publishers.
2nd printing 2023

All rights reserved. No part of this publication may be reproduced or transmitted in any form or by any means, electronic or mechanical, including photocopy, recording or any information storage and retrieval system, without permission in writing from the copyright owners.

Every reasonable attempt has been made to identify owners of copyright. Any errors or omissions brought to the publisher's attention will be corrected in subsequent editions.

Table of Contents

INTRODUCTION

What if you were to attend a sporting event and the scoreboard, which everyone in the arena is following, only shows half of what is happening on the field? What if that scoreboard only shows you the score at the end of the game, ignoring other information like period, time, penalties, current score, or anything else that might be of interest? Will your viewing experience be the same? How would you know which team is winning?

Now picture the same situation, only this time you are in the shoes of the coaches and your only source of information is the same faulty scoreboard that has been in use for decades without any update. How would you make a decision? Wouldn't you be tempted to rely on gut feel and experience alone? Or would you be looking for other sources of information?

If this sounds absurd, it's not that far from the reality of the business world.

The history of accounting can be traced back for centuries. In spite of business operations having increased exponentially in complexity, the financial reporting carried out by today's companies varies little from the system introduced by the Italian monk Luca Pacioli, in 1494.

As companies' in-market success depends more and more on intangible assets, such as culture or their employees' skill, and as their reliance on innovation to drive profit increases, the shortcomings of the financial accounting system become more and more apparent.

Developing and deploying a complementary system that works in sync with the financial accounting system while mitigating its shortcoming is gradually becoming a business imperative. Particularly so for companies that see innovation as a leading growth engine.

7

Too often, corporate leaders quickly discontinue new initiatives simply because they haven't delivered instant profits. Too often, the investment policy of large companies is skewed towards low-risk initiatives. Too often, investors rely on social media feeds to decide where to invest next. Too often, culture is being considered as the only key to success. And yet the criteria for measuring success are still a "one-size-fits-all" financial only affair.

Let us take you on a journey and help you understand how you can develop, deploy and use an accounting system which has been purposefully designed to cover all facets of your innovation ecosystem. A system that works to complement the current financial accounting system to provide you with the most accurate and timely information. Enter Innovation Accounting.

Measuring innovation can only be done if we all agree on what innovation is.

CHAPTER 1
Defining Innovation

What better place to start the conversation on Innovation Accounting than discussing what we mean by innovation. This conversation is important as innovation should not be used as a catch all word. And understanding the different facets of innovation has direct implications for the innovation measurement system, as you are going to see in the following chapters.

Innovation seems to be one of those few evergreen words. It has never gone out of fashion as it is so intertwined with humankind's development. So in today's digital world it comes as no surprise that innovation has become nothing short of a religion with "innovate or die" as its battle cry. When a company succeeds, people attribute its good fortune to superior innovation. When it fails, people say it lacked the ability to innovate.

But unfortunately, popularity has its own drawbacks. Sometimes it seems that innovation is used as a catch all concept. From political debates to the board room and from startups to advertisements, innovation seems to be on everyone's lips.

Using innovation in this way is risky, at least in the context of measuring innovation, as it might lead to confusion, miscommunication and wrong expectations.

The importance of clarifying what everyone around the table means when they say innovation became apparent to Dan during an engagement with an exhibition and trade fair organizing corporation.

Dan was invited to moderate an executive off-site workshop where the attendees had to come up with a medium-term strategic road map. From the beginning, the CEO set the stage by telling everyone that, moving forward, the company needed to be more innovative than it was. To which some of the directors replied that their respective units were already innovative enough. Only through examples were both parties able to find common ground and avoid a heated debate that would have derailed the entire event.

You see, from the directors' perspective, moving away from paper-based maps to an app and NFC sensors meant innovation. However, for the CEO that only counted as keeping up with the times. The CEO really expected to see new business models or at least new revenue streams enabled by the latest technologies, such as virtual reality. Essentially, the CEO wanted breakthrough innovation. But in the absence of a clear definition and classification of innovation in that company, the directors were only doing incremental innovation.

11

4 Types of Innovation

In his book, "*Mapping Innovation*," Greg Sattel identifies 4 types of innovation. He also makes the case against treating innovation as one-size-fits-all from a process, strategy and KPIs perspective.

The first type of innovation Greg identifies is *sustaining innovation*. This is the most popular type because most of the time companies are seeking to get better at what they are already doing. They want to improve existing capabilities in existing markets. This innovation type is characterized by a good understanding of the customer base, its problems and the ways to solve it. These incremental innovations can be thought of as variations on an existing successful theme. For example, for a company producing household cleansers, sustaining innovation might involve making a particular cleaning agent 10% stronger or pairing it with a new scent.

The second type identified by Greg is *breakthrough innovation*. Essentially, this type of innovation is characterized by a good understanding of a problem that needs solving but a fuzzy understanding of the ways to solve problems.

Let's give you an example. With the increase in popularity of smartphones a new problem appeared: screen shattering. The problem was well understood but the solution wasn't that trivial, and moving beyond bulky phone covers was proving a challenge for consumers and manufacturers alike. Enter Gorilla Glass, manufactured by Corning. The New York-based company was no stranger to breakthrough innovation in the glass industry. It produced the first glass light bulbs for Thomas Edison in 1879, supplied the windows for the spacecraft Friendship 7 (which was flown by John Glenn for the first U.S. manned orbital flight), and it was even the site of Frank Hyde's serendipitous discovery of high-purity fused silica in 1932; the precursor to the optical fibers that connect us to the Internet today.

One of the company's most recent breakthrough innovation accomplishments is the development of Gorilla Glass. In addition to being the strongest glass on the market, it's also remarkably thin; from 0.5 mm to 2 mm. Its thinness means the devices it protects are lighter, which saves manufacturers shipping costs.[1]

By 2011 Gorilla Glass was found in 200 million devices, roughly 20% of the handsets in the world at that time.[2]

Greg's third innovation type is *disruptive innovation*. These are the sort of big ideas that many of us have in mind when innovation is mentioned. They are called disruptive because they disrupt current market behavior. They render existing solutions obsolete, transform value propositions, and bring previously marginal customers and companies into the center of attention. The iPod is a prime example of this as it radically changed the way we listen to and buy music.[3] But other examples might include Uber, Netflix or Airbnb.

In a nutshell, disruptive innovation changes the basis of competition. Because of technological shifts or other changes in the marketplace, companies can potentially find themselves getting better and better at things people want less and less. When that happens, innovating your products won't help; you have to innovate your business model.[4]

Lastly, Greg talks about *basic research* as the fourth type of innovation. To Greg, basic research is needed when neither the problem (or market) nor the solution is well enough understood. Basic research is needed as path breaking innovations never arrive fully formed, they always begin with the discovery of some new phenomenon.[5]

As you can see, clarifying the type of innovation one talks about will help sharpen the conversation, align expectations and help identify the right indicators through which progress is measured.

Since breakthrough and disruptive innovation are so different from incremental innovation, they need to be measured differently.[6] For incremental innovation, metrics need to focus on efficiency: how efficient are projects going through the pipeline and how are they stacking up against forecasted and actual economic return. For **breakthrough and disruptive innovation**, given the inherent uncertainty of something that's new, the measurements must be different - this **is the focus of Innovation Accounting.**

Zooming out, you can very well view the four types of innovation as either complex or complicated. Complicated problems in general can be hard to solve, but they are addressable with rules and recipes. They also can be resolved with systems and pro-

cesses such as a hierarchical structure. Incremental innovation and basic research fall into this category. Complex problems on the other hand involve too many unknowns and too many interrelated factors to be reduced to rules and processes.

Implementing, for example, a blockchain enabled authentication solution for your company's clients is a complicated problem. It can be accomplished with good project management and the right technical skills. However, a competitor with an innovative business model, an Uber or an Airbnb, entering your company's industry is a complex problem. There's no algorithm that will tell you how to respond.[7]

13

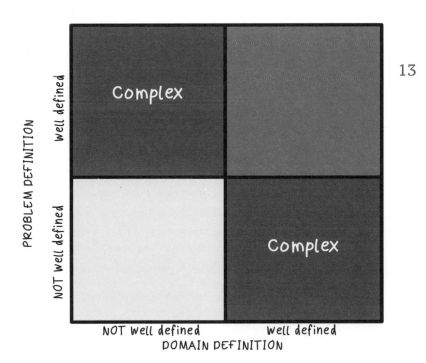

Innovation vs. Digital Transformation

Before we go much further it is probably worth taking a moment to clarify another element of the corporate growth mix, the fact that innovation should not be confused with digital transformation.[8] Making this distinction between these two activities has clear implications on the measurements used to track progress.

In simple terms, innovation is the process of creating new value, while digital transformation is the process of keeping existing business models and processes valuable in the digital age, while improving customer satisfaction and reducing operational costs.

In accounting terms, innovation contributes to the top line growth of the company while digital transformation is most effective on the bottom line.

Take your local bank for example. A digital transformation initiative might mean implementing online biometric authentication to replace the need for a physical signature on a piece of paper. Innovation could be, for example, a solution that will help you manage all the subscriptions you have connected to a credit card.

While the two activities share commonalities, such as customer centricity, iterative development and the use of high-end technologies, they differ when it comes to measurements.

Innovation measurements are designed to deal with high levels of uncertainty and help enforce evidence based investment and divestment decisions in new ventures. Meanwhile, digital transformation measurements are deployed in low uncertainty situations, focusing on the company's ability to efficiently migrate from legacy solutions and the direct outcome of that migration,[9] which in most cases directly impacts on the bottom line through reductions in operating expenses.

But designing and implementing an innovative accounting system is no easy feat since - as William Bruce Cameron famously said - *"not everything that counts can be counted, and not everything that can be counted counts."*

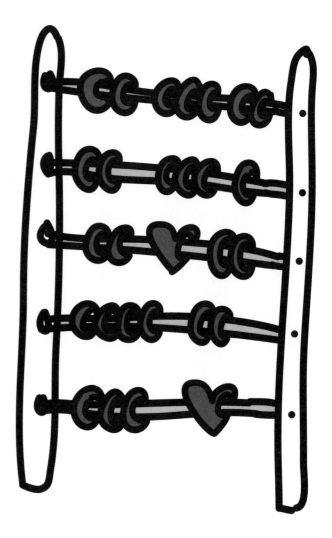

14

Worksheet - Create your definition of innovation

Getting every stakeholder in your company on the same page with innovation is the first step in creating and implementing an innovation accounting system. If you were to ask the question "what is innovation?" you would be surprised at how many distinctly different answers you will find in a group. The bigger the group, the more polarized the answers. And this is normal given that everyone is experiencing innovation differently. Some may view it from a process perspective, some from an outcome perspective, some see the cost reduction benefits of innovation while others see the new revenue generation potential.

In order to help you to align everyone behind the same innovation definition we created this simple alignment template that you can use in a workshop format.

For this workshop you will need the alignment template, sticky notes and sharpies.

You need to work through the template horizontally and iteratively starting from left to right.

You begin the workshop by asking the participants to define innovation, in their own words. After they have written their answers on sticky notes, try to cluster definitions which are similar. You will probably be left with a handful of clusters. Add them to "iteration 1" under the first question in the template.

Continue in the same manner with the other 4 questions without challenging the participants.

Now that you have initial answers for the questions, start the second iteration.

Look at the answers in "iteration 1" for each of the questions and begin challenging the participants with questions such as: why do you think this? What makes you say this? Tell me more about this.

The goal here is to reduce the number of clusters by half by creating new answers that everyone agrees with.

Continue the process for each question.

Once you are done with the 2nd iteration you can start the 3rd one. The goal of the 3rd iteration is to reach one single answer for each of the questions.

Following this process will ensure alignment amongst stakeholders and will result in a higher level of clarity of what innovation represents for your company.

From experience, we found that groups of 15+ people will require, on average, three iterations to come up with an answer that is agreed upon by the entire group. But, depending on the size and composition of your group, you might need more iterations or fewer.

How would we define innovation in our company?	What do we need to succeed in our industry?	What about innovation is important for our company?	If innovation were already happening at a high level in our company, how would we recognize it?	If our company's way of innovating were a box on the shelf of a supermarket, what would it say on the box?
Iteration 1	Iteration 1	Iteration 1	Iteration 1	Iteration 1
Iteration 2	Iteration 2	Iteration 2	Iteration 2	Iteration 2
Iteration 3	Iteration 3	Iteration 3	Iteration 3	Iteration 3

Download the worksheet here

Before setting up an innovation accounting system, you first need to agree on a company-wide definition of innovation.

An innovation accounting system is needed for new initiatives with a high level of uncertainty, such as breakthrough innovation initiatives and disruptive innovation ones.

Innovation is not a synonym for digital transformation.

Digital transformation is not a substitute for innovation. Digital transformation impacts the company's bottom line by prolonging the expiration date of the legacy business model(s); while innovation impacts top line growth by creating new business models.

Accounting is dead.
Long live Accounting.

CHAPTER 2

Innovation vs. Accounting

Claiming that investors are not data driven or that leadership teams don't look at data when making decisions about the future of their respective company won't be fair statements. The problem is not the absence of data but the quality of the data available.

Every company is obliged by law to keep a financial accounting record. Without one, a company would not be meeting its legal obligations. This accounting scoreboard is made up of three main documents: the profit and loss statement, the balance sheet and the cash-flow statement.

However, the problem with this type of scoreboard is that it's only painting half of the picture. And that half is very much rooted in the bricks and mortar economy of yesterday, putting the service-driven digital companies of today at a disadvantage. In today's marketplace, this dated scoreboard needs an update, and investors know this better than anyone.

The drive today is for information, finding a way to delve beneath the statistics of the past to bring an understanding of what is to come. After all, past performance is no guarantee of future results. Investors care only partially about how much profit was made last year. If they are putting their faith in an organization they want to know what is to come.[10]

Whatever the methodology, the underlying message has to be one which gives potential investors confidence in the future. By way of contrast, consider the decline in valuation of industrial giant GE, one which led to it being dropped from the Dow Jones Index in 2018. Despite internal restructuring and upskilling of the workforce, the company was unable to provide clarity around its future direction and investors reacted accordingly.[11]

Interestingly, GE was the last of the original Dow Jones companies to leave the index. Perhaps even more interestingly, whereas once corporate longevity was measured in centuries, at the present churn rate half of the current S&P 500 companies will have been replaced within the next ten years.[12]

So what do these contrasting company fortunes tell us? Is it a case of out with the old and in with the new? Is the age of cash accounting over? Well, not completely but perhaps it is time to let go of the hidebound view of company accounting and look towards a more blended storyboard, one which paints a truer picture of a company's direction.

If you need convincing, just take a look at some research from NYU Stern Professor Baruch Lev. Carried out over 20 years (from 1993 to 2013), this research shows how un-useful financial reports are becoming for investors.[13] If in 1993 financial reports uniquely contributed 10 percent to investors' information; 20 years later, in 2013, the same reports decreased their usefulness by almost half. At the same time, the usefulness to investors of analysts' forecasts and non-accounting SEC filings has grown exponentially.

Coincidentally or not this abrupt increase in usefulness to investors of analysts' forecasts and non-accounting SEC started from the early 2000s; a time which correlates to the coming of age of Internet-based businesses.

23

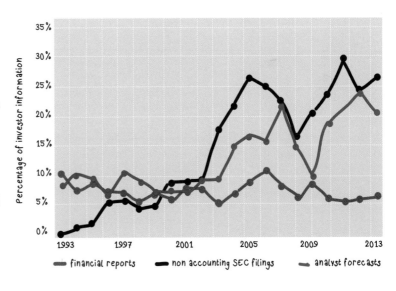

The conundrums of financial accounting

The drop in relevance of financial reports can be attributed in part to four conundrums of financial accounting:

In spite of its fact based nature, financial accounting is a poor tool for understanding the potential of a new company, or of a new idea within an existing company.

Let's face it, some of the IPOs and deals that we have seen in recent years would not have even been considered without a deep understanding of, and belief in, future potential. Take Uber for example. Despite reporting losses over the previous two years, Uber's May 2019 IPO was reported by The New York Times as valuing the company in the region of $82.4 billion.[14] And whilst markets initially discounted that valuation, at the time of writing in February 2020, we are seeing a resurgence as the company forecasts moving to EBITDA profitability in the fourth quarter of 2020.

Similarly, Twitter reported a loss of $79 million before its IPO, yet it commanded a valuation of $24 billion on its IPO date in 2013.[15] Here again we are looking at a company which has strong roots in innovation technology and for which a reliance on "traditional" accounting measurements would not have seen it even get off the ground.

The same is true for Microsoft's purchase of LinkedIn in 2016 and Facebook's acquisition of WhatsApp in 2014. In acquisitions such as these, the scoreboard looked less to traditional accounting methods and more towards what future benefits acquisitions could bring to the purchasers.

CFOs of companies such as these themselves admit that they cannot justify their market capitalizations based on traditional metrics alone. They believe that the market values could instead be viewed as the sum of the option values of the projects undertaken, or the sum of best-case scenario payoffs. One CFO said that her valuation should be considered on a per idea basis instead of a per earnings multiple.[16]

Therefore it is safe to conclude that financial accounting is not the right tool if you want to understand if a company is simultaneously searching for new growth options, while at the same time executing the existing business model(s).

Accounting-based financial reports show only the final outcome of asset deployment: revenue & earnings.

Financial accounting is totally silent on the phases an asset passes through as it is converted back into money. Financial accounting does not tell a story about the value creation process nor about the innovation process used by a company to achieve specific revenue targets.

A great example is Dell, whose pursuit of RONA (Return On Net Assets) led them to outsource most of their capabilities to ASUS. Christensen and colleagues refer to the Dell-ASUS story as a Greek tragedy. At the beginning, Dell outsourced the manufacturing of circuits and motherboards to ASUS. Later, they started outsourcing their supply chain management and computer design work. Every time Dell outsourced its capabilities to ASUS, its RONA numbers went up. They were making more money with fewer assets, which pleased the markets. The problem then occurred when ASUS decided to launch its own computers. This move was a blow to Dell, which no longer had the capabilities to respond quickly, because they had outsourced them to a company that then decided to become a competitor.

The Dell story, and others like it, is a valuable lesson for corporate leaders in the way that overemphasizing financial outcomes can demonstrate to the markets a lack of understanding of a company's value creation system.

Furthermore, the accounting based financial reports are totally silent when it comes to valuing a company's culture, ecosystem of partners and products, or the network/viral effect of their flagship product; in spite of these being the main profit drivers. Think about Apple's AppStore or Zappo's customer service culture[17] or Uber, Airbnb or Spotify virality.

Even though the most important aim for digital companies is to achieve market leadership and reach a "winner-take-all"[18] profit structure, financial accounting reports are unable to paint this picture.

Furthermore, concepts like the increase in the value of a resource with its use flies in the face of financial accounting logic, for which this actually implies negative depreciation expense in accounting terms. So the fundamental idea behind the success of digital companies, the increasing returns to scale, goes against a basic tenet of financial accounting, assets depreciate with use.[19]

25

The accounting system can't measure something that hasn't happened.

 The most valuable assets of a company are not recognized as assets in accounting terms.

This one impacts directly on the innovation process. Bringing an idea to market is not a linear process. Many unsuccessful small scale experiments go by before something sticks. The only problem with that is that, from a financial accounting perceptive, the costs incurred in those iterations are recorded.

But the savings made by not committing to a wrong avenue are not. The problem with financial accounting used in innovation management only deepens when we try to put a dollar sign before a learning gathered from a failed experiment.

Financial accounting can only measure the things that have happened - good or bad. And this issue is not only visible in the innovation department. Manufacturing companies committed to lean methodology perform major cost avoidance too. But this cost avoidance doesn't appear on any financial accounting sheet.[20]

Oscar Wilde is credited with the quote

And some argue that this is a reflection of most financial executives' mental model.

Let's look at a company's balance sheet. Leaving the intangible asset aside, assets reported on balance sheets have to be physical in nature and the company needs to own them. However, digital companies often have multiple assets that are intangible in nature. And many of them go for accessibility over ownership; deciding to rent rather than own assets. Many have ecosystems that extend even beyond the company's brand. Take for example Apple's AppStore.

Furthermore, digital companies have little to no physical products and almost no inventory. Therefore, the balance sheets of physical and digital companies depict entirely different pictures. Consider for example Walmart's $160 billion assets and its $300 billion valuation against Facebook's $9 billion dollars assets for its $500 billion valuation.

Accounting recognized assets are getting constantly commoditized through advances in technology and manufacturing. Assets such as buildings, production machinery, cars, ships and planes are more or less equally available to all competitors. A logistics company, for example, can't rise above its competitors through accounting recognized assets alone. The quality of their planes or trucks is similar (if not identical) to the one used by other companies in the industry.[21]

However, what's setting companies apart are the resources and processes (such as innovation) credited with value creation through the exploitation of accounting recognized assets. But these resources and processes are either intangible in form, not recorded at all, or even listed as liabilities.

So the depreciation in value provided by financial accounting documents to investors comes as no surprise since, understanding the paths to revenue and earnings enables investors to better evaluate the company's strategies and their execution, and improves prediction of future performance.[22] None of these are being presented in the financial reports.

Regardless of how tried-and-true the financial-accounting system is, it's overlooking an important aspect of the value creation process. None of the financially recognized assets can create customer value (which in turn drive profitability) without human intervention. Take for example, the 3D printer in an innovation lab. It is listed in the company's books under tangible fixed assets. But, by itself, the printer can't create anything of value. The printer requires a human to design a prototype of what can later be the company's next flagship product. The same story can be replicated for every other financial recognized asset.

The big issue at hand is that the financial-accounting system is recording under OPEX the human resource element and the time/process of creating customer value from accounting recog-

nized assets. So basically, from a CFO's perspective, all employees are liabilities; a fact that flies in the face of the popular "people are our greatest assets" aphorism.

Proof that executives live by the financial account system and not by the "people are our greatest assets" cliché is that when cost cutting is required, the first action is to lay off staff, cut wages or reduce spending on training.

27

By classifying employees (culture and processes) as assets, it would then be in the company's best interest to try to increase the value of these assets. This can be done by the company investing time and money, through training, mentoring, developing and improving. If the employees feel valued, their sense of job satisfaction will increase. The benefit to the employer is a more committed workforce, lower absenteeism, lower staff turnover and better qualified staff, all leading to higher productivity.

There are however blue chip organizations out there listing and treating their people as assets. These organizations are professional soccer clubs. An analysis of Manchester United PLC's (Public Limited Company) 2014 annual report submitted to the New York Stock Exchange[23] paints a clear picture as to how players are treated in accounting terms and how they are shown as assets in the balance sheet.

From the report, it can be inferred that the accounting treatment for player registrations is in no way different from any other capital asset.[24] The cost of acquisition of a player is amortized over the period of his contract through the straight-line method.[25]

It's not realistic to hope now that energy companies, for example, will start treating employees as soccer clubs treat their players. But there's one thing that The Board can start doing. They can design and deploy an accounting system which complements the financial-accounting one, and which is geared towards mitigating the shortcomings of the financial accounting system. These strategic resources will then be nurtured and developed as the financial assets are.

Enterprises effectively operating their resources and continuously innovating are able to consistently stay ahead of the game. Making their present and future competitors constantly play catch-up. Hence gaining a sustained competitive advantage.[26]

As digital companies become more economically prominent and physical companies become more digital, there is a clear need for the improvement of the science of accounting and the standards that go with it. There is a need for a complement to the established financial accounting system to meet the needs of the digital, innovation-driven economy. It's time for Innovation Accounting (IA).

Innovation Accounting

Business school education has traditionally considered net present value, payback period, and hurdle rates as necessary tools to determine which project to select. However, as we have seen above, the way in which innovation is viewed and measured will vary according to the nature of the organization and its business sector.

So whilst current financial reports are appropriate for capital and other physical projects, they don't meet the innovative ambitions of digital organizations. These companies consider scientists' and software workers' and product development teams' time to be the company's most valuable resource together with the culture and the processes.

As a result, rather than looking towards prudent allocation of financial capital, digital organizations see the raising of financial capital as a means not only of meeting funding shortfalls but also paying for acquisitions and even employee wages. In general the market agrees, thereby enabling IPOs such as those mentioned earlier in the chapter.

The digital CEO's principal aim therefore is not necessarily to judiciously allocate financial capital but to allocate precious scientific and human resources to the most promising projects, as well as to pull back and redeploy those resources in a timely manner when the prospects of specific projects are diminishing.[16]

The term "Innovation Accounting" was coined for the first time by Eric Ries in his 2011 book *The Lean Startup*." Our collective understanding of what it means to measure innovation has only improved since. Based on the experience gathered by entrepreneurs and intrapreneurs in the years following Eric's book, we consider Innovation Accounting to be an organized system of principles and indicators designed to gather, classify, analyze and report data about a company's breakthrough and disruptive innovation efforts; working to complement the existing financial accounting system.

29

Innovation Accounting
/inə-ve-sjun ə-kao-nt-iŋ/

NOUN

"an organized system of principles and indicators designed to gather, classify, analyze and report data about a company's breakthrough and disruptive innovation efforts - working to complement the existing financial accounting system".

The innovation accounting system needs to deliver a holistic viewpoint that will not only look at how teams are performing but also reveal insights about strategy, portfolio, capability and culture. But we are going to talk more about this in the coming pages.

It would probably be fair to say that organizations in both the private and the public sector are mostly being run today by managers who have not yet received any formal entrepreneurial education. Developing and deploying an innovation accounting system, therefore, needs to happen in parallel with capability development; helping leaders and managers to understand how innovation operational efficiency and effectiveness, and the work environment culture, lead to financial results.

From our experience, we've seen an inverse relationship between the knowledge and understanding of lean startup and agile which executives have, and the need for detailed financial justification in the innovation department. This however shouldn't be interpreted as: innovation mature companies don't need Innovation Accounting.

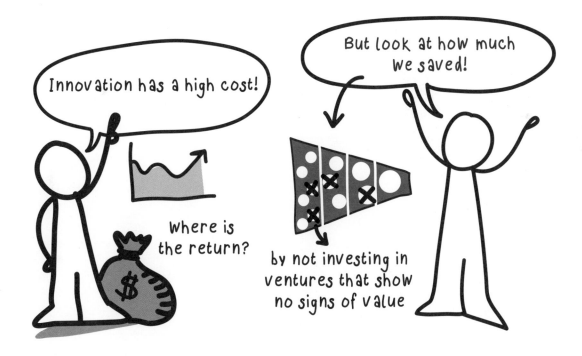

Financial accounting only paints half of the picture of how a company is doing because it only measures final outcomes, not the process used to reach it, nor cost avoidance or learnings.

In spite of its fact based nature, financial accounting is a poor tool for understanding the potential of a new company, or of a new idea within an existing company.

Financial accounting does not consider people, culture, ecosystem or process as assets.

Principles are universal.
So too, unfortunately, are myths.

CHAPTER 3

Myths and Principles of Measuring Innovation

Measuring innovation has long been perceived as the cornerstone of innovation management. A 2019 Gartner report even identified the inability to accurately measure innovation as the number one reason why corporate leaders are hesitant to invest in innovation.[27]

In this chapter, we'll take a close look at the principles of an effective innovation accounting system. Before we do though, let's look at some of the things today's companies get wrong about measuring innovation.

The myths of measuring innovation

A number of common myths tend to inform whether or how a company attempts to measure innovation. Unfortunately, these myths are only loosely tied to the real world; they don't reflect reality. Making decisions rooted in myths can be bad for business. We'll now do our best to debunk some of the more common myths around measuring innovation.

Myth #1: *R&D expenditure is a good indicator of innovation*

It seems logical for companies to equate R&D spending with innovation, or to believe that the amount of money a company puts into R&D correlates with how innovative that company is. The thing is, spending, even spending on research, and innovation are not the same things. And while a kind of common sense equates R&D with innovation, the data tells a different story.

Strategy & Business, a unit within PricewaterhouseCoopers, has published an annual report of the 1000 most innovative companies in the world for more than twelve years running. In that time, they have found no statistically significant relationship between R&D spending and sustained financial performance.[28]

This finding applies to total R&D spend, as well as R&D spending as a percentage of revenues.[29] Spending on R&D is not related to growth in sales or profits, increases in market capitalization, or shareholder returns.[30] In every annual report that Strategy & Business has published, the 10 most innovative companies are often not the top 10 spenders on R&D.

What R&D spending seems to generate is an increase in the number of patents held by a company. And while having more patents can mean more possibilities, sitting on a library of unused patents is nowhere near what it means to be innovative. If every patent represents new applications and opportunities, then simply amassing them without bringing them to market, or failing to bring them to market, in some ways represents a strange kind of complacency with the status quo.

Consider this: In the late 1970s, Xerox invented the computer mouse in their Palo Alto Research Center (PARC). And more than that, they invented a machine that could use it. Up to then, interacting with a computer meant typing in key commands. With this new invention though, users could click and drag, open and close windows, and interface with computers in a whole new way.

So why isn't Xerox widely known for being the company behind this technology? Partially because they couldn't recognize their own brilliance, and partially because someone else, a young entrepreneur by the name of Steve Jobs, could. At least that's how the legend goes.

One day, Jobs visited PARC. A Xerox engineer demoed the mouse for Jobs, and he was blown away. So much so, that he ran back to Apple and demanded a mouse, and windows, and a new way of interacting with a computer too. After some time, Apple developed the Macintosh, and the rest is history.

While a number of people have disputed the particulars of this story;[31] whether Jobs visited PARC once or twice, whether Apple was researching similar technology at the same time or not, the legend still teaches an important lesson: Innovation doesn't just mean securing patents or coming up with new ideas, it also means doing something with them. Had Xerox been able to turn its developmental genius into commercial success, Jobs said, "it could have been as big as I.B.M. plus Microsoft plus Xerox combined—and the largest high-technology company in the world."[32]

37

Myth #2: *Innovation can't be measured because innovation is creativity and creativity can't be measured*

There is a common tendency to conflate creativity with innovation.[33] Management often sees successful startups coming up with great new products, which motivates managers to pursue the development of similarly cool, new, shiny products.

Companies fall into this trap every time. They think that the best way to become better at innovation is to put a bunch of "creatives" under one roof and ask them to think of the next big thing. To be clear, awesome ideas are an important input to innovation. But just putting a bunch of subjectively creative individuals together isn't a foolproof recipe for generating those ideas. What's more, if companies stop at idea-generation, they are in for a huge disappointment. As Scott Anthony writes in *"The Little Black Book of Innovation,"* "Innovation is a process that combines discovering an opportunity, blueprinting an idea to seize that opportunity, and implementing that idea to achieve results. Remember: no impact, no innovation."

Innovation is a discipline to be mastered and managed. And it is hard work![34] But if innovation is more about discipline and routine than about creativity, it can be measured, just as any other company process can.

 Myth #3: *The success of a new innovative venture can only be measured once it's in the market*

Nothing could be further from the truth. There are many different signals along the life of an idea; signals that can indicate if an idea is heading in the right direction or not.

Say, for example, a team is working on a new product to solve a very specific problem. The team interviews potential customers about their experience with this problem, but no one they speak to seems to struggle with this issue. It seems, at least based on these interviews, that the team is solving a non-problem. If this signal isn't noticed and acted upon, the team might end up building a "solution" for a market that doesn't exist.

Understanding these signals and responding to them appropriately is how Venture Capital investors make their living. Corporations that seek to grow through innovation need to start training their managers to recognize and respond to these kinds of signals.

Performance Indicators

Result Indicators

Myth #4: *Everything is a KPI*

Myth #5: *Measuring innovation means measuring the number of ideas in the company*

39

No matter how relevant or insignificant an indicator is, they all tend to be referred to as Key Performance Indicators (KPIs).

However there is a difference between Key Performance Indicators (KPIs) and Key Result Indicators (KRIs). Performance indicators are non-financial in nature and they can be traced back to the activity the innovation team has performed day-in and day-out (e.g. churn rates, number of coaching hours booked for next month, number of customer interviews booked for next month etc.). Result indicators give a broad summary of what happened as a result of the process (e.g. net profit, return on capital employed, cumulated customer satisfaction, employee satisfaction etc.).[35]

Measuring ideas is an essential part of an innovation accounting system. Without ideas upstream, a company can hardly expect any returns downstream. But just measuring the number of ideas the company has in a backlog or the number of projects currently under development is not nearly enough.

Some companies measure product teams, but don't measure their entire portfolio. Others measure the number of ideas that their company initiates, but not how many of those ideas are still alive after two years, or what their adoption rate is in existing business units. That's why so many companies get a partial view. They focus intensely on specific business units or certain metrics, and they get *a* picture of what's going on; just not the *whole* picture.

Measuring a company's innovation ecosystem requires a wider view. In other words, it means measuring the whole, not just a few chosen parts.

 Myth #6: *All innovation measurements work successfully in any organization*

Contrary to popular belief, not all innovation measurements can work successfully in any organization. Why? First, companies vary a lot (a B2B company is pretty different from a B2B2C one). And second, for each company, innovation has a different meaning and importance. What it means to innovate in a B2B software company is not the same as what it means to innovate in an online, direct to consumer, business. Innovating in hospitality is something else entirely.

While the principles of Innovation Accounting are universal, the reality is that innovation measurements themselves need to be contextualized; they must reflect the peculiarities and particularities of the company using them. They can't just be copy-pasted from one company to another.

 Myth #7: *All innovation measurements work successfully for any type of innovation*

People tend to think of "innovation" as one thing, when, in reality, innovation takes more than one form. As we discussed in Chapter 1, incremental innovation, the little-by-little changes that improve existing products and processes, is different from breakthrough innovation which can upend entire industries seemingly overnight. Different kinds of innovation need to be measured differently. For incremental innovation, metrics need to focus on questions of efficiency: how efficient are projects going through the pipeline? And how are they stacking up against forecasted and actual economic return? For breakthrough innovation, given the inherent uncertainty of something that's new, the measurements must be different.[6]

 Myth #8: *Innovation measurements are only needed to relieve executive and stakeholder anxiety around investing in innovation*

We speak on the topic of Innovation Accounting at various events and conferences worldwide. And after every talk we give, almost like clockwork, someone from the audience approaches us, asking for help with some innovation measurements that would help them justify the existence of their team or lab to a superior.

The idea that measurements only exist to convince management is probably one of the biggest myths. At the same time, it's also one of the biggest pitfalls of Innovation Accounting.

While innovation measurements are important for executives and stakeholders, they should not be designed exclusively for their needs. When they are, they tend to focus narrowly on the financial aspect of innovation. But innovation measurements should reflect the whole innovation ecosystem and all of its processes, not just a single part (here, financial metrics). At the end of the day, innovation measurements should lead to changes in behavior; they should serve as the basis for continuous improvements.

Myth #9: *Tying innovation measurements to incentives means more and/or better outcomes*

It is a myth that money is the primary driver for staff, and that, in order to achieve better performance, organizations must design financial incentives. Recognition, respect, and self-actualization are more important drivers. In all types of organization, there is a tendency to believe that the way to make KPIs work is to tie those KPIs to an individual's pay. But when KPIs are tied to bonuses, they are more likely to be gamed for personal benefit.[36]

Every KPI can be gamed, but the ones tied to financial gains are more susceptible than others. Every measurement has a dark side, a negative consequence, or an unintended action that can lead to inferior performance.[37]

For example, one time we were coaching innovation teams in an engineering company's accelerator. Knowing the importance of lean experimenting, we said we wanted to incentivize teams to perform more experiments. As soon as we told the teams we would be measuring the number of experiments they performed each week, they began to claim that everything they did was an experiment. At that point, we had a whole other issue on our hands. We had to sit down with every team to see which of the things they've performed were really experiments and which ones weren't. This ended up being a huge time suck for us.

And this doesn't just happen in engineering. Another time, case workers in a government agency were told they'd be measured on cases closed. The result? Experienced workers flew through large numbers of easy cases, leaving the difficult ones to the inexperienced staff.[38] Not exactly the desired outcome.

Of course, the end of our list doesn't mean the end of all myths around innovation measurements. There are certainly many others. This list was based on our experience interfacing with corporate managers trying to measure innovation in their own companies. In other cases, we simply saw managers using these myths to shy away from trying to measure innovation at all.

Regardless of the situation, failing to measure innovation means having no data or evidence to support innovation efforts. And having no data or evidence to support innovation efforts often means those efforts get shelved, regardless of the promise they might have held.

41

Company-wide system

1

Abstract information

2
11011101
11011101
11011101110

Surface intangible assets

3

Highlight risk of disruption

4

Help improve the innovation ecosystem

5

Bring focus on critical success factors

6

42

Principles of an innovation accounting system

With innovation itself differing from company to company, but the need for measuring it being the same, a useful innovation accounting system needs to be rooted in principles that transcend industry peculiarities.

Principle #1: Company-wide system

Firstly, an innovation accounting system needs to *provide a company-wide framework* of chained leading indicators, each of which predicts the possible success of the ventures being evaluated. Every link in the chain is essential. When the chain is broken, the entire venture is red flagged.

Having the system deployed company-wide enables apples-to-apples comparisons between two or more ventures, allowing an evaluator to decide which venture is most worthy of continuing investment.[39] Such a system also provides a way to see any innovation project in the portfolio as a form of financial option; one with a clear potential revenue, volatility, and associated cost.

Being company-wide, the innovation accounting system needs to be understood and agreed upon by everyone in the company, from executive to innovation team members and from the Innovation Department to the financial controllers.

Principle #2: Abstract information

An innovation accounting system needs to be able to *abstract information*; a concept that our friend Matt Kerr brought to our attention. Abstraction is a concept imported from computer science. In computer science, the abstraction principle is used to reduce complexity, allowing for the efficient design and implementation of complex software systems. Abstraction is the act of representing essential features without including background details or explanations.[40]

Applied to innovation management, abstraction essentially means translating daily or weekly reports on innovation projects into the kind of insights executives require to make strategic decisions quarterly or yearly. Executives or shareholders shouldn't be expected to have the time to look into, for example, a particular team's Learning Velocity. But the Learning Velocity of a team has a massive impact on the time-to-market and survivability of an idea. Therefore, the innovation accounting system needs to be designed and deployed in a way that ensures the seamless flow of actionable data from product teams to the board.

Principle #3: Surface intangible assets

The innovation accounting system *needs to outline the specific use of the firm's growth assets, as well as the strategies deployed to extract value from accounting recognized assets.*[22]

43

This third principle mitigates the relative uselessness of financial reports for measuring innovation identified by Professor Bruch Lev, while at the same time placing more emphasis on intangibles and non-accounting recognized assets such as people and processes.

Enterprises that are constantly at the top of their game distinguish themselves from competitors by having secured a sustainable competitive advantage. To get that advantage, companies need to focus on strategic resources like patents, brand, organizational culture, or unique processes. For instance, Netflix's customer recommendation algorithm, combined with other elements, differentiates Netflix from other content streaming companies.

Perhaps ironically, most of these kinds of strategic resources and growth assets are not reported in the financial-accounting system.[41] Why not? Because investments made into them are immediately expensed and listed under costs (mainly OPEX).

The role of the innovation accounting system is to surface these spends and mark them as investments rather than simply "costs." In the process, the system would also flag any potential inefficiencies.

Highlight risk of disruption

Principle #4: *Highlight risk of disruption*

The innovation accounting system needs to be designed so that the *company's risk of disruption is clearly painted.*

The reduced cost of high end technology, coupled with the increased speed of technological advancement, has made disruption of legacy industries a frequent occurrence.

Clayton Christensen first proposed "The Disruption Theory" in his book "*Innovator's Dilemma.*" The basic idea is this: an outsider, usually a startup or small or medium business, comes into an established industry and shakes things up; usually with a digitally advanced alternative or a new business model. In the process, they threaten or replace complacent legacy players (incumbents). Examples of this phenomenon can be seen in business,[42] politics,[43] and even national security.[44] Broadly speaking, disruptions squeeze out inefficiencies, as well as those profiteering from lack of transparency, by pushing the industry forward and offering a more convenient (usually) digital option.

The Disruption Theory has seen its fair share of criticism for being biased towards the kinds of success stories that support it.[45] Regardless of where you stand on the disruption theory debate, change is inevitable. Not only is change inevitable, but as Industry 4.0 takes effect around the globe, it is impending across all industries. The fact that Uber became a market leader without owning any traditional assets (cars) can't be ignored.

But disrupting an industry means more than startups gaining market share from incumbents. Disruption is a shift in "business as usual." It's a change in money flows and value propositions. Outages bring a new wave of competition to a stagnant market transitioning to Industry 4.0.

The Disruption Theory is meant to serve both as a chronicle of the past and a model for the future. Making corporate leaders understand, aided by an innovation accounting system, that if their company is under threat of disruption, they need to deploy immediate countermeasures that go beyond an innovation lab.

Principle #5: *Help improve the innovation ecosystem*

The design of an innovation accounting system should *inform ecosystem improvement decisions*. A company's innovation ecosystem is made up of more than just processes and an idea portfolio. An innovation ecosystem encompasses human resource capabilities, partnerships and culture too. Thus, the role of an innovation accounting system is to uncover the causal relationships between inputs and outcomes. In doing so, the insight drawn from the system will prevent investments in low impact activities.

Innovation Accounting is part of innovation management but it manifests itself across the entire system. Remember: innovation isn't just one thing. And innovation accounting systems don't exist solely to determine which ventures deserve investment and which deserve the cutting room floor.

Whether your company should collaborate more with startups, double down on M&A, or invest more in capability development programs should be justified by evidence from the innovation accounting system.

Ultimately, the goal of an innovation accounting system is to help a team, manager or a CEO make better decisions.

45

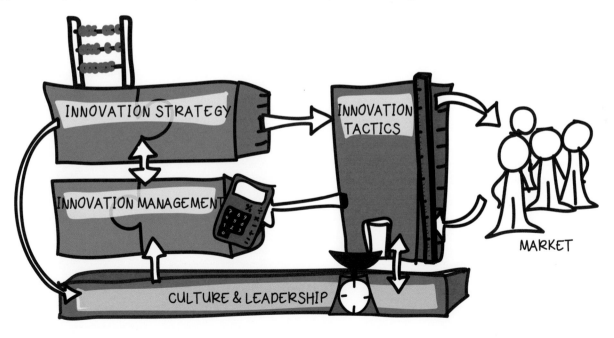

Principle #6: Bring focus on critical success factors

Of course, it's possible, and fairly easy, to get carried away when it comes to data. Since pretty much everything can be measured, setting measurements for everything that can be measured (in other words, for everything) is not the way forward. Ultimately, the innovation accounting system needs to *look at only what matters.*

What's true for product teams holds water at a company-wide level too: drowning in data is as bad, if not worse, than having no data at all. Why? Because at least teams and organizations with no data have a tendency to take action. Whether or not these actions are correct, or based on anything but a gut feeling, is a whole other conversation. Teams and organizations that collect too much data can become paralyzed by possibility, by the sheer number of options.

Since the primary role of an innovation accounting system, then, is to measure only what's relevant, only what needs to be measured, measurements should have a reason to exist beyond existence itself. Each measure should have a link to key success factors for the company, product, and/or a specific project.[46]

The Innovation Accounting System

When designing and deploying an innovation accounting system in your company, it's important to remember to manage complexity. As a rule of thumb, from our experience, a good measurement system needs to lead to behavior change or sustain an existing positive behavior.

We'll talk about how to design and implement an innovation accounting system in more detail throughout the upcoming chapters. Starting from the building blocks of the innovation ecosystem we spoke about earlier we will be focusing on how individual ventures are measured, how the innovation funnel is measured, how efficient and effective the investment in internal innovation is and how HR capability and culture is measured. Also we will be looking at how you can measure the collaboration with external players.

Today, we're in the early stages of a corporate innovation revolution. The principles outlined in this chapter form the foundation of a new way of managing growth through innovation. A way that is more fact based than faith based. A way that puts evidence in the center of the decision making process. A way that's designed to complement the shortcomings that the financial-accounting system has when it comes to measuring innovation.

STRATEGIC
innovation accounting

MANEGERIAL
innovation accounting

TACTICAL
innovation accounting

Measuring
ecosystem

Measuring
funnel

47

Measuring
teams

Measuring
Culture & Capabilities

There are six basic principles every innovation accounting system should adhere to:

1   It's a company-wide system.
2   It's made up of layers of information that abstract from each other.
3   It surfaces the investments the company is making in innovation.
4   It highlights the company's risk of disruption.
5   It helps improve the innovation ecosystem.
6   If focuses the entire company on the critical success factors of innovation.

Conversations on Innovation

Thomas Vogth-Eriksen

Group Chief Financial Officer DNV

For more than 8 years, Thomas has been the CFO of DNV, an independent assurance and risk management provider with 12,000 employees, operating in more than 100 countries. Through its broad experience and deep expertise DNV advances safety and sustainable performance, sets industry standards, and inspires and invents solutions.

Innovation Accounting: Today, large organizations face competition not only from within their own industry but also from startups and competitors in adjacent industries such as the tech giants. In this context, how is the role of the CFO changing?

Thomas Vogth-Eriksen: I've been CFO of DNV GL (now DNV) since 2012. Maybe that is not that many years, but in the digital world of today, seven years is a long time. And yes, things have changed; in some sectors, the change has been faster than in others.

Probably the biggest change however, is the speed of change. It's higher now than ever before. So you might get surprised when a new competitor, or potential competitor, is on the ground. You are surprised by the fact that you are getting surprised that suddenly.

Change is the constant, rather than anything else, so you should expect that things are changing.

I think another reflection that I have is that the digital transformation is eventually going to "kill" legacy business models based on time and material. When I say that, it doesn't mean that we will not have people in the organization; we will for sure, have people in the organization. But you can no longer price your product or your service to the customer in terms of time and material.

IA: Innovation is a cost, or at least a short term cost with an unknown long term benefit. How should CFOs deal with the "anxiety" of investing in innovation? What lens should CFOs use when looking at these investments that have an impact on the bottom line tomorrow and yet might return something in 2, 3, or 5 years, if they return anything at all?

TVE: I think this is absolutely true! The risk traditional CFOs face is that they are too focused on the history. The books only show the things that have happened. You can learn from history, but you cannot change it. The key is to learn quickly and cheaply, then adapt for the future.

The "anxiety" of investing in innovation can be alleviated by the knowledge that change is a constant and we have to always renew ourselves. Our biggest challenge, however, is that we need to invest equally in the existing business as well as in the future one.

So when innovating and looking into the future, you have to have a multi-year approach; or a multi-period approach, depending on whether you're using years or other methods. Patience is a virtue as long as you trust the innovation process and the people building the new. CFOs in general need to dare to fail, because that's the only way to learn about the market and the consumers, learning from failures. Obviously these learnings need to be systematic and scientific; only in this way can we move the company forward.

I know that investing in innovation will have a negative impact on our short term CAPEX but if we don't invest at all we can't hope to get any new revenue in a couple of years or even later.

IA: How should modern CFOs manage the two conflicting time frames: the short term time frame focused on bottom line and exploitation of existing business models, and the long term time frame focused on continuous growth and exploration of new business models?

TVE: The two time frames that you're referring to; I see them as two rooms where we need to have two distinct conversations. One is the performance room, and here we discuss performance metrics; the other is the innovation room, and here we discuss innovation metrics.

In the first one, on the performance side I think you can continue to apply a lot of the traditional metrics and we don't need to debate a lot over these. But sometimes the line between these two rooms is blurred and we have to discuss innovation during a performance meeting for example. So we need to be fast in adapting our mental model to a different time frame, where we have different metrics for success. We don't measure early stage innovation projects on revenue for example.

It is important to note that every question we have for an early stage digital product for example is connected to the potential of commercial success this project will have later on. The goal of any innovation team in the end is commercial success. But we are not going to talk about pricing, for example, without even knowing if the customers have that particular problem that we think we can solve with our solution. Basically, we are adapting our conversation to the time frame, to the two rooms.

IA: What would be your advice for CFOs that are a bit more reluctant to go down the path of being supporters of innovation & digital transformations? Or the CFOs that haven't yet started these activities?

TVE: First and foremost, I think you have to look at yourself in the mirror and understand that it's about, "change or be changed." You have to accept that change is happening without you or your company's consent. And hiding behind traditional spreadsheets and analysis, focusing primarily on the history, will most likely not be sufficient.

Then you have to create a framework for innovation that everyone in the company agrees with. A framework supported by different tools, different competencies, different ways of interacting with customers, and different ways of organizing work as well.

This framework then needs to be supported by investments, especially in competence and talent. People that are not traditionalists, innovators and entrepreneurs.

From my point of view I always see 3 potential outcomes for any project: two successful ones and one failure. Obviously the first type of success is a commercial one. But the second type of successful outcome is a good and fast failure. Maybe we shouldn't even call it failure, but a kind of good learning opportunity. And if you have a good learning opportunity, with a lot of interesting and valuable feedback from customers; well it didn't materialize in a new service or product, but it gave you a lot of learnings. Maybe that is a success in itself.

The final outcome, the failure, is a project that's stuck. I mean, that doesn't come anywhere, because nothing happens, and should be stopped as quickly as possible.

Finally I think that one of the things that a CFO needs to say to everyone else on the board is: "A longer term perspective is good for business." Actually not just for innovation, but also for the everyday existing business too. One of the things that I introduced in DNV GL some years ago, was something we call: "15 month rolling forecasting." This way every quarter we look 5 quarters into the future. My intention for my company and advice for others is to spend half of the time at board level talking about the past (the accounting books) and half preparing for the future. Unfortunately we are not there yet ourselves, but we are gradually getting there; especially with support from the CDO and our Chief People Officer.

The CFO needs to contribute to the future not only with financial resources but to force proactive conversations and move everyone away from reactive conversations. There is no point being stuck in the past, because you can't change it anyway. It's more important to learn from the past and prepare for the future.

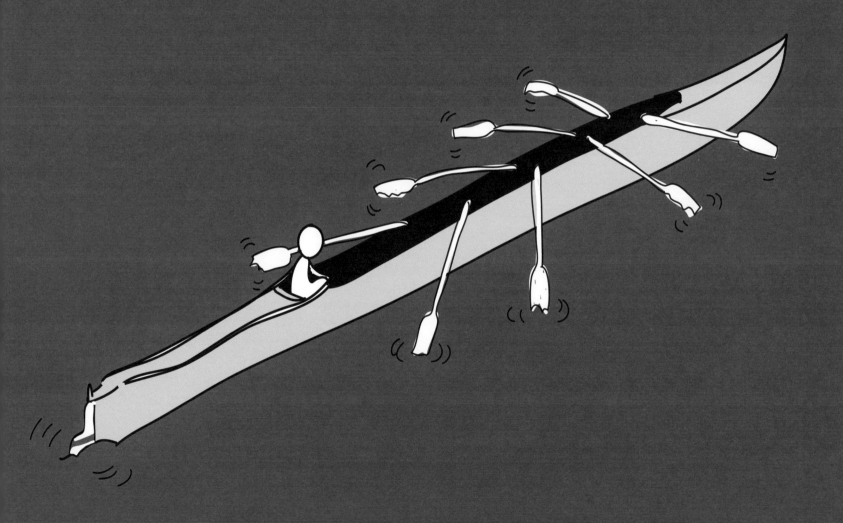

Without teams testing ideas there is nothing to steer in the first place.

CHAPTER 4

Tactical Innovation Accounting

As an innovator, particularly in a large organization you are constantly dealing with people who are solely interested in seeing the hard numbers behind your projects. You are continually bombarded with the mantra "if we can measure it we can manage it." And what reliance on that statement implies, covertly or otherwise, is a leadership who are either:

- Prioritizing control over innovation.
- Or, who don't understand the innovation value proposition; seeing it simply as another word for fun times sitting on beanbags, being casually dressed, drinking soft drinks, and playing with post it notes in a hip office while people on other floors are getting "real work" done.

To this, most innovation managers and product team leads we have encountered have a pre-defined answer: not everything that can be counted counts, and not everything that counts can be counted. This is in part true. However, relying on that statement potentially absolves innovation teams of any form of control or meaningful measurement. That way leads to unstructured development and wastage of resources.

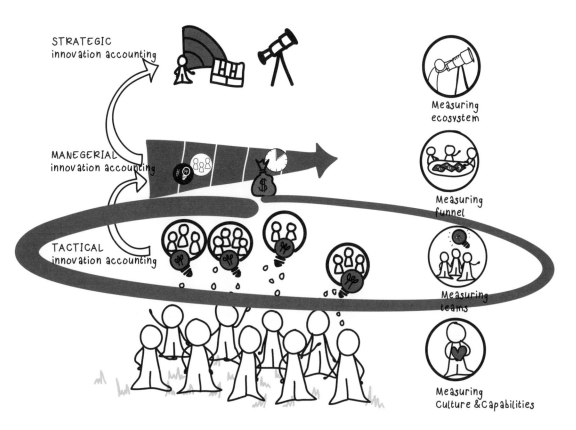

STRATEGIC
innovation accounting

Measuring
ecosystem

MANEGERIAL
innovation accounting

Measuring
funnel

TACTICAL
innovation accounting

Measuring
teams

Measuring
Culture & Capabilities

57

Hardly surprising that the result is a stalemate with both parties thinking they are right. And the problem is quite simply that the wrong question is being asked at the wrong time. The core business folks are using their frame of reference which is rooted in financial result indicators to assess the likelihood of success of an "infant" idea. On the other side, the innovation manager is most likely talking about early stage evidence of potential success; albeit with concrete results only expected to show at some time in the future.

Luckily, this situation can be defused with better communication. All it takes is for both parties to agree to speak a common language that provides the hard numbers behind a process which for some feels more like art than science.

The first step in developing that common language is to agree on a framework. Having a clear product development framework or Product Lifecycle agreed on by everyone in the company will mitigate the problem of the wrong question being asked at the wrong time. Because now everyone gets a better picture of the maturity stage a certain idea is in and knows what questions are relevant for that stage.

In recent years, many companies around the world have developed their own frameworks. To name a few companies reaping the benefit of a clear innovation process: Telefonica (Spanish telecommunication company), DNB (Norwegian bank), Pearson (British publisher and education company), DNV GL (Norwegian certification and classification society), Konika Minolta (Japanese technology company) and DHL (German logistics company). Each of these companies' innovation frameworks (or Product Lifecycles as they are also known) are slightly different from the others as they address the peculiarities of each specific company and its industry.

Take the Pearson example that we covered at large in our previous book, "*The Corporate Startup*." It uses 6 stages named as follows: Idea, Explore, Validate, Grow, Sustain, Retire.

At DHL, on the other hand, their framework is called "From idea to success in three phases." The phases of their framework are: Validate (prove that the problem exists and can be solved), Test (prove that your solution solves the problem), Gain (prove that people want to pay for your solution).

As can be seen from the examples above, every company named the maturity stages of their respective Product Lifecycle Framework in a different way. In doing so they strengthened their common language by tying the framework into existing company norms. However, irrespective of the title, the purpose of every framework is the same. An innovation framework unifies the business, enabling everybody to know and understand what phase each product or business model is in. This then acts as a catalyst for managing and measuring resources and investment decisions. More importantly, the framework unites people behind the innovation effort, engaging them in delivering change.

But remember, frameworks work best when designed specifically for the individual organization. So our comments should be seen as a guide rather than a one size fits all solution.

If your company doesn't yet have a company-wide agreed upon Product Lifecycle we will discuss how to develop one at the end of this chapter.

With a clear framework agreed upon, the next step your company needs to take in order to create an innovation accounting system for teams (tactical Innovation Accounting), is to agree on the critical success factors for each stage. Basically, this will define how success looks in each stage and what needs to happen for an idea to be progressed to the next stage of the framework.

For the rest of the book we will be using a generic framework made up of five stages: DISCOVERY - EXPLORATION - VIABILITY - GROWTH - SUSTAIN.

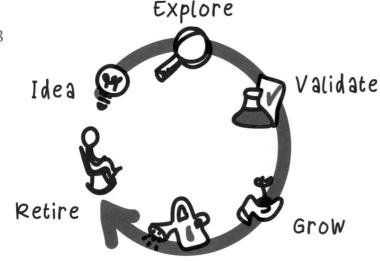

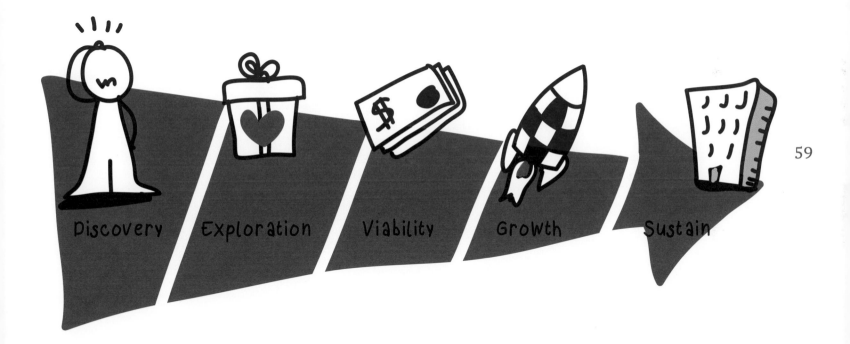

Discovery   Exploration   Viability   Growth   Sustain

Discovery

Discovery: Have we identified a problem worth solving

Remembering that one of the primary goals of innovation is to solve real problems, let's assume that the critical success factor for a team in **Discovery** is to identify a problem worth solving. The goal for the discovery stage would then be to develop empathy for the clients or end users and build a deep understanding of potential problems. Therefore, the primary areas a product team needs to focus on in the discovery phase might include:
- Identifying who may have a problem and in what area.
- Understanding how the problem impacts that group.
- Analyzing if the problem is worth solving both from a cost/benefit and customer impact perspective.

This latter would include potential customer buy-in to change, leading you to:
- Understand how many customers suffer from that problem and if this number is significant for the specific market.
- Identify if and how customers are solving the problem right now.

Responses will be reflected in the innovation accounting system by employing the following measurements:

Performance measurements:

- Number of stage-relevant assumptions identified.
- Learning Velocity. **How many learnings did the team get in a given time interval which shed light on the problem and the customer segment.?**
- Cost per Learning. **How much did the team spend to obtain one learning?** The cost can be a translation in the local currency of time spent per learning but it can also include other costs that were incurred in the process of empathy development. These costs can be, for example, costs related to travel, ethnography work, facilitated workshops or materials.

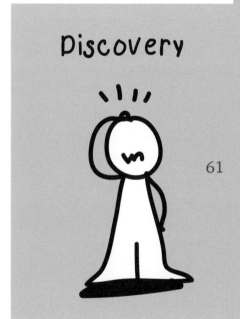

61

Discovery

Result measurements:

- Confidence. The team's activity needs to result in a level of confidence that the problem they have identified is worth solving. Hence, every week, based on the empathy work done in the field, the team needs to have an honest conversation about how likely it is that the problem they uncovered is a real problem or just a nice to have for that particular target group. In general at this stage the confidence level will be based on qualitative insights. Used properly, confidence level analysis can lead to unviable projects being dropped at an early stage or vital projects being prioritized; both resulting in a better allocation of resources.

For those looking for further guidance, although we don't want to be dogmatic or too prescriptive, we have found that the most effective methodologies for this stage are Design Thinking and Lean Startup.

Before continuing, it is worth clarifying that learnings should never be viewed as after the fact stories to cover up a failure. They are an integral part of the innovation accounting system; a system that demands learning as an idea is progressed, and demands acknowledgment of the learning as a way of measuring the potential market success of an idea. Deployed successfully, learnings can provide clarity of ideas whilst also being the conduit for unexpected ideas to come to the fore.

63

Exploration

64

Exploration: Does our solution solve the customer's problem

Moving on. The next stage a team will reach if they pass the Discovery stage is **Exploration**. At this stage, the critical success factor revolves around the willingness of the customer segment to not only have the problem solved but also adopt the solution envisioned by the team. Therefore the primary questions that need to be answered are:

- How do the customers want to have the problem solved?
- Are customers interested in the envisioned solution or in the value proposition of our future offering?

To keep track of a team's progress at this stage we recommend the use of the following:

Performance measurements:

- Number of stage-relevant assumptions identified.
- Learning Velocity in stage-relevant Business Model Canvas blocks; most particularly Customer Segment and Value Proposition.
- Experiment Efficacy showing how many of a team's experiments resulted in learnings.
- Cost per Learning.

Exploration

65

Exploration

Result measurements:

- Confidence in the interest of the customers to have the previously identified problem solved.

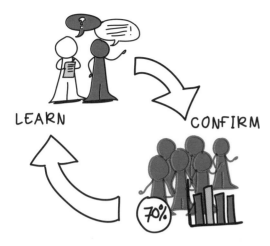

LEARN   CONFIRM

Although qualitative insights will always be necessary to understand why something is happening, the higher number of customers involved in later stages as compared to early stages make it possible to confirm those with quantitative experiments. We often see a combination of Learning Experiments providing insights that can be "confirmed" with more quantitative data. Typically there are more confirm experiments in later stages while there are more learn experiments in the earlier stages.

Keeping a discipline of continuous learning is hard. A dashboard can help both teams and managers to understand the decisions made. As we will see in the following chapter, a dashboard will also have implications for the other parts of the innovation accounting system. It can also be used in the remaining stages of the Product Lifecycle.

The dashboard should be seen as a place for a team to communicate their progress to internal stakeholders (e.g. coaches and managers) and offer a snapshot of the risk still present in their business model. At this stage the design thinking methodology, which is so instrumental in getting the team to have initial empathy of the customers' problems, gradually gives way to a more experiment-based heavy lean startup system. The teams

will find the use of the dashboard to be easier to manage and understand if deployed in conjunction with an experiment tracking template such as the Experiment Canvas we proposed in The Corporate Startup, or Experiment and Learning Cards from Alex Ostervalder's book, "*Value Proposition Design,*" or Brant Cooper's Experiment Map.[47]

The dashboard we typically co-create with our clients is made up of 3 elements which can be viewed on their own or integrated into a display dashboard. These are:

A. Experimentation overview. The team or, as we've seen in most cases, the team's coach will record the number of experiments the team has concluded in any given calendar week. This is followed by the number of intentional learnings (learnings for which the experiment was designed - the things the team knew it didn't know) and unintentional learnings (learnings obtained during the experiment on top of the ones the experiment was designed for - the things the team didn't know it didn't know) resulting from the concluded experiments. It is also worth inputting the cost of the experiment in this part of the dashboard.

B. The second part of the dashboard is made up of granular information regarding the concluded experiments and their consequent learnings. Following the Business Model Canvas or Lean Canvas the team or its coach will record in which part of the Business Model Canvas the learnings occurred. Typically, the right hand side of the Business Model Canvas needs most of the validating. It makes sense to look at each stage and the stage relevant blocks in that stage.

C. The last part of the dashboard is made up of aggregate data using the above mentioned inputs. The KPIs the dashboard will display are:
- Learning Velocity (number of learnings accumulated per week).
- Experiment Efficacy (percentage of experiments that

67

resulted in learnings). This is a particularly important indicator as it shows the team's ability to run effective experiments and highlights development needs. Teams with low Experiment Efficacy can benefit from more experiment design coaching, for example.

- Experiment Velocity (number of experiments per week).
- Intentional Learning Velocity (percentage of experiments that hit their intended mark).
- Cost of Learning (how much did the team spend to generate one piece of validated learning).

The display dashboard is there to offer internal stakeholders, coaches and the team a graphical display of the team's performance. The graphical display will show the KPIs in an easy digestible way.

A — Experimentation overview

	wk 10	wk 11	wk 12	wk 13	YTD
Number of experiments					7
Number of learnings					
- intentional	1	0	0	1	4
- unintentional	0	0	1	0	2
- total	1	0	1	1	6

B — Stage relevant BM blocks

Number of learnings by block

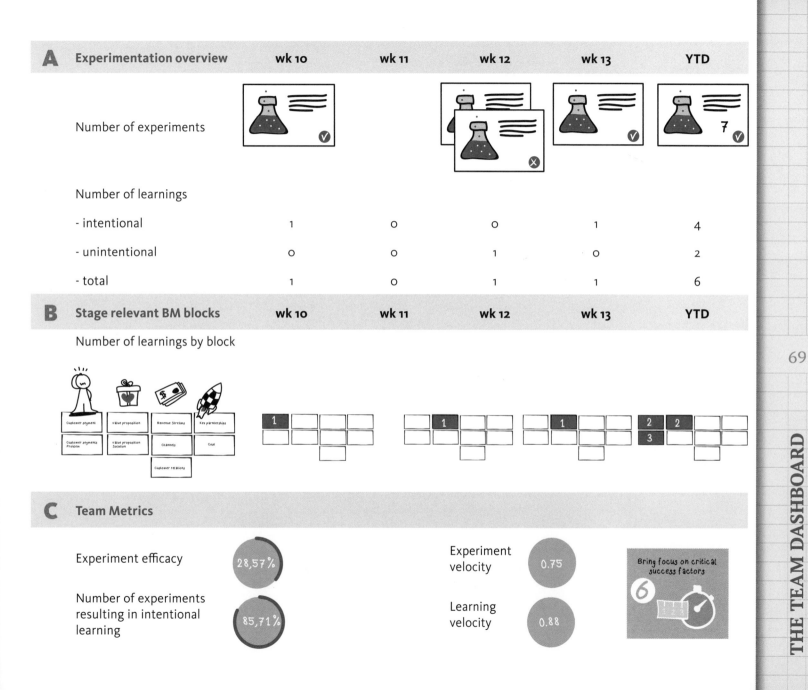

C — Team Metrics

Experiment efficacy — 28,57 %

Number of experiments resulting in intentional learning — 85,71 %

Experiment velocity — 0.75

Learning velocity — 0.88

Bring focus on critical success factors

Before we continue with the next stage of the Product Lifecycle, it's worth addressing the debate on measuring a team's Learning Velocity versus measuring their Experiment Velocity.

The lean startup mindset mythology encourages product teams to test their assumptions before launching.[48] As this mindset is gradually gathering followers in the corporate landscape, Experiment Velocity might look like a good KPI alternative to the standard ROI.

So what is wrong with Experiment Velocity?

To begin with, Experiment Velocity can be gamed, purposefully or not. Product teams, knowing that they are having their Experiment Velocity measured, might claim that every tiny thing they do is an experiment. Or, giving them the benefit of the doubt, they don't know how to design the right experiments so although their velocity is high, their impact is low.

Doing some work for a blue chip company in South East Asia using Lean Startup as the modus operandi for all product teams, we discovered Experiment Velocity to sometimes be a misleading Innovation Accounting indicator.

Look at the performance of these two teams:

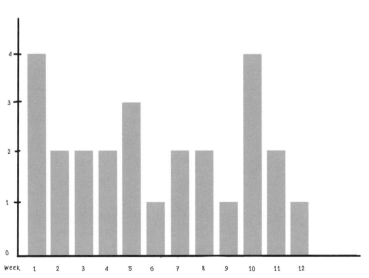

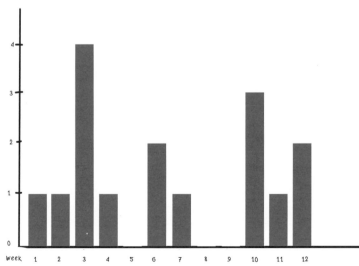

It is obvious that Team Grey did more experiments than Team Orange. The average Experiment Velocity of Team Grey was 2.1 experiments per week, while the average Experiment Velocity of Team Orange was just 1.3. If one were to consider only the Experiment Velocity as a performance KPI, Team Grey would, undoubtedly, be the winner.

But digging deeper we reached a very different conclusion. Looking at how many of these experiments have resulted in conclusive learnings I saw how Experiment Velocity can sometimes point you to the wrong conclusion.
As you can see, both teams reached the same average Learning Velocity, about 0.75 learnings/week.

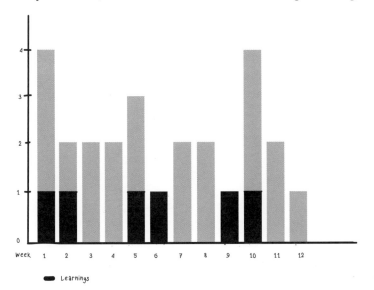

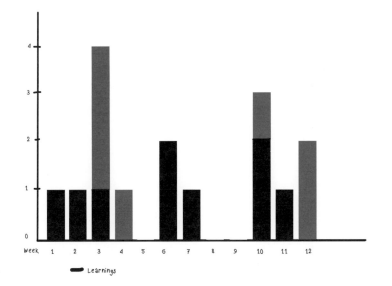

71

As the goal of product teams is to get validated learning[49] as fast as possible Learning Velocity should outshine Experiment Velocity. But it should not replace it.

Although it is true that experiments lead to learnings, it's quite hard to reach a 100% correlation. There are many reasons for experiments not generating conclusive learnings, but the outcome is the same: wasted time.

By looking at a team's Experiment/Learning ratio, one can tell a lot about the team and what type of help they need, if any.

Consider a *lower-than-1 Experiment/Learning ratio*. This means that the team in question has performed more experiments than the number of learnings they got. This can suggest they are struggling to design impactful experiments so coaching may be required. Or, at the very worst, they are trying to game the system by having high Experiment Velocity numbers.

Now consider a *higher-than-1 Experiment/Learning ratio.* This team might be running some multi-level (funnel like) experiments where at each stage of the funnel they are gathering learnings. One thing to note in this case is that this team might run multi-variable experiments which, if not done right,[50] can lead to misleading insights.

An *Experiment/Learning ratio equaling 1*, means a 100% equivalence between the number of experiments a team has performed and the number of conclusive learnings they got. This would be the ideal case.

It is important to point out that over time, as teams mature, their Experiment Velocity drops. This is due to the experiments becoming more and more complex and perhaps requiring more preparation. That is another reason why measuring the ratio is more relevant than measuring the two velocities independently of each other.

Concept box:

Runway relative to Learning Velocity.

Business schools have taught us that a runway a team or startup has, is equal to the amount of money available divided by the monthly burn rate.

However, this is only partially true. Experienced entrepreneurs will confirm that runway is in fact time available till the money runs out divided by how fast the team is learning in the market.[51]

Take for example a team that has 6 months worth of budget left and their typical iteration length is 2 weeks. Their runway is equal to 12; 24 weeks divided by 2 weeks for each learning. In simple terms this team has 12 chances of finding a sustainable business model.

Viability: Will the customer buy our solution

Continuing the journey of an innovation idea at the **Viability** stage the critical success factors for an investment decision revolve around the customer's intent to buy or adopt the product. Therefore the most important questions the teams need to provide evidence for are:
- Are customers willing to pay to have the problem solved with our solution?
- What type of revenue stream are our customers willing to accept? (subscription, one-time payment, freemium, free etc.)
- How much are customers willing to pay for a solution?
- What's the best channel to deliver the value proposition? Will customers favor one channel over another?

Hence the following are important:

73

Viability

Performance measures:

- Number of stage-relevant assumptions identified.
- Learning Velocity in stage-relevant Business Model blocks, which in this case are Channel and Revenue Stream.
- Experiment Efficacy showing how many of a team's experiments resulted in learnings.
- Cost per Learning.

Result measurements:

• Confidence in the likelihood of customers paying for the offered solution.

Viability

75

Discovery Exploration Viability Growth Sustain

As you can probably tell by looking at the performance indicators, the Viability stage of the Product Lifecycle varies from the previous stage just in the focus of experiments. However, there's another more nuanced difference in the type of evidence gathered by the experiments. As teams progress their ideas through the Product Lifecycle, qualitative insights will gradually be replaced by quantitative insights, although sometimes the question to be answered stays the same. For example, a desirability question from the previous stage for which the team already has qualitative confirmation (from interviews) can now be answered with more qualitative insight from experiments done at scale (with a landing page or ads). Adding quantitative evidence to the already existing qualitative ones will add more confidence in the business model's future success.

Also, at this stage it is worth starting to consider feasibility questions such as your company's ability to develop the envisioned solution and the compliance of the solution with your company's legal guidelines and risk model. Although the solution is in its early stage of development and in most cases is only a prototype, having early (informal) conversations with the internal stakeholders that will later help develop or deliver the solution is always a good idea. This point is particularly

important for teams active in highly regulated environments such as pharma or banking, or teams that are delivering engineering-heavy solutions such as those in manufacturing or the energy industry, to name a few.

Starting to involve other departments in the development of a new business model at this stage of the lifecycle will yield benefits later on.

We came to realize a pattern every time we worked with teams in highly regulated industries: most of the time, when we mentioned involving the legal department to a product team doing lean startup experiments, we felt the mood in the room deteriorate (to say the least). An attitude of "us" vs. "them" is, on one hand, damaging for the company culture and, on the other, detrimental for business experimenting (and building successful new products).

However, at one point we worked with teams in a pharma company. One of our early requests was to have a person from the legal department attached to each team, not on a full time basis but available to dedicate some hours per week when the team entered the Viability stage.

What we had seen happening consistently is that the teams that have a legal member on-board had a higher experiment velocity than teams with no legal liaison. They were also always more compliant and agreed faster on things. At a closer look, the benefits of involving people in the legal department in the development process of an idea at this stage are threefold:

1. Faster feedback on experiments (go/no-go on the experiment). The go/no-go feedback loop on taking an experiment live becomes almost instantaneous. Having the legal person sitting across the table and not across the campus dramatically reduces the go/no-go decision time.
2. Helps improve the experiment within legal constraints. If the experiment is a no-go, there's someone on the team that understands the context and can help fix the experiment on the spot.
3. Bolsters support for the lean startup experimentation process in the company. Having your experiment legally compliant is going to win you a lot of hearts and minds. Not only will managers stop pushing back when they hear about business experimentation but now, they will start supporting it.

Most of the time, the quality of collaboration within a team is dependent on the individual personalities of the members as modified by the team leader and not all (legal) people are alike. But regardless of how stubborn one person might be, we still think it helps having a legal representative on the team and involving them in the lean startup experimentation process. Following this experience we encourage you to have a legal person on-board every product team.

Growth

78

Growth: Can we scale our solution

Moving the Product Lifecycle on to the **Growth** stage, the team now needs to provide the proof that the idea they initially had can be transformed into a sustainable, repeatable and scalable business model. Therefore the questions the teams need to answer are:

- Can we scale the business model?
- Does it make sense to scale the business model?
- Can the channel of the business model sustain the scale?

At this stage we are looking towards a mix of financial and non-financial indicators. It is important to note here that if in the previous stages of the lifecycle the indicators were business model agnostic, at this stage teams need to employ indicators that speak for their business models' specific needs. However non-financial indicators such as Learning Velocity are relevant as the teams are still in uncertain waters. Specifically looking at the Learning Velocity indicator, it is worth noting that a decrease is expected in this measure as the feedback loops grow in length. Each result now requires more development time than in the early stages of the project when data gathering was key. In the same way, an increase in the Cost of Learning can be expected too.

Performance indicators:

As ideas reach the Growth stage, more and more people with various backgrounds and expertise are added to the team in an effort to prove the scalability of the business model. This, combined with the fact that in most cases the business models have a strong software development component, leads organizations to start using agile development as the preferred methodology. Agile project management methodologies for software development have been around since the 1990s. There are thousands of organizations using them. The Agile Manifesto,[52] published in 2001, represented a seminal point at which the software community acknowledged that requirements evolve, and cannot be fully pre-defined. Today, there are several software development methodologies, frameworks, and processes that embody the Agile Manifesto's values and principles such as, Scrum, Lean, Kanban, Feature Driven Development (FDD), Extreme Programming (XP), Crystal, and Dynamic Systems Development Methodology (DSDM), to name a few.

According to surveys from various sources,[53] projects using agile methodologies deliver sooner, are more flexible for change, and produce higher-quality outcomes. Teams and stakeholders perceive greater satisfaction due to improved communications, smoother collaborations, and increased flexibility. Furthermore, agile projects are generally seen to deliver business results faster than transitional methodologies and deliver high benefit-to-cost ratios.

However, some reports[54] suggest traditional methodologies may deliver higher results on the benefits-to-cost ratio than agile. On average, agile projects report achieving the expected business benefit more often than traditional projects. Accordingly we are going to look at some performance indicators that can be used by teams in the **Scale** stage of the Product Lifecycle. It is worth noting that these indicators will be carried on into the **Sustain** phase provided the agile development process is used; as is the case with most ideas we've worked with.

We would say at this stage that although we have deployed agile methodologies with clients on a regular basis we would not consider ourselves to be experts in this field. What follows is therefore a summary of indicators used in the agile process in order to provide a basic level of understanding on the way in which agile can help to deliver projects.

79

Growth

Performance measurements

- Sprint Velocity: Velocity is a measure of the amount of work the development team is able to perform in a given period of time. It is basically the rate at which the statements in the requirements documentation are converted into lines of code. The number of story points completed over the past few sprints gives you the Sprint Velocity, which can be used as a predictor for the value that would be delivered in the upcoming sprints as well. While it is an important metric, it cannot be used as a measure of competence or performance of the agile team. It also cannot be used as a standalone metric because, while it is a result oriented matrix that measures the quantitative output, it gives no insight in regard to the quality of development.[55]
- Lead Time: Lead Time is the period between the moment of making a request for delivering something and the actual delivery. All the processes to bring a product to completion come under Lead Time. It also includes developing a business requirement and fixing bugs.[56]
- Cycle Time: The Cycle Time is a subset of Lead Time. It measures the time for a task to go from "started" or "in progress" to "done." Normally, Cycle Times should be around half the Sprint Length. If Cycle Times are longer than a sprint, teams are not completing work they committed to.[57]
- Sprint Burndown: Before starting a sprint, a team forecasts how many story points they can complete in its course. Sprint Burndown allows a scrum master to track the completion of those story points and ensure a team will finish the planned scope of work within the set time frame.[58]
- Epic and Release Burndown: These metrics allow teams to track bigger bodies of work than Sprint Burndown can cover. One of the major benefits of Epic Burndown and Release Burndown is that they help to manage the scope creep; the addition of new requirements after the project scope was already defined.[58]

Results measurements. A framework for analytics:

The important thing to note at this stage is that, although financial indicators start making their way in the conversation, the goal is not to compare the actual numbers against certain benchmarks or industry standards as it is expected that these numbers will not be on par. What's important to understand is what the numbers are telling us. Are the numbers indicating a possible sustainable, repeatable and scalable business model or not?

To find the point where the business model becomes sustainable and the team should step on the scale gas pedal, we encourage the deployment of powerful concept by David Benetti, WPS.[59] WPS is the ratio between two growth indicators. PROM, referring to the number of users the team is able to attract through promotion, marketing, news, blogging, product placement etc., and WOM, referring to the number of users attracted through word of mouth, referrals, recommendations etc.

Calculating the WPS is fairly straightforward: simply choose a time-sliced cohort of new users (weekly, for instance) and determine whether each individual conversion (or sample thereof) was due to WOM or PROM. Divide the total WOM adoptions by the total adoptions (WOM + PROM) for each discrete period and that's your WPS for that period.

WPS = WOM / (WOM + PROM) x 100%

In English, this is the % of users that came from word of mouth activities. According to Ed Essey, Director of Intrapreneurship & Incubation at Microsoft, when WPS is between 40% and 60%, the business model is ready for scale. If it's below 40%, the business model is not ready to cross the chasm into the early majority.[60]

At this stage of maturity, if your teams haven't done it already from an earlier maturity stage, they should consider employing an analytics framework. An analytics framework is more suited than looking at individual indicators since the complexity of their activities is now higher.

Growth

81

There are many available frameworks teams can pick from. Naming a few: Dave McClure's Pirate Metrics, Sean Ellis' Growth Pyramid or Eric Ries' Engines of Growth. However we have a tendency to work with Dave McClure's framework as it seems to be the most adopted framework in the startup and product management circles.

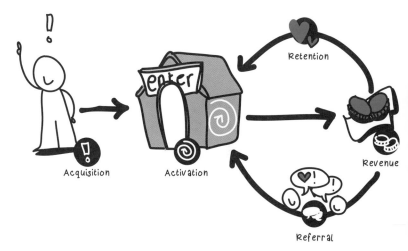

The Pirate Metrics framework gets its name from the acronym for the five distinct elements of building successful businesses: Acquisition, Activation, Retention, Revenue and Referral. These elements don't necessarily need to follow this order as much as they need to follow the logic of each business model's funnel. Also, each element of the framework can be made up by more than just one indicator. The number of indicators needs to speak to the complexity and peculiarities of the business model for which it is designed.

To illustrate that the elements do not necessarily follow the AARRR order, in his book, "*Running Lean,*" Ash Maurya introduces the happy customer loop. Depending on the types of business model and the phase that you are in, it helps you focus on the right metrics to validate.

The first A in the framework is acquisition; how do you get potential customers in front of your offering to be able to convert them to customers?

The second A, activation is all about getting your customer to do your main important activity. That is not a sign up, but rather writing a tweet or buying a product.

Moving on to the Rs; Retention, if you offer something that has enough value, your customers should be coming back to do it again.

 Referral, can you turn your customers into advocates? Some business models rely on referrals more than others. But also as a growth method, referral can prove to be an important focus.

 Revenue, finding ways to optimize and grow.

83

Since the measures depend on the business model, let's now look at some popular business models and generic applications of the AARRR framework for each respective business model. However we recommend you invest the time in building a framework that's tailored for your business model. The below list of indicators is there just to inspire you.

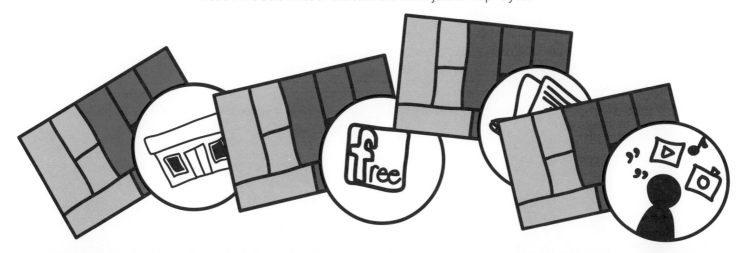

E-commerce business models (e.g. Zalando, Amazon):

Acquisition indicators:

- Number of unique visitors.
- User acquisition cost: how much does the platform pay to attract one user.

Activation indicators:

- Conversion rate: the number of visitors who buy something for the first time from the total number of visitors.
- Buyer acquisition costs: how much was spent to attract one buyer.
- Abandonment rate: the percentage of people who begin to make a purchase and don't complete it.

Retention indicators:

- Customer loyalty: percentage of customers coming back for a second item after purchasing the first one.

Referral indicators:

- Virality: number of items shared per visitor.

Revenue indicators:

- Purchases per year: the number of purchases made by each customer per year.
- Customer lifetime value: how much money is a customer spending on the platform during the time they have an account.
- Customer acquisition cost: how much does the platform pay to attract one paying customer.
- Average shopping cart size: the average amount of money spent on a purchase.

85

Subscription business models (e.g. Dropbox, Zoom, T-Mobile, Netflix):

Acquisition indicators:

- Number of unique visitors in the unit of time: how many new and unique visitors are visiting the website in a unit of time (usually per week).
- Visitors acquisitions costs: how much did it cost to attract one visitor.

Activation indicators:

- Conversion rate: the number of visitors who subscribe to the service from the total number of visitors.
- User acquisition cost: how much does the platform pay to attract one user.
- Upsell rate: percentage of basic users converting to premium features (if applicable to the business model) or becoming paying customers.

Retention indicators:

- Churn rate: how many customers are quitting their subscriptions (usually computed for 90 days).
- Usage per unit of time: how often do users come back to the service.

Referral indicators:

- Virality: percentage of users sharing the service or parts of the service.

Revenue indicators:

- Customer acquisition cost: how much does the platform pay to attract one paying customer.
- Customer lifetime value: how much is a user worth from the moment they subscribe to the service to the moment they cancel the subscription.
- Upsell average value: average value of the upsell of the premium feature (if applicable to the business model).

87

Two sided marketplaces (e.g. eBay, UBER)

Acquisition indicators:

- Number of buyer accounts created per unit of time: how many accounts are created by users interested in becoming buyers on the platform.
- Buyer growth rate: how many new buyers are being attracted.
- Buyer acquisition cost: how much is being spent to have a visitor create a buyer account.
- Number of sellers accounts created per unit of time: how many accounts are created by users interested in becoming sellers on the platform.
- Seller growth rate: how many sellers are being attracted.
- Seller acquisition cost: how much is being spent to have a visitor create a seller account.

Activation indicators:

- First buyer engagement rate: percentage of acquired buyers making the first purchase.
- First seller engagement rate: percentage of acquired sellers listing the first product or service.

Retention indicators:

- Buyer visit rate per unit of time: how often do buyers come back to the platform in a unit of time (usually per week).

Referral indicators:

Revenue indicators:

- Seller visit rate per unit of time: how often do sellers come back to the platform in a unit of time (usually per week).
- Inventory growth: the rate at which sellers are adding inventory such as new listings.
- Search effectiveness: what buyers are searching for, and whether it matches the inventory you are buying.
- Transactions made per unit of time: number of transactions made between buyers and sellers in a specific unit of time.
- Buyer churn rate: how many buyers stop visiting the platform in a unit of time (usually computed for 90 days).
- Seller churn rate: how many sellers stop visiting the platform in a unit of time (usually computed for 90 days).
- Number of purchases per unit of time.
- Number of sales per unit of time.

- Shared items: number of listings which are shared outside the platform.
- Ratings: the percentage of ratings from buyers to sellers and vice versa.

- Buyer lifetime value: how much is the platform making on average from a buyer during its entire time on the platform.
- Seller lifetime value: how much is the platform making on average from a seller during its entire time on the platform.
- Average purchase size per unit of time: on average how big is the typical transaction in a unit of time.

89

User generated content platforms (e.g. Medium, Twitter, Facebook):

Acquisition indicators:

- Number of unique visitors per unit of time.
- Visitors acquisition costs: how much does the platform pay to acquire a unique visitor.
- User conversion rate: percentage of visitors creating an account.
- User acquisition cost: how much does the platform pay to acquire a unique user.

Activation indicators:

- First engagement rate: percentage of users who interacted with the content first time.
- First generated content rate: percentage of users who created a first piece of content (e.g. uploaded a picture, created a post, wrote an article).

Retention indicators:

- Number of engaged visitors in unit of time: how often do visitors come back and how much time do they spend.
- Churn rate.
- Notification effectiveness: the percentage of users who, when told something by a push notification, email newsletter or other vehicles, act on it.

Referral indicators:

- Content sharing and virality: how much and how often does content get shared and what are the implications for growth.

Revenue indicators:

- Value of created content: how much is the content worth for the website, in terms of advertising or donations.
- Page impressions: how many page impressions are generated per unit of time.
- Ad impressions: how many ads are being viewed per unit of time.
- Ad inverter: number of ads the platform is displaying.
- Ad rate: how much is being generated from an ad.
- Content/advertising balance: the balance of ad inventory rates and content that maximizes overall performance.

91

Free apps:

Acquisition indicators:

- Number of downloads in a unit of time: how many people have downloaded the app.
- Launch rate: the percentage of people who download the app actually launch it.
- Account creation rate (if needed): the percentage of people that created an account from the ones that launched the app.
- User acquisition cost: how much does it cost to attract a new user.

Activation indicators:

- First engagement rate: percentage of users that had a first interaction with the app.

Retention indicators:

- Open rate per unit of time (usually week): how many times do users open the app in a given unit of time.
- Churn.

Referral indicators:

- Virality: on average how many other users does a user invite.

Revenue indicators:

- Paying user conversion rate: percentage of free users that have made an in-app purchase or converted to the paying version of the app if available.
- Paying users acquisition cost: how much does it cost to get a paying user.
- Upsell average value: average value of the upsell of the premium feature (if applicable to the business model).
- Monthly recurring revenue (MRR): this is taken from both purchases and watched ads. Typically, this also included app-specific information - such as which screens or items encourage the most purchases. Also look at your average revenue per paying user (ARPPU). The MRR can be later aggregated to ARR - annual recurring revenue.

- Free user lifetime value: how much is a user worth from the moment they create an account to the moment they uninstall the app.
- Paying user lifetime value.
- Ad impressions: how many ads are being viewed per unit of time (if applicable).
- Ad inverter: number of ads the platform is displaying (if applicable).
- Ad rate: how much is being generated from an ad (if applicable).

93

Media & entertainment platforms (e.g. The New York Times, YouTube)

Acquisition indicators:

- Audience size per unit of time: how many people visit the website in a unit of time, be it day, week, month.
- Audience acquisition cost: how much does the platform spend to attract one viewer.

Activation indicators:

- First engagement rate: percentage of users who interacted with the content first time (e.g. read the first article on the platform, watched the first video).

Retention indicators:

- Loyalty: how many people keep on visiting the website.
- Visits per unit of time: how often does the audience return to the platform in a unit of time (usually per week).

Referral indicators:

- Content sharing and virality: how much and how often does content get shared and what are the implications for growth.

Revenue indicators:

- Ad inventory: the number of impressions that can be monetized.
- Ad rates: sometimes measured in cost per engagement - essentially how much a site can make from those impressions based on the content it covers and the people who visit.
- Click-through rates: how many of the impressions actually turn into money.
- Content/advertising balance: the balance of ad inventory rates and content that maximizes overall performance.
- Paying user conversion rate: number of users converting from free users to paying users (if applicable).
- Paying user lifetime value (if applicable).

95

"Brick and mortar" business models

(e.g. dealership, retail shop, bank branch, dental clinic)

Acquisition indicators:

- Number of visitors.
- Number of visitors from physical channels (e.g. billboards and store front).
- Number of visitors from digital channels (e.g. ads on social media and search engines).
- Visitor acquisition cost: how much did it cost to attract one visitor.

Activation indicators:

- Customer conversion: number of visitors that purchase the product/service.
- Customer acquisition cost: how much did it cost to attract one buyer.

Retention indicators:

- Net Promoter Score.
- Participating in a loyalty scheme.
- Percentage of returning customers from the people that interacted with your offering once.
- Average duration of a visit.
- Average time between visits.
- Average time to service the customer.

Referral indicators:

- Net Promoter Score.
- Number of visitors and customers that came because of a recommendation from someone in their network.
- Number of customers that leave a positive review in relevant media (e.g. local newspapers or Tripadvisor).

Revenue indicators:

- Average spending per visit.
- Up-sell conversion: number of customers that buy additional products and services.
- Life-time value of a customer: how much does a customer spend over a longer period of time (e.g. 5–10 years).

97

Create your own AARRR framework:

We know there are many more business models out there than the ones we have shown you. And it would therefore be impossible for us to create an AARRR example for every single business model. So instead, we would like to show you how we would approach creating an AARRR from scratch. This process is really business model agnostic. For the metric framework to work, there is a simple rule to help you along. Numbers that can only "go up and to the right" do not help you in changing your product for the better. We like to call them Vanity Metrics. For example, the total number of signups since the beginning of your project is a Vanity Metric. The number can only increase over time. Good metrics are comparable. Comparable across cohorts, to metrics in the past or to other clients or customers, for example.

Acquisition Indicators:

For the acquisitions phase of the funnel we look at how users are getting in. For this stage, as with the consequent ones, you can add as many indicators as you want. However we encourage you to select these indicators based on the user's journey and only focus on the most relevant ones. The most relevant indicators for this stage need to answer these questions:

- How do we know that potential customers find your offering?
- How do we know the potential customers are liking the promise of the value proposition?

The essential metric here is the one for the action that shows potential customers buying in the promise of the value propositions. For this (and any other indicator) to work and be actionable you need to get enough relevant people in front of the promise. In some cases the acquisition action can mean creating an account. In other cases, it means downloading an app or even accepting a call with a sales representative or scanning a QR code.

Activation Indicators:

For the activation stage, the indicators you have to track are the ones answering the following question:

- How do we know that the potential customers have interacted with our offering's core value proposition for the first time?

Essentially, here you would like to see if users are carrying out the actions required of them to interact for the first time with your value proposition. This means that they should be carrying out your core activity at least once. In some complex solutions, users need to perform multiple actions to be considered activated; they need to perform multiple actions for you to conclude that they have been exposed to the value proposition of your solution.

Retention Indicators:

Moving on the retention indicators. Here you are trying to see if the audience has repeated interactions with your offering's value proposition. In other words, are they coming back to do it again? To create the right indicators for your business model in this phase try to answer the following questions:

- What are the actions that tell us that our audience likes our value proposition?
- How do we know they are consuming our value proposition on a constant basis?

Referral Indicators:

Lastly, in the referral phase of the model, you are looking at indicators that paint a clear picture of the audience spreading the word about your value proposition. Some business models rely heavily on referrals while in others this is less important. When designing your framework, for this phase, you need indicators that answer the following questions:

- How do we know that people are spreading the word about our offering?
- What is telling us that people were impressed with our value proposition and want others to know about it?

Revenue Indicators:

The revenue phase of the AARRR framework is pretty straightforward. Here you have to have indicators that are telling you about a certain financial exchange happening with your audience. Basically, you would like to see indicators here that are telling you if people buy your solution and/or if they place a monetary value on your core value proposition.

Bear in mind that, depending on the business model, the AARRR phases might come in a different order. Consider for example a fashion brand that's only selling online. In their user journey Revenue precedes Activation because customers have to buy the garment before interacting with it for the first time. The same is true for the business model of the book you are holding. First of all, you had to pay for it before you actually interacted with the content.

If your business model is a mix of any of the above, you need to consider mixing some of the measures. But the idea stays the same: the measurements need to tell you if the business model has the potential for becoming reputable, sustainable and scalable. Any breakdowns in the funnel might indicate an issue that, unless resolved, might be fatal for the business model in question.

Another important thing worth mentioning is that for the funnels we always encourage product teams to use Cohort Analysis. Other than looking at all users as one unit, a Cohort Analysis breaks them into related groups. These related groups, or cohorts, usually share common characteristics or experiences within a defined time-span.[61] Cohort Analysis allows a product team to see patterns clearly across the lifecycle of a customer (or user group), rather than slicing across all customers blindly without accounting for the natural cycle that a customer undergoes.[62]

App Launched	users	% of active users after app launch						
		Wk 0	1	2	3	4	5	6
April 3	1098	100%	33.9%	23.5%	18.7%	15.9%	16.3%	
April 10	1358	100%	31.1%	18.6%	14.3%	16.0%	14.9%	12
April 17	1257	100%	27.2%	19.6%	14.5%	12.9%	13.4%	
April 24	068	100%	24.7%	16.9%	15.8%	14.8%		
May 1	1758	100%	26.2%	20.4%	16.9%			
May 8	1824	100%	26.4%	18.1%				
May 15	110		3%					

Retention over user lifetime

Retention over product lifetime

On a word of warning, beware relying on external benchmark data unless it is fully understood and scoped. Benchmark data can be dependent on industry sector rather than a business model and can therefore mislead. For example, a subscription business model may remain unchanged across sectors whereas customer engagement will differ substantially from one sector to another.

With all these metrics to track and be aware of, it's easy for product teams to lose focus or become chaotic. In the 2013 book, "*Lean Analytics*," Alistar Croll and Benjamin Yoskowitz introduced the concept of the One Metric that Matters. In short, the discipline of One Metric That Matters, or OMTM for short, prescribes teams finding and picking a single metric or measurement that is incredibly important for the specific maturity phase of their respective business model. According to Alistar and Benjamin, this offers the teams 3 major benefits, helping them to answer the most important question they have at that time:

- Forcing the team to draw clear lines in the sand and have clear goals.
- Inspiring a culture of experimentation.
- Enabling other stakeholders to focus on the key issue that the team is trying to solve.

Some years ago we were working with a product team in the space of media and news. The team was in charge of a mobile app that they had been trying to get off the ground for more than a year before we stepped in. The first thing we did upon taking on this engagement was to set up an AARRR framework for the product. Once data started rolling in, we realized that one of the major issues the product had was very poor numbers on usage per week and a high churn. Users were coming to the app on average 1.2 to 2 times per week and by the end of 90 days about 90% of the users had either stopped coming altogether or deleted the app.

101

There were other issues we identified with the app too, but these two stuck out for us above all the others. And the churn was particularly important as when we stepped in, the team was about to roll out a massive marketing campaign; to which we argued the contrary, remembering an old, well-known saying in the ad biz that goes something like this: "Nothing kills a bad product faster than good advertising."

Basically, with a high churn number (90%) all of the advertising budget would have amounted to a very small number of users 90 days from the campaign; making the user acquisition cost huge. Therefore we convinced the team and the stakeholders to first focus on the usage per week indicator. Once that was above a certain pre-agreed limit, we would focus on churn. And once that dropped significantly, we would be able to pull the trigger on the advertising campaign.

Having the team focus on only one indicator at a time allowed us to run very clear experiments targeted at only moving the needle on that one single indicator. Since now there was only one indicator on everyone's mind, the team created an idea basket, where everyone from the team was able to throw in ideas on how to improve that indicator. This had a great effect on team culture as everyone had developed a sense of purpose and everyone felt they were listened to. From the intern to the product owner and from the testers to the designers, everyone contributed with ideas.

Many failed experiments later, the team was actually able to learn a great deal about their users and had changed the two indicators to the desired level. In the process the product also became the most engaging product in its category in that particular geography.

Sustain: Business as usual

The **Sustain** stage of the Product Lifecycle is most of the time associated in popular culture with business as usual. Here we see mature business models that the company has been offering for years. The emphasis at this stage is on profitability and efficiency. Therefore the result indicators are very much financially focused. However the performance indicators need to reflect the peculiarities of the critical success factors of the business model, the value creation process, and the profit model.

To illustrate this we are going to use a story told by David Parmenter in his "*Key Performance Indicators*" book. A distribution company's CEO realized that a critical success factor for the business was for trucks to leave as close to capacity as possible. A large truck, capable of carrying more than 40 tons, was being sent out with small loads because dispatch managers were focusing on delivering every item on time to customers.

Each day by 9 A.M. the CEO received a report of those trucks that had been sent out with an inadequate load the previous day. The CEO called the dispatch manager and asked whether any action had taken place to see if the customer could have accepted the delivery on a different date that would have enabled better utilization of the trucks. In most cases, the customer could have received it earlier or later, fitting in with a past or future truck going in that direction. The impact on profitability was significant.

An important thing to note about experimenting and use of data is that experimentation doesn't end when a business model reaches, or is in, the Sustain phase. Continuous improvement and incremental innovation are constantly needed to keep the business model profitable. With this in mind the teams need to be able to quickly generate qualitative understanding of customer-desired improvements and then quantitatively explore potential solutions. In essence the teams need to be able to learn qualitatively and validate quantitatively.

In the following chapter we will be looking at the way the data from individual teams is being aggregated, therefore showing the performance of the entire innovation funnel. Also we will be looking at the decision making mechanisms that companies need to have in place to kill unperforming ideas while investing only in the most promising ones.

Sustain

103

Exercise - Creating your company's Product Lifecycle

In this chapter we have talked about the importance of a Product Lifecycle in the context of measuring innovation. Product Lifecycles are company specific and they need to talk to the peculiarities of each company, as you have seen in this chapter.

The most important parts of a Product Lifecycle are the critical success factors for each stage. The critical success factors are things that every idea needs to have in place in order to be successful in the market (e.g. solving a customer problem or addressing a customer need). These factors are industry specific, however some commonalities can be observed.

The critical success factors are related to the focus of validation of a specific stage. Having a clear focus at each stage will help the teams focus their work and will help the managers ask the right question for the maturity stage of each specific idea. The last point is important as critical success factors need to be addressed in a time-ordered manner (e.g. a team needs to validate customer-need before they can proceed to see if the price point they want to sell at is acceptable).

As a Product Lifecycle is specific to each company, creating one starts by determining the key success factors new ideas in your company have to pass to be successful in the market.

It makes sense to select from the company's existing portfolio one or two ideas to do some forensic work on. These ideas need to be in the exploit phase (business as usual); ideas where the main emphasis is on efficiency. However you should only consider the ideas that made it to this phase in the past 2 or (maximum) 3 years.

Make sure the ideas you are analyzing are representative of your company.

#1 Run interviews with the product owners of these ideas or with their steering group. Ask the idea team, what were the things that made the idea successful? What boxes did the idea check before it reached the sustain phase? Here we would advise you to focus on both external factors as well as internal ones, but in general only consider the ones that were in the team's power to influence. For example, "the team was able to secure internal financing" is not a critical success factor. This is more a consequence of the team doing certain actions or providing certain evidence that helped them secure that investment (e.g. the team got 3 letters of intent). Also discard answers that are very specific to that one idea.

We would advise you to capture one big idea per sticky note.

You can consider speaking with "failed" ideas too. Ask them what prevented them from reaching the sustain phase. If you get to this detective work on two to five ideas, you can already start spotting patterns.

#2 Translate the things you have captured in critical success factors. For example, move from a statement such as "we had piloted the idea successfully with some clients before selling it to the mass market" to a success factor such as "prove that the customers accept the solution as a remedy to their "problem." Try to simplify the language as much as possible and keep the notes short.

#3 Proceed to drawing up a timeline on a white board. Now place the success factors on this timeline starting from left to right in the order of occurrence. See if any of the sticky notes can be clustered. Bear in mind that certain industries might have different orders for their critical success factors on the timeline. Take for example pharma where legal compliance needs to happen sooner than in other industries such fashion.

#4 In addition to this or in case you don't have any ideas to run forensics work on, follow these steps before continuing to step 5:

You could also look at the Business Model Canvas, Value Proposition Canvas and/or the Lean Canvas and look at their specific building blocks. Determine which building blocks are critical to have validated for your company. Decide what building blocks are relevant and should be focused on before others.

- Write down all the relevant building blocks, or segments, on separate post-it notes.
- Determine which 2 or 3 building blocks should have focus in the first step. We are not excluding the rest of the building blocks, we are merely trying to determine focus for each stage. For teams to understand where to start, as well as being able to ask the right questions at the right time.
- Now do the same for the rest of the building blocks one stage at a time. Discuss what segments should be the focus of each stage. Never use a post-it note twice.

If this means that it is important to zoom in to a building block to determine more focus, or have a different focus of the segment in a next stage, agree on breaking a building block up into separate segments. But be careful with doing this too often. Remember the customer segment problem example.

If you have plotted all the building blocks onto hierarchical stages, look at the whole framework and discuss if this order makes sense. You cannot test a revenue model if there is no solution experiment to test with.

#5 Separate the stages and name them. To do that, see if you have sticky notes that are similar in context. If you are able to group them, they become a phase in the Product Lifecycle. With this done you can go ahead and name the phases.

#6 The last step is made up of translating the information on the sticky notes to questions that teams can answer through their work. This will come in handy for the Venture Board work we are going to talk about in the next chapter.

What you have in front of you now is your company's Product Lifecycle with clear guidelines for teams to focus on.

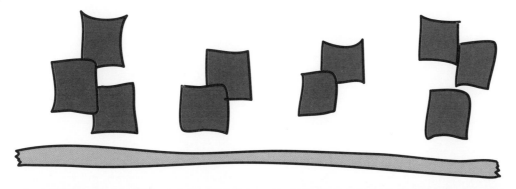

Before rolling the framework out however, we would advise you to consult other literature on the topic and see if you missed any critical success factors. Books like "*The Lean Product Lifecycle*" by Craig Strong, Sonja Kresojevi and Tendyi Viki; "*Four Steps to the Epiphany*" by Steve Blank or "*Product Roadmap Relaunched*" by Todd Lombardo, Bruce McCharty, Evan Ryan and Mchael Conors are great resources on this topic.

Another framework you can consider using to develop your company's Product Lifecycle is The NEXT Framework by Esther Gons and Timan Rebel

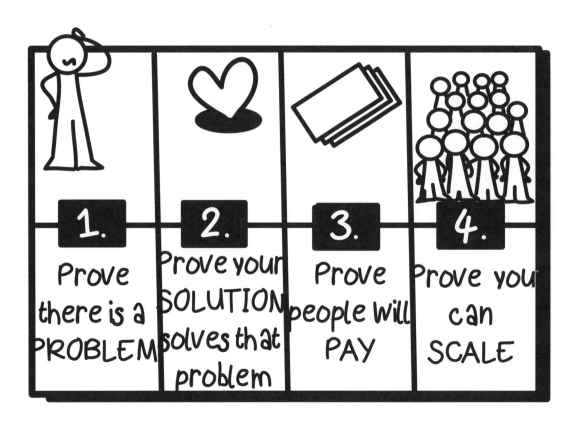

1. Prove there is a PROBLEM

2. Prove your SOLUTION solves that problem

3. Prove people will PAY

4. Prove you can SCALE

This framework was developed over time specifically for startup teams that struggled with what relevant segments needed to be looked at first and why. This resulted in a Framework with four stages, each with two building blocks to focus on:

1. Prove there is a problem

- **Customer Segment**

  Who are you solving a problem for? The smaller and more homogeneous the better. You can more easily solve their similar huge problem. In the Scale phase, you will expand the customer segment to adjacent customer segments with similar problems.

- **Problem**

  What problem is your customer experiencing? Is it a vitamin or a pain killer and is it big enough to build a solution for?

2. Prove your solution solves that problem

- **Job to be Done**

  What is your customer trying to achieve? The job to be done describes why your customer might buy from you, because the reason we hire services or buy products depends on our goals and the context that we currently live in.

- **Solution**

  How are you solving the problem of your customer and how are you fulfilling their job to be done? What type of solution do you want to build, and which features are most important?

3. Prove they will pay

- **Value Proposition**

  What value are you bringing to your customer with your solution? Even when you get the solution right, you still need to bring value for the customer to pay for your solution. You want to be Notion and not MS Word.

- **Revenue Model**

  How will you make money? A subscription or one-off payments? Who is your customer and who is only using your solution?

4. Prove you can scale

- **Channels**

  How will you reach your customer now you are scaling? Will that be outbound or inbound? Social or paid advertising? This is closely linked to how you will make money.

- **Growth Engine**

  How will you grow? Will you grow via paid advertising, repeated use, or word of mouth?

Keep in mind;

De-risking a business model is not a linear process.
Although the four stages from great ideas to scale are directional, using a Framework is not a linear process.
Validating the Job to be Done and Solution, does not mean that you don't have to look back at the Problem and Customer Segment. You are now trying to solve a puzzle with 4 pieces instead of 2. All pieces need to fit together to be able to scale.

CUSTOMER SEGMENT	JOB-TO-BE-DONE	VALUE PROPOSITION	CHANNELS
1 PROVE THERE IS A PROBLEM	**2** PROVE YOUR SOLUTION SOLVES THAT PROBLEM	**3** PROVE THEY WILL PAY	**4** PROVE YOU CAN SCALE
PROBLEM	SOLUTION	REVENUE	GROWTH

108

published under creative commons license by NEXT Amsterdam

https://next.amsterdam/canvas

Download the worksheet here

NEXT
AMSTERDAM

The abstraction principle starts with the Indicators in Tactical Innovation Accounting

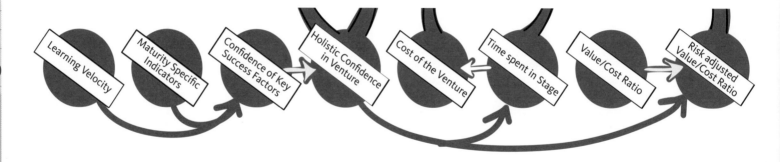

An innovation accounting system requires the company to have a clear Product Lifecycle (innovation framework) in place.

A Product Lifecycle will help teams focus on the most relevant assumptions that they need to tackle at each maturity level. At the same time having a framework in place will help the manager ask the right question at the right time.

You need to recognize both result indicators as well as performance indicators at every stage of the innovation framework. Performance indicators should offer data on how well a team is honoring the innovation process, while result indicators should offer data regarding the actual results of the team.

Conversations on Innovation

Clarissa Eva Leon

Head of Digital, Danske Statsbaner (DSB)

As an experienced transformation leader with an agile mindset, Clarissa is helping the Danish Railroad company (DSB) reach their growth goals in an increasingly digital world. A veteran of her company's commitment to the future, she set up the company's digital labs more than 4 years ago and has been leading it ever since.

Innovation Accounting: When you started the transformation journey in DBS, we suspect that some stakeholders were interested in getting numbers around innovation teams' progress. What were the initial indicators you were using?

Clarissa Eva Leon: Actually the beginning was a bit different. The first thing we did was to align on the vision and the strategy for our digital innovation journey. In particular aligning the goals of the digital labs with the overall strategic objectives of the company. Only once that was in place and agreed on by everyone, we started having conversations around indicators and measurements.

But since everyone was so new to the whole idea of innovation and in particular digital innovation in our company, we sat together and discussed what kind of indicators we should put in place. Our main concern was around putting indicators in place that won't trigger the wrong behavior.

So, what we agreed on in the beginning was to look at time-to-X type of indicators. Time-to-X we thought were relevant indicators since the expectations from the leadership level were to be fast and inspire others to buy-into a new mindset.

Therefore the primary indicators of the lab became time-to-insight, time-to-market, time-to-value. And then, on top of the time-to-X indicators we had NPS (Net Promoter Score) and something called "the problem owner satisfaction score." The problem owner satisfaction score worked very well in the context of core innovation where a leader of a business in DSB would take the role of the problem owner, while those in the labs were the solution owners.

IA: What have you learned using these indicators?

CEL: In the beginning we were very happy with our time-to-X indicators. However, soon one thing was becoming pretty apparent: we were not using them the right way. I'm not saying that the indicators were not good, on the contrary. What I'm saying is that we used them as "lines in the sand" or goal-setting instead of "self-benchmarks."

This type of use was triggering the wrong behavior. We were forcing teams to stick to predefined time-to-insight numbers and this had some repercussions on team behavior. At one point I remember we had to do a lot of overtime to get an idea to hit on the time-to-market "line in the sand"; and this was not the right thing to do.

But I guess these experiences made us better; more mature if you want.

Today we still use our time-to-X indicators. But as warning signals or self-benchmarks. We observe the time-to-X indicators for every team and in case they fall outside our benchmark we investigate further. In some cases the problems the teams are trying to tackle are too complex and require more time than usual. Or in other cases we can direct more training and coaching towards some teams.

But I think that our biggest lesson was around focusing on outcomes rather than just measuring the process. In some cases we don't even communicate the time-to-X indicators to the teams, for two reasons. We are either afraid that they will focus on the time-to-X instead of the outcome, or this might make them game the measurement only to be below the benchmark.

So now, as our transformation is gaining momentum inside the company, we are very much outcomes, results driven. Our teams have started using OKRs and this is helping them not to lose sight of the outcomes the ideas need to deliver on.

That would also be my advice for anyone doing this kind of innovation work. Focus on the outcome; always have conversations that point to the outcomes. I think you can achieve it in a lot of different ways. You can set up different indicators or different systems to measure progress but if you don't have that talk around which outcome or value you want to create, it can nudge a wrong behavior. In our shift toward outcomes, we can already see that it's triggering a different behavior than before. To summarize, I would advise anyone to never lose sight of the outcomes, the progress indicators are good but they should not dictate the conversation nor the actions.

IA: Tell us more about your outcome indicators, please. Do you have any particular ones you use more than others?

CEL: There are three things we do with respect to the outcome indicators. First of all we set a yearly ambition on the outcome we want to achieve across all labs (the long term strategy and the vision of the digital labs set the frame for this work). This gives every member of the labs an overarching goal and sense of belonging as we are all "in the same boat" even though we are working in different teams. The teams then set quarterly OKR's on how to achieve the yearly ambition. We use these to follow the progress on a weekly basis.

Then we adapt them case by case, venture by venture, if you want. If our process indicator, the time-to-X are pretty much one-size-fits-all, in terms of using them for every venture. The outcome indicators are very contextualized to each venture. Some outcomes are financial in nature, others are less tangible.

The other thing we do with respect to the outcome indicators is to adapt them to the maturity of each venture. Basically, depending where a venture is in the funnel we might have different "local" outcomes we expect of them. Obviously there is this yearly ambition outcome the teams are aiming to achieve but for a specific moment in the pipeline we either look at other outcomes or we look at indicators that prove that the team is on track to achieve the major outcome it was set up to achieve.

So it's difficult for me to tell you exactly what indicators we use as they vary from team to team. And my advice to other companies would be the same: set a yearly ambition linked to the overall strategy and vision, adapt the outcomes to each venture and always be mindful of the maturity of the idea.

IA: How often do you evaluate the progress of the ideas?

CEL: We have facilitated dialogues with the teams and in the leadership group every week. And we don't do that just to measure progress but we do it because we want to make sure they get the right amount of help, such as coaching, personal/professional development or removal of any sort of blockers.

I think that meeting them any rarer than once a week will have an impact on both outcomes and the time-to-X indicators.

Also we evaluate the teams hitting the OKR goals, on average, every quarter.

Where the strategy meets the market.

CHAPTER 5
Managerial Innovation Accounting

This chapter wouldn't have been possible without the contribution of our friend and colleague Bruno Pešec

In the last chapter we started to answer some key questions including "can we build this," "can we scale this" and most importantly of all "is this what the customer wants, and will they buy the product." Along the way we introduced a range of measures and indicators which would not only answer those questions but also help to drive projects forward.

But that's only the start of the process. Measuring innovation at a granular level may deliver the basic structure of your innovation effort but by itself it won't deliver a viable innovation accounting system.

Organizations do though need to be realistic about the way in which detail and data weave into the innovation ecosystem. You don't want stakeholders to be kept in the dark and therefore unable to make key strategy decisions. Equally, there is no reason for executives to be bombarded with the sort of detail which rightly should be devolved to those further down the information chain. Get the balance wrong and you could paralyze the organization with data overload.

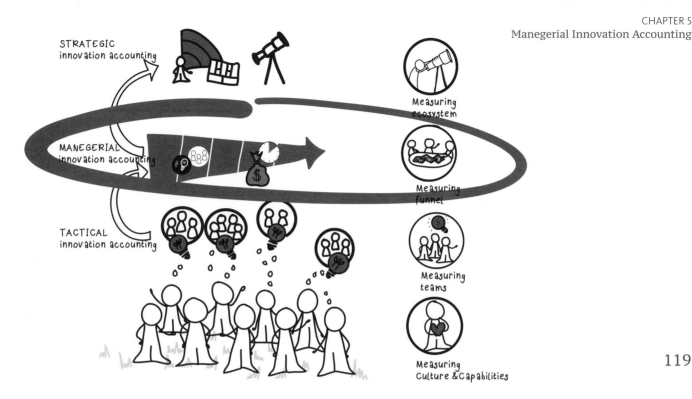

STRATEGIC
innovation accounting

MANEGERIAL
innovation accounting

TACTICAL
innovation accounting

Measuring
ecosystem

Measuring
funnel

Measuring
teams

Measuring
Culture & Capabilities

That's where managerial Innovation Accounting comes into its own, diffusing the oxygen of innovation around the corporate body. So, on the one hand it acts as a filter; providing key stakeholders with the information they need to understand the progress and performance of innovation within the organization (the abstraction principle we spoke about earlier). On the other, by targeting information appropriately it enables better and faster decision making.

This then is where we truly start to experience the benefit of innovation when viewed as a discipline to be mastered and managed.[34]

Try to think of innovation in terms of an elite sports team or a stunning piece of art. What you see is energizing and inspiring; but that's only achieved by hard work and attention to metrics and detail. In exactly the same way, innovation accounting systems require knowledge (education) and inspiration but, above all else, focus and discipline. If knowledge and discipline are lacking from the process of measuring innovation, the creativity and hard work put in by innovators are to no avail.

There is, of course, far more to entrepreneurship than systematic innovation; distinct entrepreneurial strategies, for example, and the principles of entrepreneurial management. But if you truly want your organization to succeed through innovation then system and targeted measurement have to sit at the heart of the enterprise, enabling the organization not only to live but also to breathe innovation success.

Investing in innovation

It's time perhaps for a cautionary tale; an example of what can go wrong when you measure for measurement's sake rather than contextualizing measurements.

We were called on by a European financial services company which had a few initiatives in the pipeline, none of which seemed to be progressing. Observing the innovation process in action, some things became very apparent to us. Bi-weekly meetings between the board, line managers, and innovation teams were run on a command and control basis. Teams were asked to measure progress against a series of identifiers, few of which were designed to move projects forward.

More worryingly, those running the initiatives saw their prime goal in terms of continuing to justify their existence, diverting resources to prepare for the review meetings. This reached a head when only one project remained. It then became the innovation mascot which couldn't be killed with board members increasing their intervention levels in a bid to somehow keep it alive.

This cautionary tale comes to underline again how difficult it is to see positive results from investment in innovation if the structure, the processes and indicators are misaligned.

So what's the solution? In our opinion, one of the most important actions companies can undertake to exponentially increase the likelihood of seeing results from their investments in innovation is the deployment of Venture Boards.

A Venture Board is a group of people in an organization who are in charge of a company's (or department's) innovation funnel. They are tasked with taking investment/divestment decisions on a constant basis and putting into practice the company's Innovation Thesis by only allowing in the funnel ideas that align with the strategy. Basically this group of people needs to bring into the company the Venture Capital mindset, by acting as the company's internal Venture Capital fund.

Before taking an in-depth look at Venture Boards it is perhaps worth diving briefly into Venture Capital funds with a particular emphasis on managing expectations.

Investing in breakthrough innovation is anything but a sure bet. If you allow as a comparison, it's the exact opposite of real estate investment. In the words of Fred Wilson, co-founder of Union Square Ventures, a successful New York based VC fund that has invested over the years in companies like Twitter, Kickstarter or Etsy "an ideal target for an investment portfolio is: '1/3, 1/3, 1/3,' which means that we expect to lose our entire investment on 1/3 of our investments, we expect to get our money back (or maybe make a small return) on 1/3 of our investments, and we expect to generate the bulk of our returns on 1/3 of our investments."

That's quite an optimistic viewpoint. Another Venture Capital company, Correlation Ventures, revealed that 65% of investment projects failed to deliver a return on capital. Perhaps more interestingly, only 4% of projects produced a return of 10x or more and only 10% produced a return of 5x or more.[63] That's the first lesson for innovation leaders; not all projects will succeed and if you want success you have to be prepared for failure along the way. The second lesson is that no one can select the winners, therefore many small investments are advisable instead of a few large ones.

Distribution of US Venture Returns

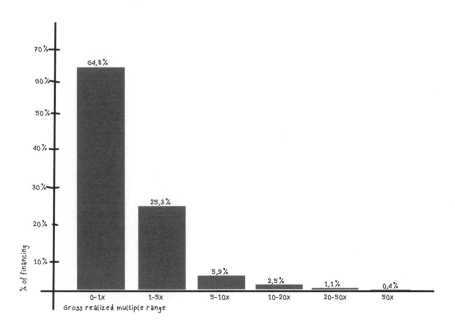

Now, admitting defeat is difficult, no doubt about it; particularly if it leads to personal doubts or fear of failure. The solution is to build an innovation culture which promotes the message that "what did you learn?" is as important a question as "what did you achieve?" and that failure is a necessary part of innovation life. As in Venture Capital, it's a portfolio game; pivot ventures when they need to pivot and shut them Down and relocate the capital when they aren't panning out.[64]

With that in mind, we're now going to move on to look at the Venture Board concept in depth; its structure, personnel and lifecycle. When you are moving on through this chapter, we recommend that you do so with two key areas in mind. Firstly, the concept of failure as an integral aspect of innovation, as outlined above. Secondly, the way in which appropriate and targeted funding can impact outcomes.

Essentially, for the Venture Board concept to work, the company needs to implement metered funding. As described by Eric Ries in *"The Startup Way,"* metered funding follows a start-up funding pathway. Ideas requiring funding are presented to decision makers, who allocate funding over a series of rounds. The funding is based on goals and milestones. In the early stages of funding, funding is learning based, and in the latter stages, funding is growth based.

In other words, at the early stages of the Product Lifecycle, investments are likely to be more weighted towards providing the team with the time to identify, research and run experiments. As the idea progresses, investments are likely to swing more towards the material, requiring investment in equipment, development and so on.

The Venture Board

So how do we structure a Venture Board which champions and drives innovation whilst at the same time being prepared to shut down unviable projects? There is no single right answer with board balance having to take into account the specific requirements of the organization and the innovation context.

As with Company Boards, representation and diversity are crucial as more people bring in more perspective in the decision making process. Richard Warr and his colleagues at NC State's Poole College of Management Gender looked at the hiring policies of the 3,000 largest publicly traded companies in the United States to see if companies with a diverse workforce were better at developing innovative products and services.[65]

According to Warr, one of the reasons diverse teams are more innovative is that they have a broader range of interests, experiences, and backgrounds to draw upon. They understand potential users of products better than less diverse teams and they tend to be better problem-solvers too.[66]

In a similar vein, Accenture Research on equality and innovation revealed that the innovation mindset is six times higher in the most equal cultures than in the least equal ones. So structuring an equal and diverse Venture Board could help to promote innovation across the organization.

124   Let's now start with a look at the Venture Board **leader**. In most cases this person is the one that's ultimately responsible for the implementation of the innovation strategy within the company or business unit. You might see a Vice President of Innovation here or a Head of (Digital) Products. Whatever the role, the leader should have enough seniority to report at board level and to champion innovation across the organization.

Appointing an **external representative** to the Venture Board brings an extra dimension to the debate. This person could be an experienced manager in another department of the company or someone drawn from outside of the organization who ideally has experience investing in startups. The role of this person is to bring an outside-in perspective, and if they come from the Venture Capital world provide more insight on how investors go about investing in startups.

The advantage is not only the specific expertise and fresh perspective the person might bring to the table but also the simple fact that it is sometimes easier for an outsider to suggest a tough decision. Internal people have a more natural tendency to be too kind to each other and not to "kill their darlings." The consequence of the latter being many "zombie" projects that keep muddling around but don't scale, scale too fast, and so on.

Having someone from another business unit within the company taking the role of an external expert will help provide cross-pollination. Furthermore, if that person is a member of another Venture Board, this might reassure teams that there is wider company interest in their project. Essentially this is solving the problem that we call: the only Venture Capital in the world problem. It is common practice in the startup world to be turned down by several investors before you land an investment round.

But the question is what would happen if you were to live in a world with only one VC investor? Can you see yourself thriving in such an environment? How many from today's most popular startups would have gone out of business in such a world? If you are an entrepreneur seeking capital to further develop your baby (business idea) you are going to knock on as many doors as it takes to get the cash. Luck might be on your side and you only need to knock once but at least you have the luxury of having more than one door to knock at. On the other hand, if

you are an intrapreneur there's only one door to knock at: your bosses. For intrapreneurs the boss might represent the only VC in their world.

126 Another important role in a Venture Board is that of the **innovation manager**; a role which brings experience and practicality to the table. We have seen instances where this role was taken by the line manager. This works as line managers are the ones that will ultimately make the time investment in the teams - giving teams the necessary time to work on their idea. This is particularly important for the early stages of the venture and for companies that prefer having teams not commit full time to their ideas early on.

Alternatively the innovation manager could be a head innovation coach or someone else in the company who has extensive experience of building new ventures, or of bringing new ideas to market. Having this person on the Venture Board allows for coaching to take place during the meeting. With their experience they can guide the teams better, coaching them and making suggestions for possible next development actions.

The role of innovation manager can also be viewed as an internal company diplomat role. The person in this role should ideally (on top of the attributes described above) be very well connected in the company with years of experience. Their connections and experience should smooth the path for the team to interact with other departments or functions.

Lastly, all Venture Board meetings should have a **domain expert** present. This person is not a permanent member of the Venture Board but the position is. The position of domain expert is important to make sure ideas can be developed and the team is not missing any critical aspects of that particular market. The person in this position is a veteran in their field.

For example, if during a Venture Board meeting in a bank the ideas being reviewed touch on the use of biometrics, an expert in the field of biometrics or data security is needed. Some meetings might require two or more domain experts, particularly if legal or financial requirements come into play.

Another thing you could consider for the Venture Board, is inviting an **executive** into the meeting. It is not reasonable to expect this person to have time to attend every meeting but when a promising idea requires a more significant investment round, say it wants to move from the Scale stage to the Sustain stage, having at least one C-level person in the meeting helps. They may well be able to move the project forward, answering questions around spin-off, team composition or the integration of the idea into a particular business unit portfolio.

127

No matter how many people you ultimately have on your Venture Board(s) or how you are going to name their roles, it is key to always include on your Venture Board one or more individuals within the following areas:

- Resource: allocating resources such as: time, money, access to customers, sales force and distribution channels.
- HR: helping ideas have the right skill mix.
- Sponsor or Patron. Someone who is interested in the integration of the ideas with a/the business unit. This particular role is key for companies that use a centralized structure for innovation such as a lab or accelerator. Our long-time friend and known innovation practitioner, Susana Jurado Apruzzese from Telefonica identified that having a sponsor for a venture is a key success factor that affects the outcome of the venture. She went as far as to use a machine learning algorithm to predict the successability of a new venture and has identified - looking at over 3 years of data - that a sponsor is a 1 or 0 factor. That is, if the venture doesn't have a sponsor it will never succeed.[67]

With your Venture Board in place, it's full steam ahead for the first meeting. Well, not quite yet. Before you leap in with both feet it might be worth injecting a note of caution. Venture Boards have the potential to deliver great outcomes but only if they act to further the interests of company innovation. So here are a few pitfalls which boards would do well to avoid.

1. Sporadic meeting. In order to build momentum, Venture Board meetings need to happen regularly. Sporadic meetings send out the wrong message, to the effect that innovation is important but not that important for us to make time on an ongoing basis. This negative impression will trickle down to the innovation teams which, not feeling a sense of urgency, will get entangled with low impact activities or the wrong activities for the maturity stage of their idea.

For companies which staff their innovation teams with part time employees (which we rarely advise) sporadic Venture Board meetings are particularly detrimental. Without regular meetings people will get pulled closer and closer to core business activities until innovation becomes a distant memory.

In DNV GL - one of the world's largest classification and certification societies, Nina Rygh, Head of Business Process noticed that: "having the Venture Board meetings happen regularly is helping both the teams and the Venture Board members. The Venture Board members will be less likely to go into a status meeting mindset since they are constantly meeting the teams. In turn, the teams will feel less anxiety when presenting to the Venture Board since they are doing it more frequently not just once every quarter or every six months. They will also get constant feedback; therefore the expectations are better aligned."

The frequency to which meetings should be held really depends on the circumstance of each company. In flat hierarchical companies active in a B2C market, we've seen three week intervals working the best. However in highly B2B regulated industries where the time needed to run an experiment is longer, 3 weeks intervals will probably not be enough for the teams to present any progress.

2. Status meeting. Another big issue we've spotted with novice Venture Boards is that they tend to transform the Venture Board meeting into a status meeting. A Venture Board meeting is a place where the innovation teams come in and present their progress and demonstrate how they are de-risking the business model. Status meetings are a bit more generic in nature.

To mitigate this, we always encourage Venture Boards to stick to predefined scripts gravitating around two questions:

1. What have you learned?
2. How did you learn that?

The first question looks at the assumptions the team has tackled since the last meeting, the second question looks to make sure the evidence can be trusted.

At one point we were offering hands-on coaching to a Venture Board in a maritime equipment development company. One of the ventures was looking at solving a particular cleaning issue for large displacement ships. In their first iteration, despite their best efforts, they were only able to validate the cleaning issue with yacht owners. Although the cleaning problem was confirmed, because the evidence came from the wrong customer segment, the assumption was invalidated as was the solution. Therefore the Venture Board disregarded the evidence and asked the team to re-do the validation but this time solely focusing on large displacement ships. On a side note, the learning regarding yacht owners was documented as it could have offered the team a good pivot opportunity in case the cleaning problem was not validated with owners of large displacement ships.

129

3. Ideation session. Much like the status meeting pitfall there is a risk that Venture Board meetings could transform into ideation sessions. Here, instead of focusing on progress and concrete evidence, the group starts talking about future plans or tangent ideas. And similar to the previous scenario, the solution is to stick to a pre-defined and pre-communicated script focused on outcomes and impact.

4. Pitching contest. Many of the ways a Venture Board meeting can go astray are interlinked. The risk of the meeting becoming a pitching contest or a meeting looking more like a Demo Day from an accelerator program can be attributed to many factors. For example, if the meeting is taking place sporadically, teams will fight for attention instead of presenting facts and outcomes. Not being strict on sticking to a predefined script might also make the session develop into a pitching contest.

To mitigate this risk we encourage the use of standardized templates. These templates can be either slide format or document format, as long as the purpose remains one of focusing the conversation and building discipline. From experience, we have seen that using standardized templates helps by removing the possibility of the teams curbing the Venture Board's opinion due to their PowerPoint and pitching skills alone. Standardized templates focus everyone in attendance on the facts and the evidence.

The template should be connected to the pre-agreed stages of the Product Lifecycle Framework. For each stage of the lifecycle, there should be a set of clear questions connected to the desired outcomes and key success factors. For each of the questions, the team will have to not only provide an answer but also state how they reached the answer. Knowing the stage-gate questions upfront also gives the teams clarity on what to focus on in order to move forward. This essentially provides transparency in the criteria for moving forward and helps to align expectations between the Venture Board and the ventures.

5. No decision being taken. Another pitfall we have seen with Venture Board meetings is that no decisions are being taken with respect to the project. A decision can take one of three forms: stop (the venture should be stopped), persevere (the venture should continue gathering evidence for the critical success factors of the current phase of the Product Lifecycle or progress to the next phase) or lastly pivot (meaning that in the face of evidence, the venture should consider making some major changes to the business model which most likely imply moving back in the lifecycle to start gathering fresh evidence).

6. Inappropriate attitude. Sometimes, in some companies, depending on the company culture, an inappropriate attitude is displayed by the Venture Board. This will influence the way teams conduct themselves, what they chose to present and what they chose to leave out during the meeting.

The atmosphere in the Venture Board should be one of inclusiveness, trust and support. The Board is not there to punish teams. These meetings need to happen regularly and should also be seen as a coaching experience for everyone involved. The communication in the meeting should be both ways, not just top down from the members to the teams. Teams need to feel a warm atmosphere where it's safe to be honest about the things that have worked and the things that haven't panned out the way they thought they would. Good and constructive decisions can only be taken in an atmosphere of trust.

7. Wrong skills. Assessing new ventures is different to managing an improvement project. The degree of uncertainty that comes with breakthrough innovation is highly different than the one in incremental innovation. Furthermore, this elevated degree of uncertainty accentuates known decision making biases:

a. Sunken cost bias: The everyday expression for this bias is "throwing good money after bad." The idea is that once we've invested time and/or money in something, we become vastly less likely to abandon it, even once it should be clear that the project will ultimately fail. The result is we frequently end up losing far more than if we had taken the hard decision to cut our losses early.[68]

b. Survivorship bias: Success stories are easy to spot. Failures that sunk quietly into non-existence much less so. That's why we commonly over-estimate the likelihood of success in risky ventures. Just ask any startup veteran who has been disabused of his starry-eyed optimism over several years in the industry if you don't believe us. This is also why we often put too much stock in the strategies of particular successful people; like dropping out of school. We remember the Bill Gates and Mark Zuckerbergs of the world and forget to factor in the vast numbers of quietly struggling dropouts when we mentally calculate how likely an action (ditching school) is to lead to an outcome (striking it rich as an entrepreneur).[69]

c. Safety bias: Safety bias refers to the all-too-human tendency to avoid loss. Many studies have shown that we would prefer not to lose money even more than we'd prefer to gain money. In other words, bad is stronger than good. Safety biases slow down decision-making and hold back healthy forms of risk-taking. One way we can mitigate the bias is by getting some distance between us and the decision, such as by imagining a past self already having made the choice successfully, to weaken the perception of loss.[70]

d. Experience bias: The tendency to take our perception to be the objective truth. We may be the stars of our own show, but other people see the world slightly differently than we do. Experience bias occurs when we fail to remember that fact. We assume our view of a given problem or situation constitutes the whole truth. This is where an external appointee can make a significant difference.

131

e. Expedience bias: We prefer to act quickly rather than take time. Expedience bias tilts us toward answers that seem obvious, often at the expense of answers that might be more relevant or useful. The privileging of immediate data can take many forms. In digital publishing, it might be measuring writers solely on traffic numbers, rather than the quality of the writing. In sales, it could be solely focusing on revenue targets, without considering how the quality of client relationships drives future business. Put another way: while it's true that what gets measured gets managed, measurement should not be confused with management.

Simplifying, decision making biases come in two flavors: logical fallacies, which are mistakes and flaws in reasoning; and cognitive biases, which are cases when we consistently see the reality differently than it objectively is. From experience, our colleague Bruno Pešec came up with a few steps for improving your decision making muscles.[71]

132
- First is in acknowledging that there are many decision making biases and becoming aware of them. You can't act if you don't realize mistakes are being made.
- Second is in using words and images to visualize the object of discussion. By doing so you are making your thinking more tangible and explicit, which in turn makes it easier to question.
- Third is in creating space where feedback can be shared candidly and flaws discussed openly. When biases appear you need to be able to discuss respectfully, without personal attacks.
- Finally, Bruno underscores these steps with a call for proactive discipline. You are always making decisions, a process you ought to continuously improve.

Sometimes it's not what you think but how you think that can make the critical difference. That's why providing managers and leaders with critical thinking training is tremendously important if the innovation accounting system is to work.

In late 2017 we made a similar point to a large European pharmaceutical consortium. They invested heavily in an internal innovation fund and they were planning on continuing investing further in the years to come. An important component of their program was the Demo Day. This Demo Day was to take place at the end of a 12 week period. During this first 12 weeks, the teams were primarily looking at validating the customer need and early desirability of their solution. The teams were therefore given coaching, investment and a clear mandate. The goal of the Demo Day was to identify, against evidence, which teams from the ones that entered the funnel 12 weeks ago should be moved on and get financing to progress their ideas further and which ideas should be discontinued.

Knowing how important the contribution of the selection jury was to the overall success of the program we made the case for intensive management training ahead of this event. Our training program had one single goal in mind: train the selected managers to understand the evidence the teams would bring. Essentially, to teach the managers to think like Venture Capital investors.

At the end of the training program we handed out feedback forms to participants. We were pleasantly surprised to read on every single form that without the training the participants believed they would have done a poor job during the Demo Day as they would have asked all the wrong questions for the maturity stage the ideas were in.

8. Poor time-management. For the Venture Board meeting to be effective, every team presenting needs to be given an equal time slot. From experience we have seen that 15 to 20 minutes are enough for the team to convey their progress and the members to ask clarifying questions. The more time is added to the hourglass, the higher the chances the meeting will become either a status meeting or an ideation session. You can think of the time constraint as a silent guardian, making sure that the meeting does not get hijacked or sidetracked.

9. No data getting recorded. For an innovation accounting system to work, it's very important that data is getting recorded following every meeting. We are going to talk about which data should be collected and recorded in the following pages, but for now remember that a Venture Board meeting where no data is being recorded is as terrible as a meeting where no decisions are being taken.

Venture Boards are the interface between a company's strategy and its tactics. They make sure the innovation strategy is being executed while at the same time providing feedback on that strategy. The Venture Board meeting is where a company knows if their innovation strategy holds water in the market or it needs to be changed.

We are not saying that without the Venture Board meetings the company will not get feedback on their strategy, we are just saying that without these meetings the feedback will be slow and it will only be visible in the financial accounting books. Venture Board meetings also shorten the feedback cycle on the innovation strategy; they serve as an early warning system of the strategy not working well. All this, while mitigating one of the conundrums of the financial accounting system discussed in the earlier chapters: accounting-based financial reports which show only the final outcome of asset deployment: revenue & earnings.

Therefore for Venture Boards to work they require an Innovation Thesis and a clear definition of innovation. The Innovation Thesis will help the Venture Board take investment decisions along the entire Product Lifecycle. The definition of innovation dictates which ideas/teams are to be treated as new innovative ventures and which are just incremental improvement projects or digital transformation initiatives.

133

Concept box: Innovation Thesis

The Innovation Thesis is the outcome and the actionable document of the innovation strategy. Just like Venture Capitalists have investment theses that specify the types of startups and markets they're prepared to invest in, every large company must have an Innovation Thesis.

An Innovation Thesis sets out a company's view of the future alongside strategic innovation objectives. The Innovation Thesis needs to help everyone make more deliberate investment decisions, both internally (own product development) and externally (investing in startups). The thesis will always be used by more people than just the ones that created it. Thus clarity is a must. Also, a thesis serves as a "decision companion" catering for the needs of people at each hierarchy level across the entire Product Lifecycle.

A synthesized thesis should be formed of three parts; statement, antithesis and thesis - each section addressing the particular needs of specific target users. The statement part of the thesis is centered around providing a macro view of the company's innovation ambitions, communicating the big picture without going into too much detail.

Following the statement is the antithesis, created to paint a clear picture of the things the company is deliberately not going to invest in. If the statement part is primarily useful for executives and stakeholders, the antithesis part is helpful for top and middle management on the basis that this group typically makes the vast majority of investment decisions.

A precise antithesis can also prevent innovators from coming up with ideas not in-sync with the company's purpose or vision for the future.

As the thesis needs to be useful in the decision making process at every stage of a product's lifecycle – and not just in ideation or idea selection – it needs to cover problem spaces, business models and technologies. The antithesis problem spaces segment then outlines what areas the company is not interested in exploring. As a product matures and it passes the problem-solution-fit stage, the antithesis needs to set clear rules on the type of business models the company is not motivated to pursue.

As the product matures, the antithesis needs to stipulate the type of technologies the company will not back. In this part, the document should not name particular technologies, but provide a broader outline by mentioning characteristics of technologies (e.g. requires on-premise infrastructure, are not secure enough and so on)

In the final document, the antithesis is followed by the thesis. The thesis specifies what the company will support and for consistency and ease of use, its structure should follow the same rationale as the structure of the antithesis as the thesis and antithesis users are the same. (For more details on how to create an Innovation Thesis we encourage you to take a look at our previous book "*The Corporate Startup*.")

What is being measured

In the previous chapter we demonstrated how result indicators could help to define and measure each stage of the Product Lifecycle. We also highlighted the way in which, particularly in the early stages, the result indicator correlated with confidence levels on the desirability, viability and feasibility of the project.

With that in mind, we now encourage Venture Boards to add one more column to the templates we presented in the previous pages. This column will be used by the Venture Board to rank the confidence they have in the evidence the team presents for each of the questions in each of the stages of the Product Lifecycle.

The confidence the Venture Board has in each answer can't be calculated in a clear cut manner; it can only be estimated. The quality of that estimation will be dependent on the people doing the estimation. This is another reason for training Venture Board members, giving them the skills they will need in order to provide meaningful judgements and guidance.

Every company should agree on its own scale for confidence. From experience we have seen that 1 to 10 or 1 to 100 work the best. Probabilities refer to teams honoring the process and help visualize the progress made over time.

Once the confidence in a venture reaches a certain level the team can be progressed to the next stage of the lifecycle, effectively confirming that the Venture Board is prepared to invest further in the project. The confidence level after which a team has progressed to the next stage has to be predetermined by the Venture Board. More often than not we have seen this being determined on a case by case basis. That's not surprising as each project will have different parameters and outcomes. Nevertheless, as a rule of thumb we always encourage Venture Boards to set up the minimum threshold under which no teams are progressed whatsoever. This will make life easier for both the Venture Board members and the teams.

By asking the holistic question "How likely is it for the team to progress to the next stage?" the Venture Board is essentially asking "How likely are you to find evidence to move forward?" Hence the Venture Board is building in the expectation of finding evidence from the market and stakeholders, instead of focusing on nonessential activities. We would recommend Venture Boards look to score their holistic estimation of a venture as follows:

135

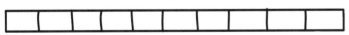

Not confident   Confident

10%

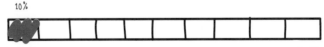

Not confident   Confident

- 10% We don't see the team moving forward.

10%

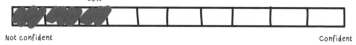

Not confident   Confident

- 30% There is not enough evidence that the team will move forward.

30%

Not confident   Confident

- 60% There is some evidence that the team will move forward.

60%

Not confident   Confident

- 90% There is strong evidence for the team moving forward.

90%

Not confident   Confident

You might wonder why we don't just add together or average confidence for each individual question and use that in generating a holistic view. Since the questions are inter-connected but can also be viewed individually, using a sum or multiple scores would not provide a meaningful result.

Instead, we propose assessing both individual confidence and a holistic view of the team. That way we are still aware of what the biggest risk with this venture is (the question with the lowest score), and we are making a meaningful assessment of the team's likelihood of finding evidence to progress to the next stage.

If there is a big disconnect between these two, that's a trigger for further reflection and questioning. For example, if the individual confidence score came out at 70% and yet the Venture Board's holistic view was around 30% there is a case for further discussion. What do the Venture Board see? Do they have some information that transcends what the team knows? What are they basing their assessment on? What has led to one key success factor being at odds with the rest of the scores, thereby potentially holding back progress?

It's important to remember that the likelihood of progressing to the next stage can be seen to be quite volatile, especially when in the initial stages of the idea. That is why it is important to focus on the evidence that's uncovered by the team and how it changes the possible outcome. Also bear in mind that the question of progression has implications in the way a venture will be valued and the "healthiness" of the innovation pipeline.

Also don't worry that much about using qualitative estimations; qualitative estimation of risk is an established and accepted approach in the field of project management.[72,73] Furthermore, the Venture Board members don't judge the overall likelihood of success of the venture they assess; but they only look at individual parts of the venture and the venture's likelihood of making it to the next financing round.

Experience has shown that confidence degree estimations will get better with time, particularly once Venture Board members build their experience in judging the worth of projects. This can be aided through training and is another reason for considering the appointment of an existing Venture Board member from another area of the company to a newly formed board. They can then bring their expertise to the new board. We would also recommend that new Venture Boards deploy methods like the Delphi Technique or the Six Thinking Hats to help them to reach consensus.

Aside from formal training, one other way of helping Venture Board members to build their skills is for the company to seek out partnerships with local startup accelerator programs. We've seen this work well, particularly when Venture Board members are able to go and observe, coach and even judge teams on the accelerator program.

Venture Board responsibilities don't end with delivering value judgments on the likelihood of ideas progressing to fruition. They also need to track and manage the costs associated with each venture. These may include time costs (for example how many hours has the team spent working on their venture), or expenses incurred in the course of the project.

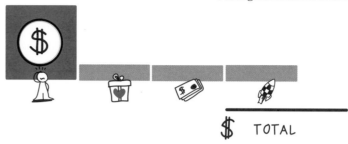

For the innovation accounting system to work, and for it to inform other actions in the company, the Venture Board should consider tracking how long each venture spent in each of the stages of the Product Lifecycle. The time spent in each stage of the lifecycle by each respective team is an important indicator for the Venture Board, not only because it impacts the average time to market of ventures in the company but also because it shows the coaching and capability needs of teams.

137

Consider a team that's struggling in the Discovery stage of the lifecycle. The Venture Board may see that the indicator "time spent in stage" is growing out of proportion or is greater than the average for that stage. In general, one of two things might be at play: either the team is dealing with an extremely complex problem, or they need some help with customer/problem empathy. The latter can be addressed by the Venture Board through coaching.

However if a venture's time is significantly greater than the average for the stage, it can also imply that the team is doing their very best to avoid having their idea discontinued. The Venture Board's role is to always free up resources for non-promising ideas; this indicator is there to draw their attention.

The cost indicators (hours and development cost) and their respective sums are there to offer the Venture Board a holistic view on that particular venture. These indicators will obviously paint a picture of the company's Cost of Innovation when aggregated at pipeline level. Furthermore these indicators will have an impact on the decisions that the Venture Board will take moving forward.

Measuring innovation is not only about measuring costs. At the end of the day, Venture Capitalists invest in startups for a profit or a certain (social) impact. Therefore this layer of the corporate innovation accounting system needs to also consider the value that the ventures will bring, and in a wider context the "healthiness! of the innovation pipeline of which we will talk later in the chapter.

To get a better understanding of the value a certain venture brings, it's time to introduce a new measure: the venture's estimated Value to Cost ratio, which serves as a proxy for an estimated ROI.

Calculating the Value to Cost ratio is not complex. However, since it can have a measurable impact on proposition outcomes, we are now going to work through the calculation on a step by step basis and then provide examples.

In essence, the ratio requires an estimate of the minimum, most likely, and maximum project value and cost. These are then used to calculate a weighted average.

Admittedly estimation isn't an exact science, particularly when each project will have its own variables. For our purpose we are borrowing an estimating model from the PERT technique developed by the U.S. Navy in the 1950s, originally used to estimate time intervals.[74]

Let's start with estimating value. Your first port of call has to be to your own organization's definition of what constitutes value. In many organizations, value is dictated by revenue so you'd need to apply the agreed revenue formula to each business model.

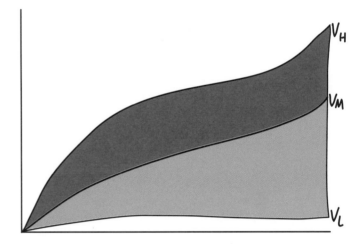

However, more and more businesses are also moving to a more elastic interpretation of value, bringing in measures such as sustainability or climate impact. If so, these would also need to be factored in to ensure that your value calculation is in line with that of the organization and therefore each proposition can be measured against existing products or services. For the same reason, calculations should be consistent across projects and across measurements. For most organizations we would also recommend looking at a realistic timeline of three or five years.

Once you understand how value is to be calculated, your next step is to create estimations at three levels: the lowest, V_L; most likely, V_M; and highest, V_H.

The lowest estimated value represents the worst case scenario. The highest represents the best case scenario - but it should be realistic. These two variables define your range, between which the most likely value should be placed.

Be critical when estimating V_M. Ask a barrage of questions: Has your organization ever done something similar? How did they fare? Has anyone in your country done something similar? How did they fare? Has anyone in your industry done something similar? How did they fare? Question everything.

Once you've finished with estimating value, you can finally move to algebra. The formula for calculating the weighted average of the project value, V_{WA}, is:

$$V_{wa} = \frac{V_l + 4 \times V_m + V_h}{6}$$

The weighting factors (1 for lowest value, 4 for most likely value, and 1 for highest value) are taken from the PERT estimating equation. Now moving on to cost, we can apply the same logic to the estimated weighted cost (C_{WA}). Make sure that you apply consistent logic and the same time frame when computing a business model's lowest estimated cost (C_L); most likely estimated cost (C_M); and estimated highest cost (C_H). The formula for calculating the Cost Weighted Average is:

$$C_{wa} = \frac{C_l + 4 \times C_m + C_h}{6}$$

With those two figures to hand, the Value to Cost ratio is simply the Value Weighted Average over the Cost Weighted Average.

$$VCR = \frac{V_{wa}}{C_{wa}}$$

139

And that's it; almost. The estimated Value to Cost ratio (as well as the indicators that make it up) now need to be risk adjusted based on the evidence the team has brought forward.
To do this risk adjustment is fairly easy. The Value to Cost ratio, or any other indicator that makes it up (value or cost), needs to be multiplied by the Venture Board's holistic view of the venture in question. Essentially you are going to discount the Value to Cost ratio by how risky the Venture Board considers the venture to be at that moment in time. Obviously, in the light of new evidence the risk adjustment will change, either going up or down. This is an important point to understand; your ratio is not fixed for the lifecycle of the venture. Rather it will flex as the project matures or as new evidence comes to light.

Let's look at an example. Project Alpha has been estimated to bring in a realistic value of $40m (VM) within a scale with the lowest value at $30m (VL), and the highest at $65m (VH). Cost estimates over the same time period range from $5m (CL) to $10m (CH) with a realistic estimate of $6.5m (CM).

However at the moment, the holistic view the Venture Board has of Alpha is that there is not enough evidence to move them to the next maturity level. Accordingly they have decided to apply a risk discount of 70% since the confidence level currently sits at 30%. Following our above logic, the risk adjusted Value to Cost ratio of Alpha will be computed as follows:

Value weighted average =

$$V_{wa} = \frac{(30(V_l) + 4 \times 40(V_m) + 65(V_h))}{6}$$

$$42,5$$

Cost weighted average =

$$C_{wa} = \frac{(5(C_l) + 4 \times 6,5(C_m) + 10(C_h))}{6}$$

$$6,83$$

Value to Cost ratio =

$$VCR = \frac{42,5}{6,83}$$

Adjusting for risk - VCRrisk =

$$VCRisk = 6,22 \times 30\%$$

$$1,86$$

So what do these numbers tell us about the viability of Alpha as a project? Remember that Value to Cost is a proxy for Return in Investment. It's not perfect and it's full of assumptions but it is the best we have at this moment. If the Value to Cost ratio is below 1, even before being adjusted for risk, then we are looking at something that should most likely be discontinued.

In the case of Alpha the venture is promising a 6x return. However, if we consider the risk weighting the return becomes almost 3 times smaller. Based on this indicator alone the venture should be allowed to gather evidence in the current stage of the lifecycle but it should under no circumstances be allowed to progress to the next stage until further evaluations have taken place.

As a word of advice for Venture Boards, if the Value to Cost ratio and/or risk adjusted Value to Cost ratio are below 1 they should most likely discontinue the venture immediately. A value between 1 and 2 indicates that there is a small gain to be made. This is fairly typical of incremental innovation projects. Values above 10 should either be taken with a pinch of salt or nurtured as potential internal unicorns. Given the Venture Capital outcomes we showed you in the beginning of the chapter, getting to 10x return is going to be tough going.

This particular way of looking at individual ventures will, on the one hand, help the Venture Board to make investment decisions by comparing ventures on VCR, risk and risk adjusted VCR. This is particularly important when the company can't finance the entire pipeline and they need to make hard decisions on who's getting the investments and in which order. On the other hand, these measures serve as a good way to communicate to the C-level of the company the potential impact the innovation pipeline might have on the company's top line providing the pipeline is supported; but more on this in the next chapter.

Remember! We don't encourage anyone to start computing a venture's estimated Value to Cost ratio and consequent financial indicators before the venture is at least in Product-Market Fit. In the very early stages there is just too much uncertainty for realistic estimations to take place.

The templates for the Venture Board can look something like the following:

141

Stage: Discovery

KEY SUCCESS FACTOR QUESTIONS

Who is the customer for the proposed idea?

Not confident — Confident

What is the problem you are trying to solve?

Not confident — Confident

How many potential customers are out there suffering from this problem?

Not confident — Confident

How is the customer having the problem solved today?

Not confident — Confident

HOLISTIC VIEW ON THE TEAM:
How likely is it for the team to progress to the next stage?

EVIDENCE

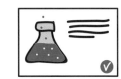  

  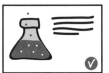

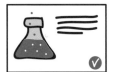  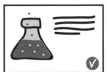

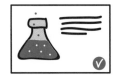 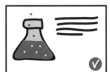 

Not confident — Confident

10% we don't see the team moving forward.
30% there is not enough evidence that the team will move forward.
60% there is some evidence that the team will move forward.
90% there is strong evidence for the team moving forward.

HOURS WORKED ON THE VENTURE
IN THIS STAGE (TO DATE):

TIME SPENT BY THE VENTURE SINCE IT
ENTERED THIS STAGE (TO DATE):

DEVELOPMENT COSTS INCURRED FOR
THIS STAGE (TO DATE):

Discovery

$ TOTAL

143

Bring focus on critical
success factors

6

Notes by the Venture Board

Suggested action by the Venture Board

Persevere

Progress to next stage

Discontinue

Stage: Exploration

KEY SUCCESS FACTOR QUESTIONS

Does the potential customer want to have the problem solved?

Not confident Confident

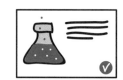  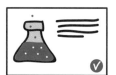

EVIDENCE

How do the customers want to have the problem solved?

Not confident Confident

Does the customer accept your solution or value proposition of your envisioned solution?

Not confident Confident

Who are you competing with to have the customer's problem solved?

Not confident Confident

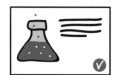  

HOLISTIC VIEW ON THE TEAM:
How likely is it for the team to progress to the next stage?

 Not confident Confident

10% we don't see the team moving forward.
30% there is not enough evidence that the team will move forward.
60% there is some evidence that the team will move forward.
90% there is strong evidence for the team moving forward.

HOURS WORKED ON THE VENTURE IN THIS STAGE (TO DATE):

Months

TIME SPENT BY THE VENTURE SINCE IT ENTERED THIS STAGE (TO DATE):

320

DEVELOPMENT COSTS INCURRED FOR THIS STAGE (TO DATE):

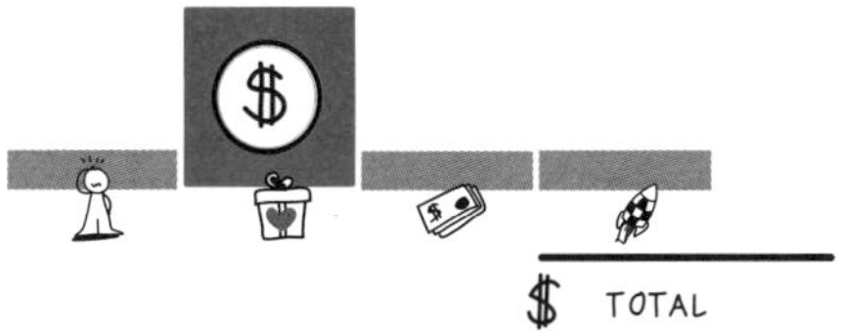

$ TOTAL

$ ACCUMULATED DEVELOPMENT COSTS (TO DATE):

320 ACCUMULATED HOURS WORKED (TO DATE):

Explore

Bring focus on critical success factors

6

Notes by the Venture Board

Suggested action by the Venture Board

Persevere

Progress to next stage

Discontinue

Stage: Viability

KEY SUCCESS FACTOR QUESTIONS

Are the customers willing to pay to have the problem solved? If so, how? (What type of revenue stream are the customers willing to accept, e.g. subscription, one time purchase etc?)

Not confident ——————————————— Confident

How much are customers willing to pay to have the problem solved?

Not confident ——————————————— Confident

What's the best channel to deliver the value proposition to them? Will customers favor one channel over another?

Not confident ——————————————— Confident

Is there early evidence we can build the proposed solution?

Not confident ——————————————— Confident

Is our envisioned solution ethically and legally compliant?

Not confident ——————————————— Confident

HOLISTIC VIEW ON THE TEAM:
How likely is it for the team to progress to the next stage?

EVIDENCE

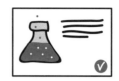 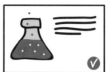 

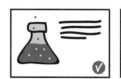  

Not confident ——————————————— Confident

10% we don't see the team moving forward.
30% there is not enough evidence that the team will move forward.
60% there is some evidence that the team will move forward.
90% there is strong evidence for the team moving forward.

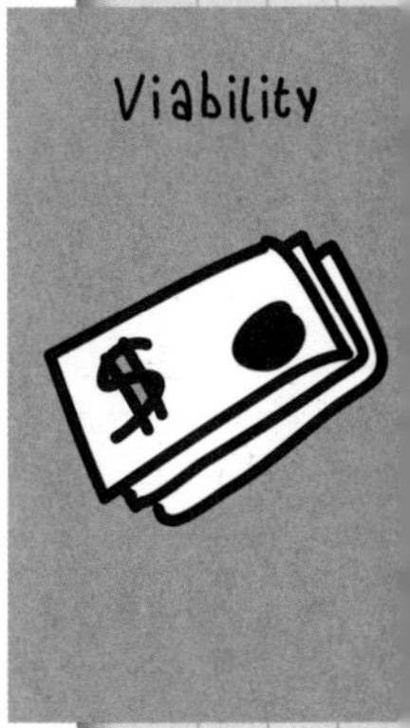

HOURS WORKED ON THE VENTURE IN THIS STAGE (TO DATE):

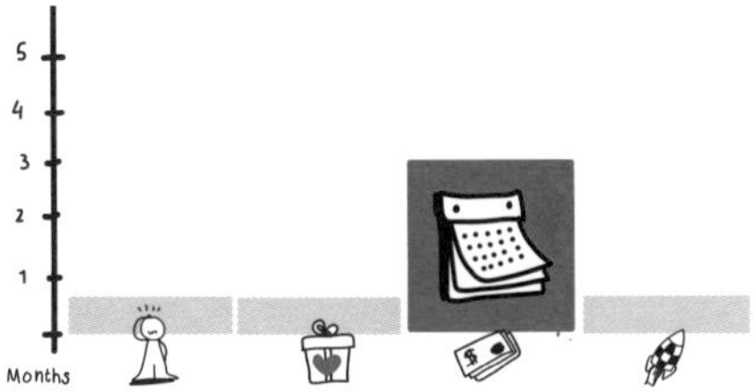

TIME SPENT BY THE VENTURE SINCE IT ENTERED THIS STAGE (TO DATE):

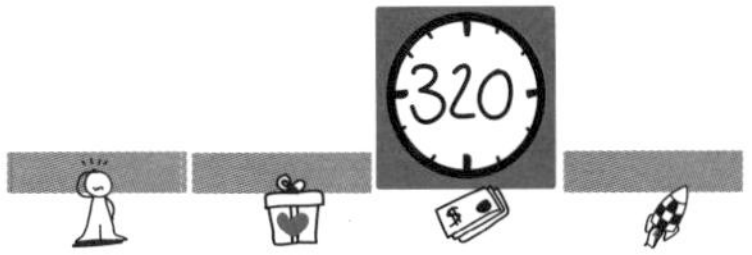

DEVELOPMENT COSTS INCURRED FOR THIS STAGE (TO DATE):

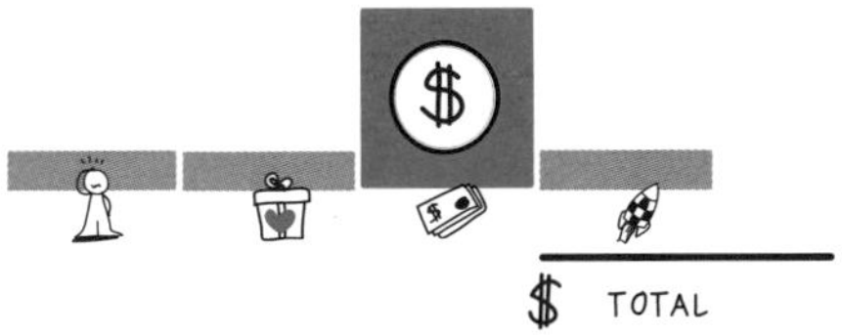

$ TOTAL

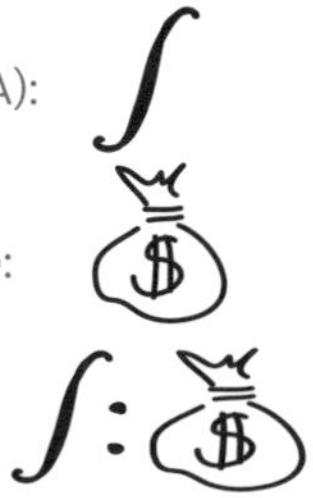

WEIGHTED AVERAGE VALUE (VWA): ∫

WEIGHTED AVERAGE COST (CWA): $

VALUE TO COST RATIO (VCR): ∫ : $

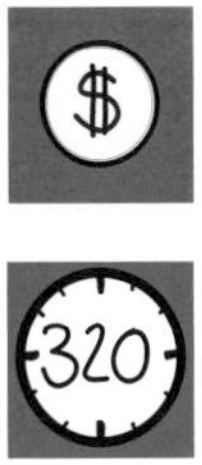

ACCUMULATED DEVELOPMENT COSTS (TO DATE):

ACCUMULATED HOURS WORKED (TO DATE):

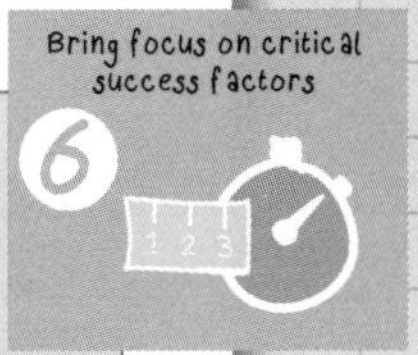

147

Bring focus on critical success factors

6

Notes by the Venture Board

Suggested action by the Venture Board

Persevere

Progress to next stage

Discontinue

Growth

Stage: Growth

KEY SUCCESS FACTOR QUESTIONS

Can the business model be scaled?

Not confident ⬚⬚⬚⬚⬚⬚⬚⬚⬚⬚ Confident

EVIDENCE

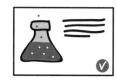 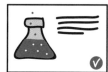 

Does it make sense to scale the business model?

Not confident ⬚⬚⬚⬚⬚⬚⬚⬚⬚⬚ Confident

Is the business model still going to be ethically and legally compliant at scale?

Not confident ⬚⬚⬚⬚⬚⬚⬚⬚⬚⬚ Confident

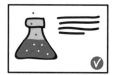  

Can the channel of the business model sustain the scale?

Not confident ⬚⬚⬚⬚⬚⬚⬚⬚⬚⬚ Confident

 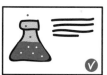 

HOLISTIC VIEW ON THE TEAM:
How likely is it for the team to progress to the next stage?

Not confident   Confident

10% we don't see the team moving forward.
30% there is not enough evidence that the team will move forward.
60% there is some evidence that the team will move forward.
90% there is strong evidence for the team moving forward.

148 VENTURE BOARD DASHBOARD

HOURS WORKED ON THE VENTURE IN THIS STAGE (TO DATE):

Months

TIME SPENT BY THE VENTURE SINCE IT ENTERED THIS STAGE (TO DATE):

320

DEVELOPMENT COSTS INCURRED FOR THIS STAGE (TO DATE):

$ TOTAL

Growth

WEIGHTED AVERAGE VALUE (VWA):

WEIGHTED AVERAGE COST (CWA):

VALUE TO COST RATIO (VCR):

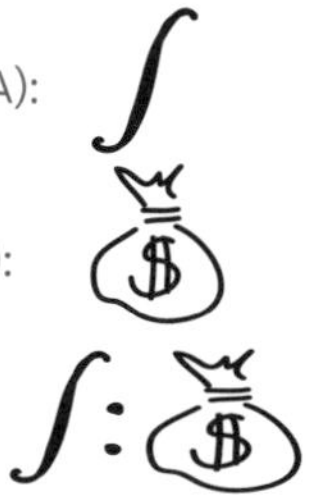

ACCUMULATED DEVELOPMENT COSTS (TO DATE):

ACCUMULATED HOURS WORKED (TO DATE):

149

Bring focus on critical success factors

6

Notes by the Venture Board

Suggested action by the Venture Board

Persevere

Progress to next stage

Discontinue

Note that these are just generic templates based on the life-cycle presented in the previous chapter. We encourage you to create your own templates starting from the key success factors that speak to your company and your industry.

Do bear in mind that some stages of a project will take longer than others. Gathering evidence in some stages will be quicker than in others. Complex experiments done in the more mature phases tend to take longer than experiments in the early stages, as we have seen in the previous chapter. So it is not reasonable to expect that every, say, three weeks, a team will have made enough progress to move from one stage of the lifecycle to the next. It therefore makes sense to ask yourself how a meeting will look for a team that's been in the same stage for a long time?

Are they being asked any new questions? Well, not really. For a team in any of the stages, the questions and key success factors stay the same for as long as they are in that stage. Every time they attend the meeting however, they need to present more evidence making the case for their idea to progress to the next stage. The job of the Venture Board is not to decide whether or not an answer to a question is correct but to decide if the evidence/learnings the team is presenting can be trusted.

The funnel dashboard

There are two key aspects of the innovation accounting system at this level of organizations:

1. Getting data on individual ventures to increase the quality of the investment/divestment decisions.
2. Aggregate the data of the entire funnel to get a better picture of the company's innovation effort. This will later be transferred to the upper echelons and will serve as input into strategy, as well as to take decisions regarding broader aspects of the internal innovation ecosystem such as capability development and training.

So far in the chapter we've only covered the first aspect. Now let's turn our attention to the second one.

Having data from multiple ventures is key to be able to inform strategic decisions with respect to a company's innovation efforts and direction. But this data needs to be aggregated for it to be useful and to paint an accurate picture. To do this, at Venture Board level we encourage the use of the following tool: the funnel dashboard.

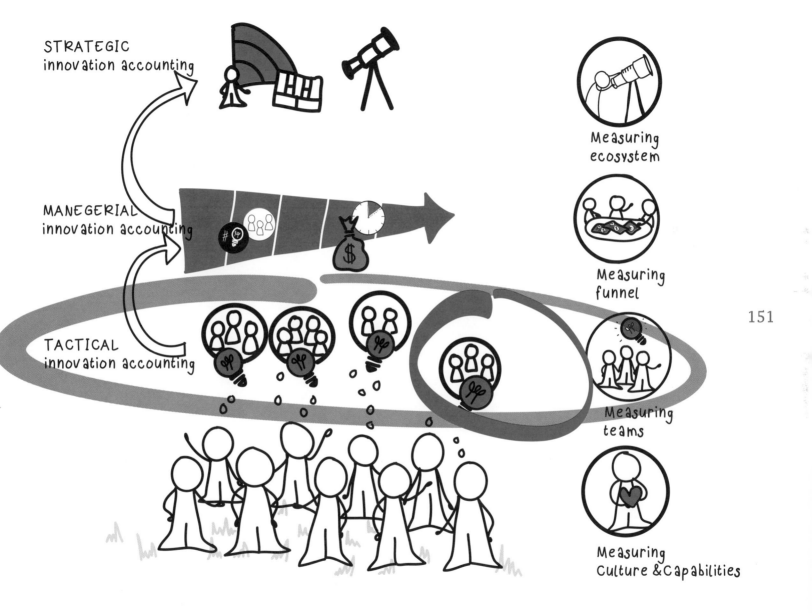

STRATEGIC
innovation accounting

MANEGERIAL
innovation accounting

TACTICAL
innovation accounting

Measuring
ecosystem

Measuring
funnel

Measuring
teams

Measuring
Culture & Capabilities

151

DISCOVERY

Number of ideas in stage

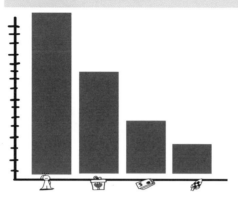

EXPLORATION

Number of ideas progressed

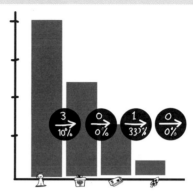

Average work hours cost per stage (to date)

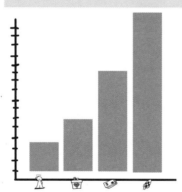

Average development cost per stage (to date)

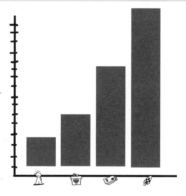

Cumulated development cost per stage (to date)

 320

 1130 1456 2101 3145

Cumulated work hours cost per stage (to date)

$ 20.000 300.000 540.000 998.003

VIABILITY

Number of ideas stopped

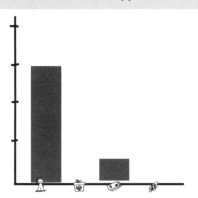

Total average cost per stage (to date)

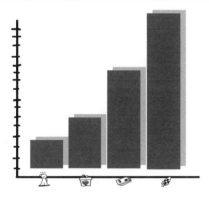

Total cumulative cost to date per stage

GROWTH

Average time spent in stage

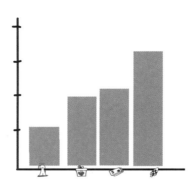

Average estimated risk adjusted
Value to Cost ratio
(VCRrisk)

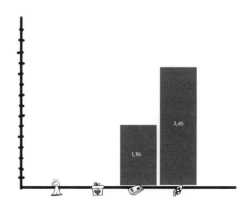

By aggregating data from multiple ventures into a single chart, organizations are able to make strategic decisions in respect of the overall innovation effort, funding and training requirements. Let's take a closer look at the dashboard and see how every indicator is computed and why it is relevant for the innovation accounting system.

Number of ideas in stage.
This is a simple count of the number of ideas you have in development at each stage of the Product Lifecycle. Not only does this give you a bird's eye view of the health of the pipeline it also can also act as a starting point for a gap analysis of the state of innovation across the organization.

As a rule of thumb more ideas are better. Depending on the organization, you could delve further into the data, perhaps dividing the number of ideas into portfolio buckets (core ideas, adjacent ideas, transformational ideas) or looking at separate data streams for different divisions.

Number of ideas stopped at this stage.
Keeping a tally of the number of ideas which have stopped and the stages at which they stopped can help organizations to better understand their own innovation maturity levels. Remember, there is nothing wrong with stopping ideas. As we highlighted earlier in the chapter, failure should be seen as a learning point and the more ideas, potentially the greater chance of innovation success. To drill down further you might want to add a reason code indicating why the idea stopped. This may include the fact that the opportunity just isn't there, or sufficient evidence couldn't be gathered, or organizational priorities changed and there are other ideas that have to be

tended to. Although this indicator is cumulative, do be cautious about how far back you maintain the data in this area. For example, if the organization's innovation efforts are dramatically reorganized, past data may well not give an indication of future success.

Number of ideas progressed to the next stage.
Understanding how many ideas progress to the next stage helps to build an understanding of the health of your pipeline.

Percentage of ideas progressed to the next stage.
Dividing the number of ideas which have progressed to the next stage by the sum of all ideas progressed and stopped gives a quick check of overall progress (e.g. We have 10 ideas that have progressed to the next stage, and 20 that have been stopped. Then the calculation would be 10 divided by 10 progressed plus 20 stopped, which gives us 10 divided by 30, or 33%). If the resultant percentage is high, you should question if you are being too relaxed and letting everything pass; too low and you should investigate if you are taking on ideas that are poor or if you are inadequately supporting your teams.

Average time spent per stage
The average time spent per stage indicator gives you an idea of how fast ventures have moved from one stage to the next or have been discontinued. This indicator should correlate with how much time employees are allowed to spend on innovation. For companies that allow full time commitment to ventures, this indicator will be lower than for companies that only allow a portion of time to be spent on innovation.

However, results can be skewed by teams which are working slower than would be expected, indicating a resource or training need. This indicator is computed by adding the time spent in a stage by all ventures that have been in this stage (whether they are progressed or discontinued) divided by the number of ventures.

(e.g. 3 ventures entered PS Fit. Venture 1 stayed there for 4 weeks and it progressed to PM Fit, Venture 2 stayed there for 8 weeks and it was discontinued, Venture 3 stayed there for 6 weeks and it progressed to PM Fit. This makes the average time spent in stage: (4weeks + 8weeks + 6weeks) / 3 = 6 weeks.)

Cost indicators are there to paint a picture of the investment made by the company in its pipeline at every stage of the Product Lifecycle. In the dashboard these are lagging indicators - painting a picture of what has happened, incurred cost. For early stages such as Empathy and Problem Solution fit, you can expect to only have time costs. However to make things easier to compute you can transform the time cost into monetary cost by multiplying the time spent with the average salary of an employee in your company.

At later stages, once the experiments become a bit more complex and the effort to progress an idea becomes a bit more costly, you can expect to be able to include time and expense costs which can be identified from the Venture Board templates.

The cost indicator is probably one of the most important for anyone interested in improving their innovation ecosystem; although lagging, it is packed with insight. Tracking the cost of each stage can aid in improving the innovation processes (such

as the Product Lifecycle) or improving the human capability in the company (such as offering more training to the teams; training that will help them validate their ideas faster which in term will drive the cost down).

Furthermore, both the cost indicators and the time indicators can help the company self-benchmark; giving them an idea of how the internal ecosystem and knowledge pool has improved over the years and has helped the company launch ideas faster and more cost effectively. Self-benchmarking is connected with the second principle of the innovation accounting system presented in previous chapters, specifically that the innovation accounting system should help with innovation ecosystem improvements.

The average estimated risk adjusted Value to Cost ratio (VCRrisk) is pretty straightforward to compute, being the sum of all VCRrisk of every venture in a particular stage divided by the number of ventures in that stage.

This particular indicator is useful as it gives a snapshot of the potential of the innovation pipeline. This might be useful for the Venture Board as well as other stakeholders in the company including the board. As we mentioned earlier in the chapter, values below 1 are more likely to be incremental projects, whilst values greater than 10 should be taken with a pinch of salt. This indicator can also be used when looking at individual ventures. The Venture Board can compare the VCRrisk of a certain venture against the average of the stage and take appropriate measures. If the VCRrisk of the venture is way lower than the average, further investigation will be needed; same if it is way higher.

155

Concept box: Opportunity Cost

Most companies don't have an infinite number of resources at their disposal. Sometimes there needs to be some hard decisions taken when it comes to investing in certain ventures and not investing in others. Although in most cases the company's innovation strategy and/or vision will dictate where resources get allocated, there are still cases where decisions need to be made for ventures which are equal in the eyes of the strategy/vision. This is where leaders might want to consider Opportunity Cost.

In the simplest terms, Opportunity Cost is what the company could have gained if it had invested in another venture rather than the one it chose to invest in. It's the loss of a potential gain. Although there is no specifically defined or agreed on mathematical formula to calculate Opportunity Cost, there are ways to think about opportunity costs in a mathematical way. Furthermore there are actually some great tools for this in the finance department. Concepts like the Cost of Capital and Net Present Value (NPV) take opportunity costs into account for cash costs.

One formula to calculate Opportunity Cost could be the ratio of what you are sacrificing to what you are gaining by taking that investment decision. If we think about opportunity costs like this, then the formula is very straight forward: What you sacrifice / What you gain = Opportunity Costs

The inputs for both the numerator and denominator come from the values reported by the teams to the Venture Board. Depending on the company the value might include just the potential value of the venture, the potential value and the potential cost of the venture, and even the confidence the Venture Board has in the ventures in question.
No matter what you end up using in your formula, what's important to remember is that, when deciding about financing a certain venture to the detriment of another, it is advisable to consider Opportunity Cost too, on top of strategy, vision and/or portfolio balance imperative.

As ideas progress from the scale phase and move to the exploit side of the organization, we encourage leaders to keep the metered funding and exploration mindset alive. The best way to take investment decisions beyond the scale phase is through the use of real options. These provide us with a mechanism for valuing uncertainty and discovery, while providing a safeguard against over-committing. It's by no means a perfect valuation methodology, prone to human and managerial errors, but it is more fitting to the world of innovation.

Reminder box: Real options

Viewing innovation projects as investment opportunities has several effects. First, it acknowledges that we have the agency to decide how, when and if we want to invest into it. In other words, we have options. By pricing an investment opportunity like an option, we can learn more about its value than if we were just to use discounted cash flow analysis. To do so, we can leverage the field of real options analysis and valuation.

In their 2011 book "*Competitive Strategy: Options and Games*," Chevalier-Roignant and Trigeorgis define real options as *"the flexibility arising when a decision maker has the opportunity to adapt or tailor a future decision to information and developments that will be revealed in the future. A real option conveys the right, but not the obligation, to take an action (e.g., defer, expand, contract, or abandon a project) at a specified cost (the exercise price) for a certain period of time, contingent on the resolution of some exogenous (e.g., demand) uncertainty."*

What makes this approach attractive is the fact that it recognizes the value of learning through experimentation, and provides a way beyond go/no-go investment decisions. For example, we can opt to postpone (defer) an investment in favor of running more experiments, or upon finding other lucrative opportunities, decide to expand an option with new markets or products and services.

The approach can be roughly divided in two stages. We begin by understanding the business situation and framing the option credibly. That means using past data (e.g. market performance of similar initiatives), learning we have accumulated so far (e.g. from experiments and research), and discussing with various stakeholders of interest. We want to describe key value drivers (e.g. elements of your revenue formula), and milestones which require management decisions and investments (e.g. developing a new product, market introduction, market expansion, etc.). The output will be some sort of decision tree, illustrating the relationship between all decisions.

157

Then we move to actual valuation. Discounted cash flow (DCF) analysis and net present value (NPV) calculations are used to determine the base case, followed by one of the option valuation models. Black-Scholes option pricing model is perhaps most widespread, but for this case the binomial model is more appropriate. In essence, we go through the decision tree and evaluate each node (decision point) Copeland and Tufano offer an accessible example in their Harvard Business Review article "A real-world way to manage real options."

Using a real options approach is best reserved for initiatives that have reached product-market fit and are considered for scaling. If you opt to use the binomial model for valuation, then you can use conventional spreadsheet software to build your model. Your finance department most likely already has spreadsheets for DCF analysis and NPV calculation, and can help you structure your options.

If you wish to dig deeper, we recommend the 2017 article "Real options theory in strategic management" by Trigeorgis and Reuer for academic understanding, and Bruno Pešec 2021 book *"How to value innovation projects"* for practical application.

For the innovation accounting system to work at this layer, the templates we presented above, as well as the dashboard, should be filled in every time there is an interaction between the Venture Board and the ventures. This will help keep the information fresh and accurate, allowing for better decisions to be taken. However, for this not to become a logistical burden that will lead to the system being ignored, we have found that splitting the work between the ventures and Venture Board is the way forward.

In many companies where we have implemented this system, the teams were in charge of filling in their answers on their respective templates ahead of the meeting with the Venture Board as well as their incurred costs, time worked and estimated value and estimated cost parameters (if applicable for their maturity level). The numbers should therefore reflect the changes that have happened since the last meeting.

During the meeting with the Venture Board, risk related sections are updated on each template followed by an update of the dashboard. These actions are done by one of the Venture Board's members either at the beginning of the meeting or at the end.

A cautionary word for companies willing to implement Innovation Accounting comes from our long-time partner (and close friend) Tristan Kromer, in the form of something he refers to as The Rudder Fallacy.[75] In his metaphor Tristan basically says that no matter how much a helmsman in a rowing boat is turning the helm, if the rowers don't produce forward movement by rowing, the boat won't be moving. For an innovation ecosystem this means that no matter how good your measuring system is, if there are no projects in the pipeline (or if the teams don't honor the process) the company won't make any progress.

The abstraction principle applied to the Indicators
in Tactical Innovation Accounting and
Managerial Innovation Accounting

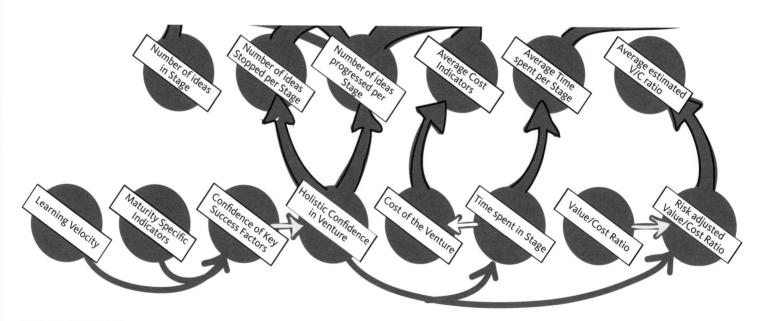

Having a Venture Board is a critical element in an innovation accounting system. A well working Venture Board displays an attitude of support and trust, evaluates on relevant indicators and serves as early feedback on the overall strategy.

The Venture Board's role is to assess the likelihood of individual ventures making it to the next stage of the innovation framework. The Venture Board does this by weighing the in-market evidence presented by the teams.

Data from individual teams can be aggregated to show the performance of the company's innovation funnel on cost, time spent and potential future revenue. Or as our fried Bruno Pešec says:

'Managerial Innovation Accounting is the bridge between strategy and execution'.

Conversations on Innovation

Susana Jurado Apruzzese

Head of Open Innovation, Academia Telefónica

Susana has been with Telefónica (one of the world's top 10 telecommunication companies) for more than 20 years. She started her career in information systems modeling and software development but for the past 8 years she has focused squarely on innovation management. In this role she helped design and develop the company's intrapreneurship innovation model, later being involved in operationalizing it too. Over the years she's held many positions in the company including, at the time of the interview, the position of Head of Innovation Portfolio. Susana has also authored countless articles on corporate innovation management, some of which have been published by major outlets such as Harvard Business Review.

Innovation Accounting: Starting from the HBR case study "Telefonica: A Lean Elephant" and continuing with initiatives like Wayra; in the corporate innovation space, Telefónica is a company to be reckoned with. When it comes to internal innovation, the company prides itself on being able to do more innovation with fewer resources, using a very disciplined approach they call Lean Elephant. How is that working?

Susana Jurado Apruzzese: We started working with a new innovation process in 2012. In just 18 months after deploying the new way of working we were twice as fast as we were before. This speed combined with metered funding allows us, within the same timeframe, to test 45% more ideas than we were capable of before. And we were investing on average, 48% less budget in each venture than before.

IA: How did you achieve that?

SJA: We have a very clear process of investing and divesting in ventures. And the venture teams have a very clear process of bringing their ideas forward. We try to build an innovation culture based on discipline; essentially sticking to the process and the guidelines. And most importantly, every decision we are making is rooted in data.

IA: What are some variables you're considering when making an investment or divestment decision?

SJA: What I'm sure everyone knows is that when managing innovation you are going to face high levels of uncertainty. You have to reconcile with the fact that you are not going to have 100% certainty when you're making decisions. But you're still going to have data available that will help you.

We gather data for each of our ventures. With this information we are able to better manage individual ventures but also be able to compare them against one another. For example we usually compare ventures in terms of the opportunity they represent. This is basically the potential business impact forecast we have for each of them.

But this is not the only indicator we use in our decision making process. We also look at the resources each of the ventures is consuming versus the opportunity they represent. Or, based on the evidence the team is bringing, we try to estimate the probability of success of each venture, and then we compare it with the opportunity.

We consider other things like, for example, the duration we have estimated for each of the stages based on our past experience and then compare this to the actual time a venture is staying in that stage. If there is a venture that is taking more time in a particular stage, we have to understand what's happening there. Maybe it's because the idea is stuck and the team is not progressing; therefore we should probably look to invest in other opportunities.

Risk evolution is another data point we use when taking decisions. When we talk about metered funding, we talk about investing incrementally as ventures progress with validated learnings. Therefore the risk should be decreasing as there is less uncertainty. We have to make sure that this is happening and act accordingly.

We also track other things too. For example, cost of failure or the validation speed.

The validation speed is particularly interesting. In our stage-gating process we have different stages defined, so basically what we try to find out is how fast we are in each of them. So we measure how fast the ventures move from one stage to the next one. This information is critical for our executives further up the line as they try to understand our time to market and Cost of Innovation.

IA: So who is taking the go/no-go decisions and who's compiling all the data that's informing these decisions?

SJA: In short, the data is being compiled by us, the team called Innovation Operations and Strategy. The decisions are being taken by everyone involved, the ventures included. However we have stage-gate committees. These are made up of representatives from every unit including HR and financing. This way we ensure the right amount of investment goes in each venture. The fact that the venture will have a future once it reaches maturity is ensured by having a sponsor early on in the process. This person is in constant contact with the venture and its progress.

IA: What's happening when you discontinue an investment?

SJA: In general we try to make the most of the learnings. So when ventures are "killed," we relocate the people in other ventures or even encourage them to test a new idea from the beginning. We don't fire them or just say "Okay, look for another place in the organization." Basically what we are telling them is that this is not the end of the world. Life goes on. You were working on a venture that is not progressing, but you get the opportunity to work and test other ideas that might progress, or join a team of another venture that is progressing, and it's growing because it's showing promising results. You show them that we all have learned something, so it's okay, and you also have a future here. Again we make it very clear that it's not the end of the world and above all it's not about them as it is about the idea and the business model.

IA: Any advice for our readers that want to apply the same process in their own organizations?

SJA: Remember that you have to look globally to your innovation funnel, and you have to consider not only how a particular venture is doing but how the entire funnel is doing. You have to make sure you have ventures in different stages so that there is a constant flow of ideas from the company and back into the company. And very important, you also have to make sure the ideas in the funnel are aligned with the company's strategy; otherwise why bother making the investment to begin with?!?

Also in the context of considering the entire funnel it's important to always look at the cost of opportunity when you're making an investment decision. You are making the decision if you're going to invest or continue investing in this one venture, but you have to ask yourself, am I missing a potentially bigger opportunity? You're trying to understand if this particular venture is the best one to place your available resources in.

Innovation: a fancy expense or an investment for the future?

CHAPTER 6
Strategic Innovation Accounting

Innovation doesn't matter. Yes you read it right, the purpose of a company is not to be innovative. So much so that, according to the 2020 World Economic Forum Manifesto, the universal purpose of a company is to engage all its stakeholders in shared and sustained value creation. In delivering that value outcome, a company serves not only its shareholders, but all its stakeholders – employees, customers, suppliers, local communities and society at large.[76] As you can see there is no mention of innovation.

This shouldn't sound strange to you at all. In one of the previous chapters we said that the job of a product team is to bring to market a new and successful product, not to run experiments. On the other hand, running experiments seems to be the most effective way of bringing new ideas successfully to market.

In essence therefore, long-term success relies on focused value creation whilst staving off potential disruptors. How do you achieve that? Well the most effective way of achieving value creation is through innovation. And the most effective innovation management comes from managing and developing your existing portfolio alongside a funnel of new ideas.

In other words, portfolio management is key to growing and creating value through innovation. It's a point which was highlighted by McKinsey & Co. research which concluded that companies that manage their portfolios more actively earn higher returns with less variance. They are also less likely to be acquired or go bankrupt.[77] On the other side of the coin, research has also found that CEOs who undermanage their portfolios are more likely to be fired.[78]

So far in this book we have seen how the innovation accounting system helps teams to improve outcomes and managers to take better investment/divestment decisions.

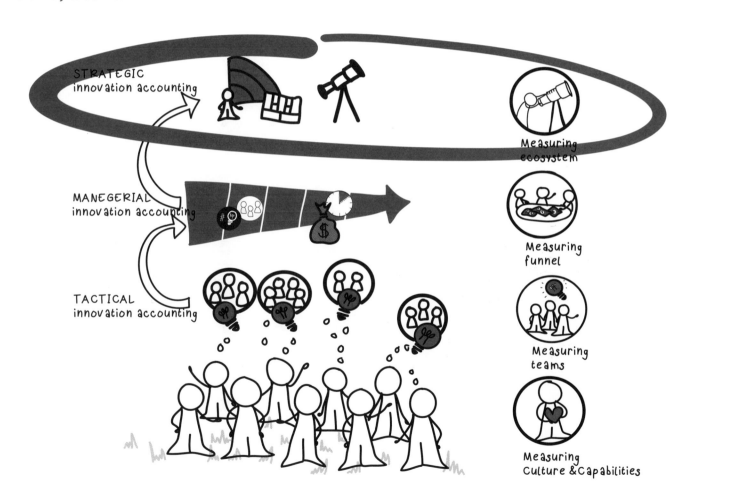

169

Now, following the abstraction principle, let's see how we can use Innovation Accounting to assist both executives in developing strategy and investors/shareholders in assessing the current and future potential of a company.

The Innovation Accounting Executive Dashboard

Whilst there are many innovation metrics that can be deployed to understand the healthiness of a company's innovation ecosystem, some can harm the company and the overall innovation effort if not enough thought goes into putting them into practice. The indicators used need to paint a clear and reliable picture that anyone can understand. They need to provide the answer to key questions and they need to be mutually supporting to do that.

Large corporations often have a tendency to distill innovation performance down to one simple metric. This totally ignores the complexity of bringing a new idea to market or the connection between that particular result indicator and other performance indicators. To mitigate against this, and to help you paint a clear picture of the efficiency and efficacy of your company's innovation ecosystem, we suggest using a dashboard. In the following pages we will be looking in detail at each of the indicators that make up the Innovation Accounting Executive Dashboard

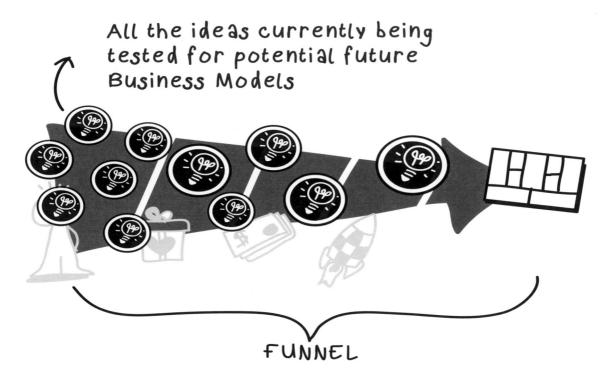

All the ideas currently being tested for potential future Business Models

FUNNEL

Concept box: Portfolio vs. Funnel

We'd like to take a few moments to clarify two terms that we sometimes hear being used as synonyms, although they are not: funnel and portfolio.

To put it simply, an innovation funnel (or funnel in short) represents the flow of ideas to be tested. These, once validated, go on to make up your company portfolio. You could say that the funnel is tactical in nature, where the portfolio is more strategic.

Another distinction we need to make between funnel and portfolio is the one of attrition. The funnel's attrition rate is higher than that of the portfolio. That's because funnels are constantly being revised with go/no-go decisions by the Venture Boards.

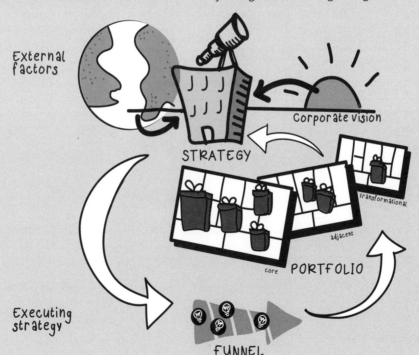

What are you trying to understand?	What questions should you ask?	Indicator
If my company is under the risk of disruption	Do we have a diverse enough portfolio of business models?	 Portfolio Distribution (PD)
	Which offerings are becoming less attractive and by how much? Where is possible disruption coming from?	 Portfolio Fade (PF)
If innovation is driving growth in my company	How well do our investments in innovation convert to new revenue?	 Efficiency of Innovation Investment (EII)
	Are we launching profitable ideas?	Innovation Profitability Ratio (IPR)
	Are our new ideas more profitable than the existing ones?	 New-to-Existing Profitability Index (NEPI)

What are you trying to understand?	What questions should you ask?	Indicator
How does my company's future look	Are we investing beyond our today's core?	Investment Distribution (innovation funnel distribution)
	Is our innovation accepted by the market?	New Product Vitality Index (NPVI)
How efficient is my company's innovation ecosystem	How much are we spending on innovation? How important is innovation for us?	Cost of Innovation (CI)
	How long does it take us to bring an idea to maturity?	Average Time to Sustain (ATS)
	How many ideas do we need to invest in to reach a certain objective (financial or otherwise)?	Average Funnel Conversion Rate (ACR)

173

Portfolio Distribution and Investment Distribution

The place where the tactics and the strategy come together to build your company's future is the portfolio, so it's only logical to start the dashboard here.

The portfolio of tomorrow is reflected in the funnel of today. For your company to connect the two in an effort to stay profitable (and meet all stakeholders' expectations), a clear strategy needs to be in place. Therefore it is safe to conclude that leaders need to have a transparent overview of both the innovation funnel and portfolio in order to take ownership of the strategic agenda.

This picture of the funnel and the portfolio answers two specific questions: what is your company's current risk of disruption and is the company actively pursuing growth beyond its core.

The easiest place to start building this picture is by creating a map of all of your business models. By judging where each one sits in terms of Product Lifecycle maturity (oX) and their distribution in the portfolio (oY) it is easy to create a snapshot which can then be used as a basis for both analysis and strategy decisions. To better understand how to create this picture for your company, we have prepared a step by step guide at the end of this chapter.

INVESTMENT DISTRIBUTION   PORTFOLIO DISTRIBUTION

Transformational · Adjacent · Core

Discovery · Exploration · Viability · Growth · Sustain

With the overview in hand you need now to only compute the Portfolio Distribution (PD) and Investment Distribution (ID). Both indicators are really straightforward.

Portfolio Distribution expresses in percentage how many of your company's existing ventures are core offerings, how many are adjacent and how many are transformations. The resulting figures paint, on one hand, a picture of the risk of disruption, and, on the other hand, provide very clear input to the strategy.

From experience we have seen that there isn't a clear benchmark for the Portfolio Distribution. Every company has its own ideal Portfolio Distribution which takes into consideration both its macro and micro context. However we strongly encourage self-benchmarking. Tracking Portfolio Distribution year on year shows you how your company is changing and by how much.

Ideally the portfolio's change rate needs to be above a certain threshold for your company to outperform its competitors. McKinsey & Co's research[77] spanning over 10 years has identified that companies which keep their portfolio mostly unchanged over the period (changes <10%) barely moved the needle in annual total returns to shareholders (TRS).

On the opposite side of the scale, the same research had some surprising findings. Companies that tended to refresh their portfolios by more than 30% actually produced slightly negative TRS.

The research concluded that the ideal portfolio change rate sits between 10% and 30%. Companies in this bracket delivered results that were "just right"; outperforming the others in TRS by, on average, 5.2 percent per annum.

175

Here again we encourage you not to be dogmatic about these numbers and take into consideration all the factors that are at play within your company.

Similarly to the Portfolio Distribution, the Investment Distribution shows you where most of your company's efforts are going. The Investment Distribution is computed using the same logic as the Portfolio Distribution. The difference is that it is applied to your innovation funnel rather than existing portfolio. Specifically Investment Distribution identifies core, adjacent and transformational ventures as a percentage of the total number of new ventures your company is currently investing in.

The Investment Distribution figures tell a story of your company pursuing growth beyond today's core and can be viewed as a window into your future. That's why this figure can be so important to investors who want assurance of future growth. Self-benchmarking the Investment Distribution can reveal changes in your company's innovation strategy. The current Investment Distribution can also be compared with the vision to understand if there are any discrepancies. Take, for example, a company that wishes to move away from its current core business as it knows it is about to get disrupted by a new technology. If the Investment Distribution is not showing a high percentage of ventures in the transformation bracket, it is safe to conclude there's a discrepancy between what the company should be doing and what it actually is doing.

In many conversations we have had with leaders over the years we have been asked about the best distribution of investment across the portfolio map. In other words, how should companies spread their efforts across core, adjacent and transformational innovations? First of all, we don't believe in a one-size-fits-all ratio. We believe that this ratio is impacted by many factors, including appetite for change/innovation, industry speed, risk of disruption, barriers to entry in the industry, and so on.

Research carried out in 2020 by KPMG in partnership with Innovation Leader revealed that on a sample of more than 100 companies worldwide with revenues over $50 bn., the distribution of investment in innovation was 50% core, 30% adjacent and 20% transformational.[79] But if you try and stick to that mix then you could find yourself missing out on vital transformations or trying to change too fast. That's where true leadership comes in; understanding your company's context and developing strategies accordingly.

So far we've focused solely on the distribution of investments in the innovation funnel relative to their future position in the portfolio. But this is not the only lens through which you can look at your company's innovation funnel, although this is the most straightforward. You can consider any of the following lenses in case you are looking for a more rounded picture.

Lens 1: Dead horses and unicorns

If you want to look at your funnel from the perspective of potential future profitability, we would encourage you to use what we call a "stable overview." Let us explain why we use the term "stable" first and then we will show you how to go about creating your own "stable overview."

In the startup world, highly successful startups that reach a valuation of $1 bn. are called unicorns. Meanwhile,

incremental innovation is usually referred to as "faster horses," inspired by Henry Ford's quote: "if I had asked people what they wanted, they would have said faster horses."

With that in mind, we propose segregating ideas in the funnel according to their risk adjusted value-to-cost ratio in the following types:

Dead horse: ideas that have a value to cost lower than 1, meaning they are not profitable.

< 1x

Faster horse: ideas that have a value to cost ratio from 1 to 2. Essentially these ideas are either only going to break even or going to offer limited profitability.

1–2x

Work horse: ideas that will offer anything from 2x to 10x return.

2–10x

Unicorns: ideas that have a risk adjusted value to cost of 10x and above.

>10x

You can now take your stable of ideas and create a graph. Use the oY axis to identify where each idea sits on the range of "dead horses" to "unicorns." The oX axis shows the level of confidence which your Venture Board has in each idea. It's also advisable to create a separate diagram for every maturity stage you want to analyze as this will allow for real "apples-to-apples" comparison between ideas that are of similar maturity.

It won't take long for you to spot a pattern. Ventures will tend to follow the right path as they mature. This is expected, as the value to cost estimate is getting more realistic as the maturity of the venture increases. A proxy for a venture's maturity is the confidence the Venture Board has in the venture.

We would encourage you to only look at ventures which are past a certain maturity level. Ventures which are too "early stage" would be too volatile to produce a meaningful picture (the value to cost ratio and the confidence can vary wildly from week to week).

As you can see, the only information required to create an accurate picture of the funnel already exists in the Funnel Dashboard we spoke about in the previous chapter. Color coding can also be used in order to highlight the expected portfolio direction of each of your initiatives. For example, core initiatives could be color coded blue, adjacent red and transformational yellow.

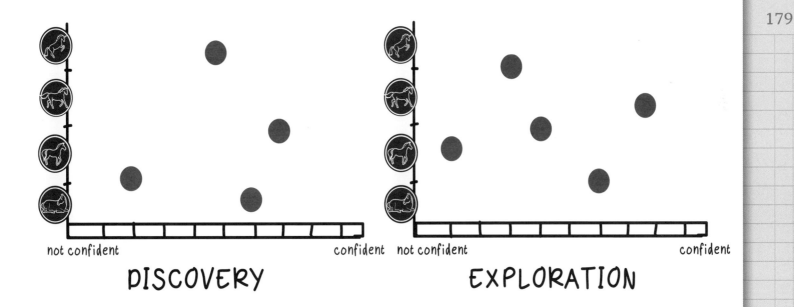

not confident   confident   not confident   confident

DISCOVERY   EXPLORATION

Lens 2: Investment per strategic priority

Another lens you can use to analyze your innovation funnel is the one on distribution of investments relative to strategic priorities.

As we've seen earlier, your strategy should be influencing the funnel. One of the questions that you should constantly ask is: is our company's Innovation Thesis being applied? To check if that's the case in your company, you can calculate the percentage of ventures or money invested in respect of each strategic priority[80] outlined in your company's Innovation Thesis.

A negative answer to this question, particularly if a high percentage of ideas don't connect with any strategic priority, is a cause for concern. Possible causes could be: the Thesis not being communicated, being incomprehensible or the Venture Board not applying the Thesis in the decision making process.

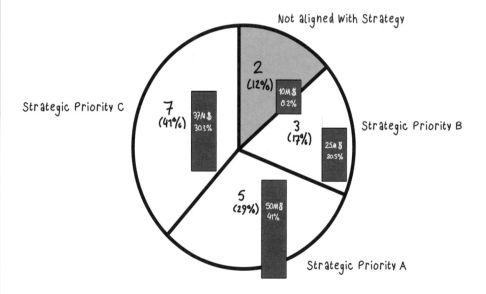

Strategic priority
- number of ideas
- total investment
- percentage of funnel

Lens 3: Addressable market size

Another lens you can use to look at the innovation funnel is the one on addressable market size. Essentially you try to understand the target market for each of your innovation funnel initiatives. Aggregated at funnel level, this view can be useful in understanding the long term potential of your innovation exercise.

Furthermore this lens can help you understand if your current innovation investments are following the Innovation Thesis; in particular with respect to the market size the thesis states that ventures should be in. Say for example your company only wishes to pursue initiatives in markets bigger than $150 mil. and they make this very clear in the Thesis. Analyzing the funnel through this lens will help you understand how many ideas in percentage terms follow this Thesis guideline. A high percentage of ideas not following the guidelines can prompt questions around how well the thesis was communicated, understood and put into practice.

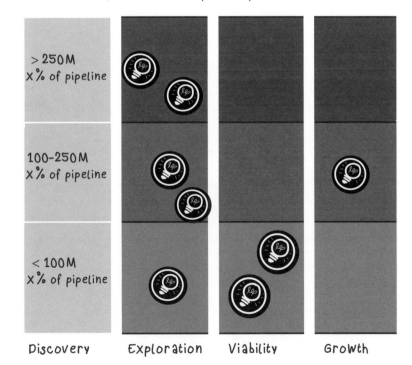

types of innovations and not all types produce the same top line growth. For example, if new innovations are just re-makes of existing products, product improvements or line extensions then they may only sustain the same market share and have limited top line growth. Alternatively, innovations introduced into new markets could deliver 100% accretive growth.

In a conversation we had with John Patrin, Innovation and Growth Director for DuPont he identified the following pros and cons of NPVI:

Pros
- Simple single number related to innovation and the percentage revenue obtained from newer products.
- Easy to measure; NPVI tracks innovations launched within the last 5 years, quantifying innovation revenue as a percentage of total revenue.
- A common metric in large B2B companies and therefore, because NPVI is summarized as a percentage, it is easy to compare against other companies.

Cons
- Provides only a partial view of the revenue picture; innovation revenue is only a percentage of the total revenue and one needs to know all the revenue components to understand the interplay between the components and their growth contribution.
- The percentage is market dependent, for example markets with short replacement cycles (consumer electronics) can be very high versus markets that have long adoption cycles (medical) which can result in very low NPVI.
- The percentage can depend on the market and technology maturity, for example mature markets or technologies may have little innovation potential (i.e. tires).
- Company NPVI definitions vary, making comparisons difficult (i.e. minor product iterations or ingredient changes can be counted in one company and not in another).

One of the result indicators that we've seen being used a lot to summarize the innovation prowess of a company is the New Product Vitality Index (NPVI) so it's only logical to look at it next. The NPVI indicator was first coined by 3M and is commonly measured as the percentage of total revenue from innovations launched in the last 5 years.[81] A high percentage (i.e. 30% for B2B Companies) is generally considered to correlate with a healthy innovation practice. It is often assumed that a high and increasing NPVI will generate growth because the company's new offerings are delivering value and being adopted by customers. Although on paper NPVI may be considered a good measure for a company's innovation ecosystem's performance, in practice it provides an incomplete growth picture. For example, from 2011 to 2015 3M had an NPVI of 32-33%, yet the revenue compound annual growth rate over this time frame was only 0.6%.[82]

The challenge with NPVI is manyfold. First, NPVI is a result indicator, an aggregate of many innovation activities and not a future predictor of growth. Second, NPVI is the result of all

- Can be gamed and result in an increase in incremental innovations proliferating the number of products, adding manufacturing and supply chain complexity while also increasing the stress on the marketing and sales channels.
- Innovation revenue is too generic and does not provide any insight about the innovation portfolio components. For example, not all innovation revenue has the same topline growth potential. Innovation revenue resulting from adjacent markets is accretive whereas revenue from CORE innovations may be replacement, cannibalize other products and have low to no growth.
- Typically reported on an annual basis and not used to continuously improve innovation ecosystem performance.

We are not saying that NPVI is a useless indicator; we are only concluding that NPVI can't be used as the sole indicator when assessing the innovation performance of a company. However, to mitigate against some of NPVI's shortcomings companies might want to consider:

1. Agreeing on a definition of innovation as we discussed at the beginning of this book. This will align everyone's expectations and will make sure that everyone understands the same thing when talking about "new products."
2. Aligning expectations with the risk of disruption. Historically speaking, most companies were disrupted because of their inability or unwillingness to expand beyond the core business. In other words they had too much focus on execution and not enough investment in the future. Cautionary tales like Blockbuster vs. video streaming, or Kodak vs. digital photography are there to warn leaders of the dangers of fully committing to business as usual. Before deciding to use the NPVI part of the ecosystem's dashboard, the leadership team needs to decide where they are expecting the new products to be created, and where NPVI is measured. Ideally, measuring NPVI will become a proxy for the risk of disruption (therefore fitting Principle 4 of an innovation accounting system: surface the risk of disruption). If NPVI is measured for adjacent and transformational initiatives, low numbers may indicate that the company is not investing enough in new, beyond the core, ideas or it lacks the skills to bring beyond the core ideas to market.
3. The leadership team may well therefore decide to take NPVI samples from each of the 3 areas of the portfolio. These indicators (NPVI Core, NPVI adjacent, NPVI transformational) can provide added clarity to investment strategy and outcome.

183

In simplistic terms, your New Product Vitality Index is directly connected with your innovation funnel. But, as we have commented above, to solely rely on this index can lead to distortions in perception. These distortions can have a significant impact on not only future strategies but also in providing meaningful data to investors.

So NPVI, like many other metrics, has its limitations. However, by running it alongside other measures it can become a useful indicator for any leader looking to make data informed decisions with respect to their company's innovation ecosystem.

To understand the ideal measure for the New Product Vitality Index (NPVI) in your respective organization, you could start by looking at another indicator: Portfolio Fade (PF). Portfolio Fade represents the degree to which certain offerings in a portfolio are being eroded; you can think of it as a churn/attrition rate. The key to good portfolio management is in understanding how offerings "drip" from the portfolio. This understanding helps leaders to make better investment decisions. Here again Portfolio Fade will vary according to the industry and company maturity. Knowing a likely range which is specific to your company could help to move away from a dogmatic pursuit of the "70-20-10 portfolio golden rule."

184

For example, in 2013 the North American market for luxury sedan vehicles was dominated by European manufacturers. Audi's A7 had a market share of 14%, BMW's 6 Series 15%, Jaguar's XJ 9% and the Mercedes Benz CLS 13%.[83]

Fast forward to 2016 and the situation was completely different. Audi's A7 went down to 8%, BMW's 6 Series now had a market share of 5%, Jaguar lost 4% and Mercedes Benz went down from 13% to 5%.

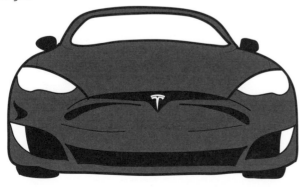

Why? Well in 2013 Tesla had only just launched the Model S so their share of the market was minimal. By 2016, however, Tesla's share had grown to 35%.[83] A Portfolio Fade calculation would not only have highlighted which offerings were becoming less attractive to the marketplace, it could also have highlighted the need to investigate the cause of any attrition.

It might be tempting to say here that leaders already know the answer to the Portfolio Fade question; that it comes from gut instinct or product knowledge. But thinking you know is one thing, translating that into accounting terms that can be used to define strategy and report outcomes is quite another.

So how do you calculate your Portfolio Fade? First of all you need to define what you will put into the mix. In practice we've seen companies look to understand the Portfolio Fade of a certain offering (e.g. a certain vehicle class) or for certain business model bundles (e.g. personal credit which is made up of loans, mortgages and credit cards).

When you know what you are measuring, you then need to decide what period you want to take the measurement over. This could be anything from 12 months to 5 years.

Then you need to decide on the unit of measurement to be used. This can be either market share, as we have shown above, or units sold.

For a more granular view, the Portfolio Fade could be computed in monetary units, perhaps looking at either revenue or margin from the units sold. However, we advise against this as revenue and margin are not so clear cut indicators for an offering's decrease in desirability. Remember, they can be influenced by gains in efficiency, raw material prices, or even brilliant marketing.

Computing Portfolio Fade is pretty straight forward from here, simply looking at the movement between the beginning and end of the analysis period.

Knowing how much a portfolio is eroding and the degree to which this gap is bridged by new innovations is only a part of the picture. Leaders also need to understand the Efficiency of the Innovation Investment (EII).

Innovation expenditure falls primarily under the operating expense (OPEX) of a company. Because OPEX makes up the bulk of a company's ongoing costs, leaders typically look for ways to reduce OPEX without causing a critical drop in quality or production output.[84] And innovation is always a prime target when OPEX cuts are needed as initiatives with longer-term payoffs will naturally be reviewed critically in challenging times. So much so that an Ivalua report[85] revealed that 67% of UK businesses agreed that innovation was being blocked by a focus on cost reduction.

185

Portfolio Fade is a great indicator for leaders as it forces the conversation of how you can grow beyond the core and whether you should be investing in more than just incremental innovation. In our example above, the 2016 Audi A7 delivered incremental improvements over the 2013 model. However, these were not enough to convince clients in the face of Tesla's Model S breakthrough proposition.

It is common for leaders to be skeptical of spending too much on long-term opportunities when there is a short-term performance gap that must be closed to assure the survival of the company.[80] Therefore understanding the Efficiency of Innovation Investment (EII) is key. EII answers a critical question for any leader: how well do our "innovation dollars" convert to new revenue?

The answer to this question can always serve as a good justification for ongoing investment in innovation. In particular, when facing innovation-skeptical stakeholders.

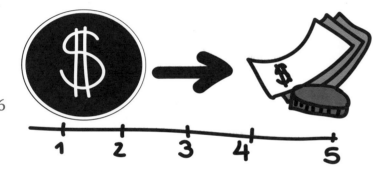

On top of that, the Efficiency of the Innovation Investment is a good complement to your New Product Vitality Index result. If NPVI is telling you how much you are making today from products you launched in the past X years, EII is here to tell you how much you've spent to generate that new revenue.

The formula for EII is: current year's total revenue from products launched in the past X years, divided by the sum of the costs of innovation in the same X years. You need to make your own decision on the time frame, considering your company's needs. However we would advise you to use either a 3 or a 5 year time frame.

Take, for example, a company that reported at the end of 2020 total revenue from new ventures launched in the past 3 years of $18 mil. The same company has incurred costs in innovation of $3 mil. in 2020, $1 mil. in 2019 and $4 mil. in 2018; making their total innovation cost for the period 2018-2020, $8 mil. In this case the EII is 18/8 = 2.25 (if you want the result as a percentage, you can just say that the Efficiency of the Innovation Investment is 225%).

In plain English, this means that for every dollar of cost incurred for innovation in the period 2018-2020 the company generated $2.25 of new revenue in 2020.

If your EII happens to drop below 1 or 100%, it means that you are paying more for innovation than you are getting back as revenue. The innovation theater warning light should now be flashing red.

When computing the Efficiency of the Innovation Investment for internal innovation, the costs can be found in the funnel dashboard we've discussed in the previous chapter. The cost you need in order to compute EII is the sum of all the costs incurred in the innovation exercise. These are the costs incurred by: live ventures, ventures that reach the sustain phase and discontinued ventures. You need to look at these costs for the same time period you want to compute EII for.

Note that no OPEX and CAPEX costs of running the ventures in the sustain phase should be included.

In case you want a more holistic view on EII, you can consider including in the calculation the revenue and costs associated with other innovation related activities such as mergers and acquisitions (M&A), investments made in startups (CVC) or joint ventures, in addition to internal innovation.

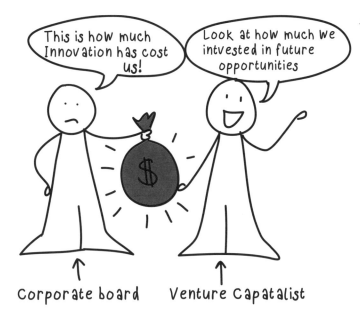

Also, if you just want to zoom-in on the EII for a certain innovation vehicle such as CVC, you can use the same logic of the EII formula but only applied to the outcomes and costs of CVC.

It is worth remembering that Venture Capital companies' investment efficiency is not given by picking only the winning tickets (startups) but by methodically investing and following up several investments. Only a handful will be successful. But these successful ones will ultimately cover the loss incurred in all the other ventures and account for the profit of the fund too. This again highlights the importance of mindset shift when investing and managing innovation.

The Efficiency of Innovation Investment indicator (EII) is a lagging indicator. However this indicator is great for self benchmarking, trends analysis and understanding how the innovation ecosystem is maturing over time and contributing to growth.

As you can probably tell, the key for an accurate computation of EII is in clearly defining and computing the Cost of Innovation (CI) for your organization. As with many other things, we encourage every organization to create its own definition. However, you need to make sure you are consistent every time you use that term.

In our experience, we've defined the Cost of Innovation as the total cost of the innovation funnel for a set time period (the sum of all costs for: live ventures, ventures that made it to the sustain phase and discontinued investments). In other words, how much did the company spend on trying to bring new ventures to the sustain phase in a given time frame. We therefore derive CI from the funnel dashboard.

Bear in mind that CI is a useful indicator on its own too, not only as an ingredient for other indicators. For example, CI can be easily benchmarked to tell you how high innovation sits on the leadership's agenda and how this position is changing over time. This is especially true if you view CI as a percentage of revenue.

Just measuring how many ideas your company is working on, how much they cost or how much revenue new ventures generate, is not enough to claim innovation as an activity worth doing. Leaders and investors also need to be interested in innovation margins.

At one point we were involved in the transformation of a large energy advisory and certification company located in western Europe. The biggest challenge this organization had was that, in spite of their commanding market share, their profitability was flat. The main reason behind this was that the majority of the business models in their portfolio were the time-and-material type. Essentially, they were sending highly trained engineers to run different projects for their clients. The company got to a point where no matter how many new people they hired to serve new clients, thereby growing their revenue, the profitability stayed the same.

The leadership team turned to innovation for a solution. They were particularly interested in new business models that were scalable and weren't time-and-material based. These new business models had to solve the problem of increasing revenue without increasing OPEX.

For the leadership team to understand if their investment in innovation was getting them closer to their objective, we suggested the use of two indicators: Innovation Profitability Ratio (IPR) and New-to-Existing Profitability Index (NEPI).

The Innovation Profitability Ratio helps leaders to understand the profitability of new ventures, answering the simple question: is our company launching profitable ideas?

This indicator is essentially the "operating profit margins" indicator from financial accounting but considered only for new ventures.

188

Your internal finance team should find this indicator easy to compute. The only thing you need to consider is what constitutes a new venture. In most cases it is advisable to consider new ventures as ideas that reached the Sustain phase of the Product Lifecycle Framework no later than 3 or 5 years ago.

With the Innovation Profitability Ratio figure in hand, you can now use it for self-benchmarking and to run trends analysis. For example you can see if there are any fluctuations from one fiscal year to the next. These can prompt you to dig deeper into internal factors that might have caused these fluctuations. These internal factors might be changes to the company's Innovation Thesis, for example. Or they could be as a result of a change in the Venture Board's decision making process. Obviously external factors can lead to fluctuations too.

As you've seen, IPR is a useful indicator on its own. But probably a more interesting thing you can do with the IPR is compare it to the profitability of existing offerings (offerings in the company's portfolio older than 3 years). We call this ratio New-to-Existing Profitability Index (NEPI) and it answers the following questions: are our new ventures more profitable than our existing ones?

To compute NEPI you only need to divide IPR by the operating profit of ventures older than, say 3 years (if 3 years was part of your definition of IPR).

Take for example a company that has reported an average IPR of 20% for ventures that reached Sustain in 2020, 2019 and 2018. At the same time, the same company has reported at the end of 2020, an average operating profit of 5% for all the other ventures except the new ones mentioned above. The 2020 NEPI of this company is therefore 20/5 = 4.

If the NEPI is above 1 it means that your new ventures have better profit margins than the existing ones. Conversely, if it's below 1 it means older products have better profit margins.

Also note that the NEPI figure is telling you by how much new ventures are more profitable than the existing ones. In the example above the ventures the company brought to Sustain in 2018, 2019 and 2020 were on average 4 times more profitable than older ventures.

Much like the other indicators we have covered so far in this chapter, NEPI can be easily used for self-benchmarking and can help drive improvements in the innovation ecosystem. Some things that might impact NEPI are the company's Innovation Thesis and the Venture Board's decision making process.

Used in conjunction with NPVI, you can now see if the innovation is an activity worth doing. If NPVI was telling you how much new revenue you are getting, NEPI is telling you how much more profitable this new revenue is.

IPR and NEPI should be constantly monitored by the leadership team (at least yearly). And similar to the other indicators we spoke about, these two indicators need to be deployed and used carefully and in context.

Your company needs to agree and understand how these indicators best fit within the context of your specific industry, internal peculiarities and above all, strategic vision. To exemplify this we are going to show you a tale of how innovation profitability can be shouldered aside by the company's strategic vision.

Cloud infrastructure is a hot topic for companies around the world and even more so for technology companies which are heavily invested in "the battle." In Q3 of 2020, Amazon's AWS had 32% market share, followed by Microsoft Azure with 19%, Google Cloud 7%, Alibaba Cloud 6% and other providers totaling 37%.[86]

Although Microsoft had a great Q4 in 2020 with Azure growing almost 50%,[87] things weren't always like this for the cloud solution. For years, despite being a mature solution, Azure was barely offering 3.5% profitability.[88] And the situation isn't any better over at Amazon or Google, with the latter even refusing to disclose the profitability of their cloud solution in 2020.[89]

'We believe in a future with cloud infrastructure'

189

However, the profitability of the cloud solution for each of these 3 players is not the primary source of concern. Leaders in these companies view cloud as an imperative for their strategic vision and a fundamental pillar in their respective companies' futures. That's why they made the strategic decision to continue investing in spite of low profitability figures.

So far, we've covered a lot of ratio type indicators. However, a word of caution is needed when talking about ratios. You need to be careful about why the value of a ratio is changing as it might be rooted in either poor decisions or it might lead to undesired behaviors. Let's look at EII for example. Since it is a ratio of NPVI to Cost of Innovation, do you decrease innovation expenditure to increase the ratio? Probably not the best idea, but it can have a quick impact on the result. Or do you increase the number of "incremental innovation" ideas that are sure bets, to improve new product sales? That might be good for the short-term but you run the risk of missing out on longer term profitability.

Ratios in general are tricky, in particular ratios in innovation management where there are so many moving parts. Our advice to you is two-fold: never base a decision only on one indicator and, if in doubt, always look at the company's (innovation) strategy for answers.

We just looked at how well the company's innovation dollars convert to new revenue and also how profitable new ventures are. But none of the indicators above are telling us anything about how long it takes your company to generate this new revenue or how many ideas it needs to invest in, in order to get one idea sustainably generating revenue. The answers to these questions can be found by looking at two more measures; the Average Funnel Conversion Rate (ACR) and the Average Time to Sustain (ATS) of a typical venture.

The Average Funnel Conversion Rate (ACR) paints a picture of the average "survivability" of an idea going through the company's innovation funnel. Essentially this answers the question of how many ideas are expected to reach maturity if the company decides to kick off a certain number today. This will help manage expectations for innovation investment.

The ACR is a critical indicator for the Cost of Innovation as the overall Cost of Innovation for the company is not only given by the cost of the handful of successful ideas that reached maturity but by all investments made in trying to grow through innovation.

Another important aspect of having a clear picture of a company's ACR is that it helps shift the mindset of "picking the winners" to "innovation is a numbers game that needs to be played at scale."

Computing the ACR is pretty straightforward once the funnel dashboard can be interrogated. In the funnel dashboard presented in the previous chapter, we spoke about an indicator called: Percentage of ideas progressed to the next stage. ACR can be computed by multiplying all values of "Percentage of ideas progressed to the next stage" from your innovation funnel.

Let's consider again the Product Lifecycle presented earlier. Let's assume that a company is progressing only 20% of its ideas from Discovery to Explore. Another 50% of the ideas from Explore are usually making it to Viability. From Viability, in general 75% make it to Scale and from these, 90% make it to Sustain. Under these circumstances ACR = 0.2 x 0.5 x 0.75 x 0.9 = 0.0675 which translates to 6.75% of the ideas the company is initiating make it the Sustain phase. For leaders, it means that if they kickoff 200 ideas today they can expect about 13 of them to make it to Sustain.

As exciting as this indicator might look, we want to make you aware of a couple of things. Firstly, you can only compute ACR if you've had enough ideas go through your funnel. If you only had, say, 10 ideas, the percentage of ideas progressed to the next stage you can compute is just not statistically significant. Plus the performance of the funnel could have been easily influenced by other factors external to the teams' or Venture Boards' capability. In essence the more a company invests in innovation the more accurate the indicator will get.

Secondly, as we've already established in Chapter 2, it's very important to clearly define what innovation is for your company. If innovation is not clearly defined you might end up with purely incremental projects in the funnel. Needless to say incremental innovation has a higher survivability rate than the more disruptive form as it has less inherent risk. This will obviously increase the ACR which will lead to a false sense of security and success.

As with previous indicators ACR is best used in helping you to benchmark and track progress. Fluctuations in your ACR value might be rooted in a range of factors including: team capability, Venture Board capability, tools, culture (e.g. psychological safety where teams feel safe to fail therefore trying to invalidate ideas rather living under the spell of confirmation bias) or even governance (e.g. time allowed for employees to work on ideas).

Knowing how many ideas reach the sustain phase of the Product Lifecycle paints only half of the picture of your company's ability to bring ideas to market. The time it takes for a product to reach maturity complements very well the picture painted by ACR. As famous startup investor Paul Graham says: "I've seen a lot of startups die because they were too slow to release stuff, and none because they were too quick."

Enter the Average Time to Sustain (ATS). ATS represents the time it takes on average for a venture in the innovation funnel to reach the sustain phase from the moment it was created.

191

This indicator can be computed from information available in the funnel dashboard. Computing the ATS is pretty straightforward: you look in the funnel dashboard and you sum up all the values for "average time spent in stage" indicators, for all stages before the sustain phase.

Similar to most indicators in the innovation accounting system, ATS should help a company self-benchmark, always striving to get better year after year. With a clear benchmark figure for ATS, leaders can start having more focused conversations around: capability development for both teams and Venture Board members, overall process improvements, efficacy of the decision making process and supporting tools/artifacts.

However, you need to bear in mind that ATS is not influenced solely by internal factors but also by external ones or by the peculiarities of the industry the company is in. B2C companies will usually have an ATS smaller than a B2B or B2G.

We know what you're thinking: isn't ATS the same as time-to-market? ATS should not be confused with the infamous time-to-market indicator, an indicator which in our opinion is highly inappropriate for companies that use the lean startup approach to bringing new ideas to life.

Let's explain. Most companies these days have seen the benefit of using lean startup as the driving methodology for innovation.[90] A fundamental piece of this mind-set methodology is in-market testing; either through qualitative inquiries or through quantitative experiments. Some of these experiments require in-market testing of certain prototypes which in some cases can even be considered a minimum viable product (MVP).[91] However the time it took a team to launch an MVP doesn't necessarily constitute the team's time-to-market as the results from the MVP might suggest the need for a pivot.[91] Or sometimes the MVP is required very early in the Product Lifecycle for the team to uncover the evidence needed to progress.

So this leaves one asking: what is time-to-market? Is it the time to launch the MVP? What if the MVP fails and the team pivots to another idea which is more successful? Is time-to-market the time it took the team to generate first revenue? But what if they perform a fake-door experiment[92] where they take pre-orders without even having a solution ready? Take Dropbox, for example,[93] when the young startup created only an explainer video and asked people to fill-in a form to show interest in their idea without having any product developed.

As you can very well see, Time to Market is an antiquated indicator in the age of rapid experimenting brought on by the lean startup methodology. Therefore measuring the time it takes a venture to reach maturity (the Sustain phase of the Product Lifecycle) constitutes a more focused replacement.

Implementation

What you've read so far might seem a lot to implement by one individual. And this was never the point. We've made the case time and again that innovation management is a team sport.

To be able to actively monitor a company's portfolio, as well as constantly updating the indicators in the dashboard above, you need a team. The team should include innovation management experts as well as internal controllers or auditors that can help pull the numbers from your company's financial statements.

You also need to establish a good cadence for updating the dashboard and the portfolio. Doing it sporadically will diminish the usefulness of the data. And with infrequent reviews it will be hard to determine causal relationships between actions in the ecosystem and outcomes. The cadence needs to be tailored for your company and be sensitive to its internal and external contexts.

But above all else, the entire executive team needs to support the activity by showing interest in the findings and taking actions rooted in this data.

Conclusions

In this chapter we've looked at a number of metrics which will not only help you to understand your innovation funnel and portfolio, but also to identify trends and action points. With each metric the key message is not to see it in isolation. Just as you need a diversity of people to deliver a rounded product, so too do you need a diversity of metrics to really understand and develop your company's future.

We started this chapter claiming that innovation doesn't actually matter; we still stand by our words. Innovation doesn't matter. Understanding your innovation ecosystem is, however, a way of not only staying relevant in a changing world but also leading the change. For leaders it is important to understand that the success of the overall ecosystem trumps the success of individual initiatives.

193

Worksheet - Mapping your portfolio

The primary purpose of a business is to drive growth and performance while generating value for a range of stakeholders. Although it's common for managers to focus on financial performance, good managers seek to exploit new opportunities to create additional value beyond today's core.

Good portfolio management can also mitigate a company's risk of disruption. Disruption usually takes place when a company is so blinded by past success and investments that it can't escape the massive gravitational pull of the core business.

Succeeding in today's hyper competitive environment requires a mindset shift from the company's leaders when it comes to portfolio management. Leaders need to start thinking in terms of business model portfolio and not only product portfolio.

Let's give you an example from the toy industry which perfectly illustrates the importance of business model portfolio thinking: the bankruptcy of Toys"R"Us®. At a stroke this deprived toy manufacturers of their main distribution channel.

In the wake of the Toys"R"Us® bankruptcy, according to the Wall Street Journal, toy manufacturers can no longer rely on a global toy retailer like Toys"R"Us® placing large orders on a consistent basis.[94]

Even manufacturers such as Hasbro, which has an incredibly diverse product range, were affected by the closure of one of their main distribution channels.

As a result, toy manufacturers had to shift their business model by considering direct sales to end consumers in parallel with shifting to smaller production batches.

Hindsight is a great thing, but if those manufacturers had looked at their portfolio through the lens of business models rather than just products, the risk of disruption would have been immediately visible.

This tale serves as a warning for leaders in other industries where portfolio diversity is seen only through the number of products, totally disregarding the business model perspective. It's a point we brought up as part of the company wide transformation for a major European bank. In a conversation with this client's Retail Banking leadership team, we brought up the topic of business model portfolio thinking. This followed an observation that despite the company having 100+ credit card products, they were pretty much using the same business model across the board. Shifting the leaders' view from products to business models proved crucial when they started investing in new initiatives.

Managed wisely, business model diversification can help executives improve performance and advance the purpose of the enterprise. As you've seen in this chapter, we propose a business model portfolio map over a product portfolio map as it depicts the risk of disruption better.

So how do you create your map? The simple answer is one step at a time!

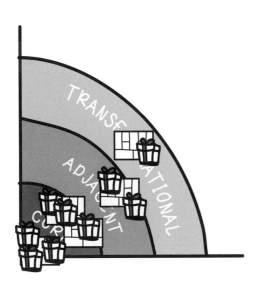

Step 1 - Analyze the business model of each product in your current company lineup. Doing this is as easy as creating a business model canvas for each product in the line-up.

Step 2 - With all the business model canvases in front of you, you can now proceed to create clusters. Each cluster should contain business models that are almost identical in customer segment and value proposition. (e.g. all the consumer mortgage products a bank is offering can be clustered.)

Step 3 - With the business model clusters created, you now need to go and find out the net income (also known as accounting profit) of each cluster.

Step 4 - Identify the CORE of your company's portfolio. This is the cluster that offers the highest net income. Place that cluster in the CORE section of the map.

Other clusters which are similar in both value proposition and customer segment with the most profitable identified earlier will also be considered as part of the CORE. (e.g. Following the banking example, let's say that the mortgage cluster is the most profitable. Other clusters such as consumer credits or consumer credit cards are also part of the CORE.)

Step 5 - Identify the ADJACENT business models. This is done by looking at the remaining business model clusters in front of you. Take the ones that vary from the core in either customer segment or value proposition. (In our banking example, a mobile payment app might be part of the ADJACENT segment as it varies from the CORE in value proposition.)

Step 6 - With the ADJACENT part of the portfolio map completed you can now turn your attention to the TRANSFORMATIONAL one. The TRANSFORMATIONAL business models vary in both customer segment and value proposition from the CORE. Continuing on the banking narrative, this might be an application that's helping customers file their tax returns or better understand spam risks.

Step 7 - On the horizontal axes now add your company's Product Lifecycle. As soon as you have this ready you can populate it with the ventures that are in the funnel. Make sure you consider both the maturity stage and type of business model when placing the ventures in the funnel on the map.

With the map created, you can now analyze the distribution of business models and feed this information into the strategy formation process.

In highly diversified conglomerates or corporations we encourage you to create one business model map for each business unit (e.g. in a bank structured on business units such as retail banking, wholesale banking and wealth management, each business unit should have its own portfolio map).

With the map created you can now analyze the distribution of business models and feed this information into the strategy formation process.

The abstraction principle applied to the Indicators
in Tactical Innovation Accounting, Managerial
Innovation Accounting and Strategic Innovation Accounting

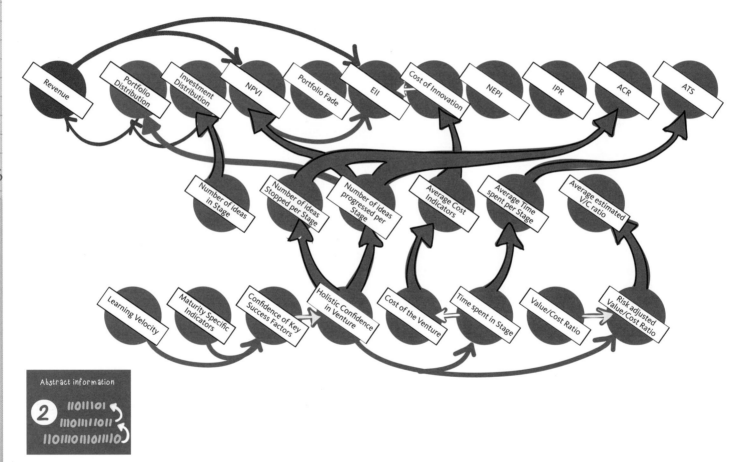

Abstract information

The innovation funnel of today represents the portfolio of tomorrow. To build a comprehensive innovation strategy it is important to paint a clear picture of the risk of disruption by looking at the Portfolio through the Business model lens rather than the product lens.

The overall performance of the innovation ecosystem cannot be measured by one single indicator. You need an interconnected and mutually supporting mix of indicators to build a clear picture of the efficacy and efficiency of your innovation ecosystem. Ask yourself these four main questions:

- Is my company under risk of disruption?
- Is innovation driving growth in my company?
- How does my company's future look?
- How efficient is my company's innovation ecosystem?

Leaders need to focus on the ROI of the innovation funnel as a whole and not the ROI of individual teams.

Conversations on Innovation

Alexa Dembek

Chief Technology and Sustainability Officer, DuPont

With her core beliefs around customer centricity, strategic alignment, relentless communication, and collaboration, Alexa Dembek is DuPont's Chief Technology and Sustainability Officer. She is an experienced strategic leader with a passion for science-based innovation contributing to business growth.

Innovation Accounting: What's the biggest driver for innovation in your company?

Alexa Dembek: Every company has different drivers. For us at DuPont, innovation led growth is a really important driver to create value. Value delivers on the purpose of the company "To empower the world with the essential innovations to thrive" which aligns with sustainability.

This might not be the same for other companies. For example, some companies might be looking at innovation to achieve geographic expansion. Some might look at capital expansion.

DuPont has a legacy that stretches over two centuries and what worked for us in the past and what's working for us, is innovation led growth. We're constantly reinventing ourselves to be relevant for what's coming and what the needs of the future are. Our fundamental strategy, therefore, is to align with market and technology trends. And then we look at how to adjust our internal capabilities for the problems we would like to tackle.

IA: What's the biggest challenge when it comes to communicating growth through innovation to the other peers on the board? How do you interact with the CEO or the CFO for example?

AD: So what we have all agreed on is to drive both the speed to market and the impact of our growth investments. The challenge is always, how do we make sure that we can tie the investments that we're making to top and bottom line growth. And that's where we spend a lot of our effort, making sure that both the scale of the investment is right and then the speed to delivery is right too. And both of those vary depending on where we're at in the market. Some markets have a very fast cycle. Some markets are the opposite - with very long cycles. Therefore the investment requirements as well as the speed is different. So we have to look at it very carefully when analyzing our performance. We never take a one-size-fits-all stance when measuring these things.

At the end of the day what matters for everyone are three things: top line growth, bottom line growth and return on invested capital. What will vary is the cycle time, how we look at speed and also how we look at what the investment is or needs to be.

Our investments in innovation and R&D, at the enterprise level, have been steady at ~ 4% of sales. So the key indicators aren't just the spend, but what is the outcome we get based on the investments we made. And these outcomes are both growth - as I said earlier - and keeping the company relevant by delivering on our purpose in the years to come.

IA: What kind of indicators do you use to show investors or other shareholders that the money spent on innovation is well spent? Is it just the final outcome, the top line growth, bottom line, or do you have anything else that justifies the investments?

AD: Each business has a strategy for how they're going to achieve their objectives in their respective markets. A key element of our success is in aligning innovation investments with each one of those strategic priorities. So there are some questions that are always front of stage for us:
What are the important and invaluable problems in each of our opportunity areas we have identified?
What is it going to take to win and what are our investment profiles to be able to deliver in those areas?
So that's what we spend all of our time, doing it with speed at scale.

And then the investments come from that discussion. This is not just a year over year, it's part of our DNA, our culture if you want. We do this on an ongoing basis.

We always stay focused on the market and customer problem - not what others are doing. We look at what's our unique and differentiated solution. What can we deliver to be able to help solve these important problems in the market. So we're very market-focused, everything's about market and customer focused.

IA: What are you doing when, in spite of proper investment and strategic clarity the return is just not there at the end?

AD: We always view every outcome, positive or negative, as learnings and we do our best to leverage what we learned as we develop the next strategy. To do that we encourage our colleagues to not fall in love with projects, but fall in love with growth. Projects will come and go but our quest for growth, our quest for solving important problems is what's timeless. And that's where we try to focus the conversation, win or lose. And once we're aligned across the company and with all the businesses on what the problems that need to be solved are, it makes everybody really energetic and excited to go and work on important problems.

The real point for me is to make everyone fall in love with the outcome. Don't fall in love with the process.

IA: Beyond the financial result indicators you mentioned, are you looking at other non-financial indicators? And if you do, how well are these received by the financial people in the company?

AD: Yes for financial performance, the things that really matter are those three, top-line growth, bottom-line growth and return on capital for all investments. However we have many non-financial measures as well and I'd have to say that our CFO values them equally.

Most of our non-financial metrics are ESG (Environmental, Social, and Governance) and culture relevant. DuPont's 2030 sustainability goals are nonfinancial. So, every year, there are many things that we have to improve beyond just the financials in order to drive a much broader impact. How are we driving diversity, equity and inclusion of which culture is a dimension for example. Or our work in sustainability, our work in the community, our work on reducing greenhouse gases or our work on water stewardship are things we constantly focus on and they are all included to deliver our 2030 goals.

We have in total nine goals in our 2030 sustainability roadmap. And each of those is very quantifiable including diversity, equality, inclusion and representation. We have very quantifiable measures in areas which are traditionally difficult to quantify. For further reference the readers can look at our GRI report from July 2020 where we outline everything we track around non-financial impact.

To conclude I would say that for DuPont, it's an "and" profit, "and" purpose. The measurement side is obviously much more quantifiable on the financial metrics. But the nonfinancial metrics are just as important, therefore we track them too.

IA: Given your experience of measuring innovation led growth, what are some guiding principles or "do's" and "don'ts" that you would encourage other business leaders to follow? Are there any tips?

AD: Well, what's been successful for DuPont is looking at innovation through two lenses. One is the retrospective view. So looking back in time on what's been delivered and the outcomes we had.

The second is the forward view. This looks at anticipating progress. The measure is different here than in the retrospective view. Here we focus more on uncertainty reduction and how we win. Are we learning fast enough in new markets? I think that's been key for us and we overvalue our learnings from places we weren't successful in. We host this annual Dead Project Day around Halloween, and this gives us a chance to be reflective in a fun and not a threatening environment where we can say, "what did we learn from things that we had to stop and pivot, and how do we use those learnings to be even faster in the future?"

The other thing that we've had to spend a lot of time on is the cultural dimensions of risk taking and empowerment. And I think everyone these days knows those cultural dimensions are critical.

Think of it as an
opportunity! We use
your innovation and
you make changes that
fit our wishes.

1+1 = 3. The accounting logic of partnerships.

CHAPTER 7
Measuring Startup Collaborations

This chapter wouldn't have been possible without the contribution of our friend and colleague Peter LePiane

How do you react when your marketplace starts drifting away from you? Do you do nothing, hoping that customers will return once they have sampled the alternatives and realized the value of your offering? Do you instantly embark on a company-wide reset, potentially sacrificing continuity of service or product in the chase for differentiation? Or do you perhaps reach out into the business sphere, looking to partner with another organization in order to reconnect with your customers?

And even if your marketplace is stable, are you contemplating any of the latter two scenarios in order to stay ahead of the curve or to connect with a new audience? It's a challenge facing all organizations at one time or another. How you react could determine the future direction of your business, including the development of product lines.

Interestingly the challenge isn't solely related to products. The same can be true of customer interactions or even of product flow. Let's give you an example. In 2017, Hellmann's (the mayonnaise brand owned by Unilever) identified a need to engage with a new audience which was becoming increasingly important in the marketplace; digitally-savvy millennials.

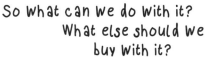

Recognizing that a new digital audience required a new digital approach, Unilever identified an opportunity to deliver a new model through a partnership with on-demand delivery service Quiqup.

Targeting shoppers who were likely to make impulse purchases, the collaboration enabled consumers to choose a recipe and get all of the fresh ingredients delivered to them within an hour. Commenting on the new offering, Joanna Allen, Global Brand VP for Hellmann's, said: "As a brand that originated in a deli, it's an important opportunity for us to return to direct-to-consumer servicing" while Bassel El Koussa, Quiqup CEO & Co-Founder, added: "Today's consumers have come to expect businesses to offer fast, flexible and efficient delivery options because they recognize the scarcity of time and want to make the most of what they have. Our technology enables Hellmann's to remain relevant to new audiences and adapt to changing digital consumer lifestyles."[95]

205

The Quiqup tie-up isn't the only collaborative partnership enjoyed by Unilever which has its own startup partnering platform, The Unilever Foundry. It is just one example which we could have picked from thousands of stories across business that demonstrate the benefits of partnering with external expertise in order to enhance product development, consumer choice and service.

In fact this rise in collaborative relationships is one reason why in 2017 the International Organization for Standardization (ISO) released a standard for Collaborative Business Relationship Management Systems; ISO 44001. Building on the earlier 2006 PAS11000 Collaborative Business Relationships model, the ISO standard has been designed to apply to all business systems and collaborations from governmental organizations to micro businesses and from one-to-one direct relationships to multi-business relationships.

In this chapter we are concentrating on collaborations between corporations and startups but many of the issues considered and solutions explored will equally apply to other collaboration models. With that in mind, typical corporate/startup collaborations may include:

- Paid or Free pilots.

- Joint Ventures such as new product development, market research or technology research.

- Venturing (buying a stake in a startup).

- Acquisitions.

	Limited resource commitment by corporate	Substantial resource commitment by corporate
Substantial resource commitment by startup	Joint Venture	Acquisitions Venturing
Limited resource commitment by startup	Free Pilot	Paid Pilot

We will be examining these in more detail as we move through this chapter. When deciding on the optimum collaboration type, one of the key factors to take into consideration is the potential commitment of resources to the project. Areas for consideration here include costs, time, and product sharing, alongside intangibles such as reputation and market access.[96]

Entities also need to consider implementation vehicles and models including acceleration programs, shared workspaces or open access to technology. Again we will be examining these considerations for each of the above collaboration types as we explore key metrics and accounting parameters for collaboration.

Why Collaborate?

Make no mistake, startup collaborations are not single-sided deals; they have to work for both partners if they are to be effective. It is vital therefore that chief executive officers of both corporates and start-ups share common strategic goals of delivering innovation whilst at the same time growing their respective companies, improving their competitive positioning, and generating revenue.

Nothing should be ruled out in the pursuit for differentiation. That's why some corporations even find it beneficial to partner with potential disruptors.

Although this might sound counterintuitive, a collaboration between an established entity and a disruptor startup can enable the established business to overcome the challenge of disrupting from within, whilst bringing industry knowledge and accelerated development potential to the startup business. Such are the benefits of collaboration that a BSI study[97] in respect of the fore-runner of ISO 44001 revealed that 79% saw adherence to the collaborative relationship standard as increasing their competitive edge, whilst 62% reported an increase in customer numbers.

Now is perhaps the time to make one thing crystal clear; successful collaborations take work and understanding. No two organizations are alike and, regardless of the shape of the collaboration, working together requires organizations to build an understanding and acceptance of each other's culture, strengths, and working methodologies. And that understanding shouldn't be confined to management levels. Chief executive officers of start-ups often find themselves talking, not to the chief executive officers of corporates, but to employees much further down the hierarchy who also have to have a deep understanding of the way in which potential synergies will evolve. Complications also commonly arise from a clash of cultures: for example agile versus waterfall. Different work ethics and

different risk appetites might also, further down the line, spin the collaboration out of control unless clear terms of reference are agreed at the outset. We'll come back to the challenge/risk matrix later in this chapter.

207

Another benefit for startups entering into a collaboration with a legacy company is riskless internationalization. Working with a multinational established organization offers a startup the chance to expand into other countries by partnering with the corporate's local subsidiaries. Furthermore, leveraging areas such as brand recognition, marketing, and distribution channels can again help the startup to rapidly develop. Moreover, collaborative pilot exercises can enable the startup to rapidly test and validate their business model.

The benefits for startups don't stop here. Partnering with a corporation can also present some intangible benefits such as the development of case studies/testimonials or garnering in-depth knowledge of the sector, both of which could help with future sales drives. Particularly so, as corporate decision-makers tend to look for references as well as industry experience before signing on the dotted line.

For corporations, usually the most cited benefit is **innovation**. We probably don't need to highlight here the importance of innovation as an antidote to disruption or the securer of future competitive advantage. We also don't need to go into the importance of taking advantage of shifts in the marketplace, whether caused by technological or societal developments in existing or adjacent industries. However, with the current tendency for corporates to focus more on incremental (48%) or adjacent (26%) innovation rather than transformational (28%) innovation[98] corporates may find that external collaboration is required in order to drive change. Startups, being free of corporate governance chains, have more freedom to develop truly disruptive solutions.

Although usually not the primary driving force behind a collaborative initiative from the corporate side, **new revenues** that result from a partnership cannot be ignored.

Although **the benefits** of collaboration are different for each party, the potential rewards are substantial enough to bring the two together and make them work through their differences.

For startups, **revenue** is often the primary incentive, especially if the startup is an early-stage company. Big corporates can be willing to invest considerable amounts of money in a partnership, provided they see the potential benefits. This capital infusion can free start-ups from the need to seek further outside investments; enabling them to concentrate on their business model. Corporates may also be willing to take a long-term interest; thereby helping to stabilize a start-up and enabling it to reach break-even or even profitability earlier than planned. Such an approach allows the start-up to achieve sustainable growth, independently from scarce Venture Capital.

Furthermore, start-ups tend to be more **customer-centric** as they are not as process-driven as established corporates. With less baggage, startups can adapt and customize solutions more easily, allowing the corporation to serve and know its customers better. Working with customer-centric and innovative startups enables a corporation to better track changes in **market trends**, **purchasing behaviors** and **technology usage** that ultimately may bring about the disruption of the corporation's core industry.

On top of the tangible benefits described above, corporations are drawn to startups for the intangible benefits they bring. For example, working with start-ups can spark a more **entrepreneurial culture** in an otherwise hierarchical organization.

Even if the benefits of collaboration are clear for both sides, as mentioned above there are some **challenges** and risks that need to be overcome.

The primary challenge for a ***startup*** is associated with managing **sales cycle times**. As start-up teams are small, each bet on a corporate deal equates to a risk of running out of cash if the deal doesn't come through. Shorter sales cycles equal a higher survivability rate for the startup; something which may well conflict with a more extended corporate sales cycle.

Furthermore, start-ups often feel the relationship is treated in a top-down way instead of at eye level. Despite agreed synergies, they can find it challenging to be perceived as serious businesses. In order to overcome this perception, they may make compromises that they wouldn't otherwise have made.

209

There is another danger which arises from startups being all too willing to accede to corporate requests; a lack of challenge of key agreements. Startups may not have the resources to fully investigate and consider all of the clauses within a contract, but they ignore this aspect at their peril. What may be a standard clause for a corporate may be a make-or-break demand for a smaller startup. We are thinking here about areas such as the post-collaboration ownership of jointly-developed intellectual property, ongoing client servicing, or even future development rights. It may seem tedious to spend time examining areas such as these at the start of a project, particularly if the first phase may only be a free pilot, but, unless agreement is reached at the outset the startup may find itself tied to an agreement which renders it unviable in the long term.

On the *corporate* side, collaboration challenges tend to revolve around internal issues. The **not-invented-here syndrome** is ever-present in innovation, even more so when the innovation comes from the outside. It can be difficult for a corporation to internally adopt innovations that were developed in collaboration with start-ups.

Another challenge for the corporations is **budgeting**. We are not saying that money is an issue. But the annual nature of the budgeting cycle in most corporations is. When a corporation wants to engage a business unit to work with a startup and carry out a pilot for example, that particular business unit hasn't got any budget to go ahead and start that engagement. The budget in corporations is usually decided the year before and it's done on an annual basis, so unless the open innovation organization or the venturing team of the corporation pays for the pilot it will be very complicated for the collaborations to happen.

Furthermore, business units may not be aligned on the collaboration's goal and its possible outcomes before its kickoff. This can lead to **conflicting requirements** and delays further down the line, as well as feeding into the innovation acceptance/rejection culture of the corporation.

This brings us to an important observation. Whilst we have seen a gradual acceptance of failure as a bi-product of innovation, there is still a residual perception that failure is a cause for censure rather than a learning point. In fact, 27% of executives still see it as unacceptable to invest in an innovation project that fails.[99] This can lead to a culture in which failure has a heavy cost for those involved. Thus, unlike what happens in start-ups, failures are both avoided from the outset and not openly acknowledged when they happen.

It is, therefore, a key challenge for C-Level managers hoping to build an internal culture of innovation in their blue-chip company on the heels of the startup collaboration, to structure and sensitize their organization to take collaborative approaches seriously and give projects the support they need to become a success. This re-education also needs to extend to shareholders; helping them to appreciate the play-off between short-term interests and long term benefits.

Collaborations can come in many shapes and sizes. However, success stories are always rooted in each side being sensitive towards the interests, expectations, incentives, culture and work ethic of the other. Aside from clearly defining roles, rights and responsibilities, a collaboration also needs to consider the ever-present **risks** for both sides of the partnership.

*For the **startups***, from our experience, the biggest risk represents **getting engulfed by one single customer**. Focusing on a single custom solution for a single large corporate client may distract a start-up from working towards their universal, scalable vision, and limit growth prospects in the long run. On the opposite end of the scale, some corporations may not pursue a strong collaboration with a startup, and rather consider the smaller company as a source of **free consultancy**. This practice by the corporation tends to gobble up a lot of the start-up's resources.

211

Another risk on the startup side has to do with the follow-up from a collaboration: **prematurely scaling** the solution after successful proof of concept or the signing of the first deal. So a word of advice for entrepreneurs should be that successful sales to innovation departments or first clients do not mean that the solution should be scaled or indeed offered elsewhere in an unchanged form.

As corporations are complex organizations and collaborating with a startup might be interesting for several internal stakeholders, several corporate departments might start to formulate different requirements for the partnership. This often leads to **delays**, which eat into the startup's financial runway.

Lastly, in the case of collaboration getting too close and the dependency on corporate decision-making too strong, there is a high risk of the startup **losing its agile spirit**.

Corporations will not be protected from the risks of a collaboration by their size alone. Some risks, such as mission creep, apply equally to corporates and startups; other risks have more impact for the corporate side of the relationship. The most cited of these being **reputation damage**. When something goes wrong in a partnership, reputation damage has far greater consequences for the corporation than for the startup.

Depending on how much was invested in the collaboration, **lost investment** is also a risk that corporations need to consider. Many start-ups fail (about 80%), and many seemingly obvious projects turn out not to have a useful or profitable application so the investment risk for corporates is high.

We mentioned above the danger for startups if corporate employees are not fully engaged with the project. This extends to changing culture and practices to bring a more entrepreneurial spirit to the corporation. Corporate employees are used to following the beaten path and tend to regard failure as jeopardizing their careers. In a partnership with a startup they might feel threatened by the start-up's unfamiliar culture and remain overly protective of the status quo **without fully committing** to the partnership's goals. This is a risk not only to both parties but also to the success of the project.

When corporates engage, in particular with high-tech start-ups that propose solutions that the corporate is not yet ready to adopt, the so-called **maturity misalignment** can occur. In order to avoid this, it is advisable to agree on a technology readiness scale similar to the one NASA has been using,[100] ahead of the partnership's kickoff.

Collaborations can come in many shapes and sizes: incubation, acceleration, paid demos, joined ventures or free partnership. However, success stories are always rooted in each side being sensitive towards the interests, expectations, incentives, culture and work ethic of the other.

As you have seen above, partnerships are complex undertakings with challenges and risks but also with benefits that can extend beyond the immediate project. In order to mitigate the risk and start to lay the foundation of a successful partnership, corporations and startups would do well to start by running through the following checklists.

- The first item on the **startup's checklist** revolves around the target of the partnership: What is the target of the partnership for them as a startup? What is the target of the corporate partner? Are the two targets achievable at the same time? Is the partnership, in its current state (e.g. paid demo), going to lead to both parties achieving their targets?

- The second item on the list has to do with the way the success of the collaboration will be measured. How will you as a startup measure the success of the collaboration? How will the corporate partner do that? Are the two measurements contradictory or not?

- The third item on the startup's checklist is budget: Do you, as a startup, have enough runway to deliver on the collaboration's goals? Is the budget that's being allocated on the corporation's side (time, resources, other materials) sufficient to achieve the goal of the partnership?

- The fourth and last item the startup needs to be aware of is the person they are in contact with on the corporate side: What buyer persona are you speaking with? Is this the only person you are in contact with? Is the person the right one to achieve the goals of the partnership? (Make sure you speak with at least two people in case you are in contact with just one person from the corporation and this person changes jobs or leaves the company, putting the collaboration in jeopardy. At the very best, the collaboration might still happen, but you are going to spend countless hours figuring out who the new person in-charge of the deal is. This will impact your "runway." This risk is greater at the beginning of the collaboration before any agreement is signed.) Do any of the people you are in contact with have enough influence to shield the collaboration in case priorities get reshuffled on the corporation's side?

Make no mistake, the startups are not the only ones needing a collaboration checklist; corporates need one as well. However, the corporate checklist is slightly different from the startup one and it should be structured to take account of the nature of the collaboration and the lead individual or department. What follows is therefore only a suggestion:

- The first item on the ***corporation's checklist*** is similar to the first one on the startup's checklist, the target of the collaboration. However the questions differ: What are the goals of the collaboration? Are the goals of the collaboration aligned with our company's (innovation) strategy? Is the startup's target for the collaboration competing with our target?

- The second item the corporations need to be clear on before going into a partnership is the internal reasoning behind the collaboration. To get clarity on this, the corporation needs to find answers to the following questions: Does it make sense for us to collaborate with a startup to achieve our goals or can we achieve the same results using internal resources?

- Thirdly, the corporation needs to get clarity around the best way to collaborate (and consequently achieve their targets). What form should the collaboration take in order for us to achieve our target (e.g. paid demo, joint venture, free demo etc.)? Is this form of collaboration going to help the startup achieve their goal too?

- The fourth item on the corporation's checklist revolves around resources and their allocation: What resources are needed for this collaboration to succeed? Can we allocate the necessary results for the collaboration to succeed? Do we have the necessary resources at our disposal?

- The next item on the list has to do with the way the success of the collaboration will be measured. How will you measure the success of the collaboration? How will the startup partner do that? Are the two measurements contradictory or not?

- The sixth item on the list touches on the internal stakeholders from the corporate side: Who will be the stakeholders responsible for driving the collaboration? Are these people the right ones for the collaboration to succeed?

The checklist is there to ensure the best fitting collaborations go forward on both the corporate side as well as the startup side.

But having a checklist before going into a collaboration is not going to be enough if the corporation is not mature enough to collaborate with startups. At the end of the chapter we have included an assessment that will help you understand the current maturity level of your corporation's collaboration "game." Taking the assessment will also help you pinpoint the areas for improvement.

Collaboration between two companies will never be easy, regardless of how much they need each other. The success of a collaboration depends on one hand on mutual understanding (each side appreciating the risks and the differences the other faces in embarking on collaboration) and on the other hand on thorough preparation before signing on the proverbial dotted line. And the work doesn't stop there. Having a robust measurement system in place enables organizations to better define, manage and progress collaborative projects.

How to measure your startup collaboration
In order to better manage and measure your startup collaboration projects, it is important firstly to understand what needs to be measured at program level before applying those parameters to individual collaboration types.

Let's first focus on program level.

From experience, we encourage you to have a funnel view when analyzing your startup collaboration program(s). There are many ways to segment a funnel but let's, for now, consider the following generic stages:
• Demand.
• Live.
• Outcome.

In the **Demand** phase of the funnel, a company can analyze the extent to which the startup is actively looking to collaborate with the company and vice-versa.

The **Live** phase of the funnel measures ongoing collaborations. This gives organizations on both sides a snapshot of ongoing progress as well as an indication of future outcomes.

The **Outcome** phase of the funnel consists of tracking the impact completed collaborations had on the company.

Now let's look in more detail at the demand, live and outcome phases for each of the collaboration types mentioned towards the start of this chapter and highlight some indicators that can be tracked for each phase.

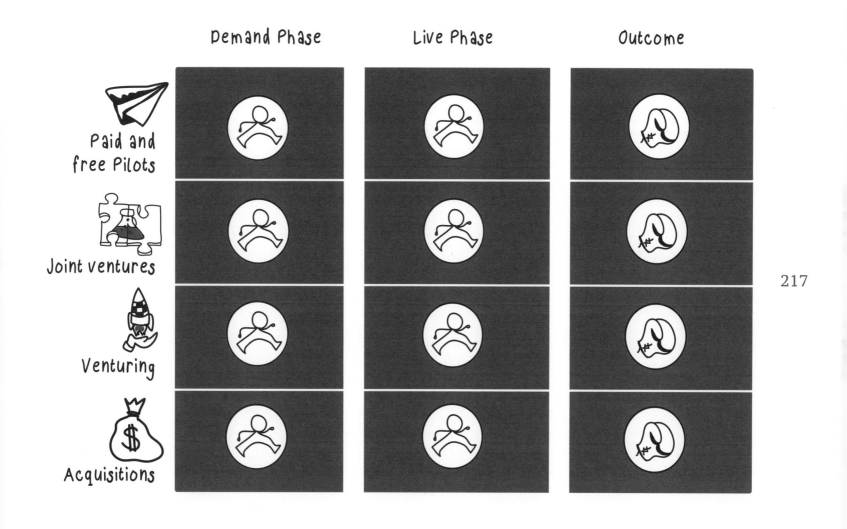

Paid and free pilots

218

Paid & Free Pilots
Demand Phase

For this type of collaboration and this phase of the collaboration funnel, it is advisable for the company to track the following performance indicators:

- Number of requests received for either of these two types of collaborations per unit of time.
- Number of requests sent for either of these two types of collaborations per unit of time.
- Average cost of attracting one demo; this might include the travel budget of the startup collaboration team or certain event sponsorships.

Paid & Free Pilots
Live Phase

For this type of collaboration and this phase of the collaboration funnel, it is advisable for the company to track the following performance indicators:

- Percentage of initiated demos from total proposed (for added clarity this should be ideally computed separately for each type of demo).
- Invested capital per unit of time (for paid demos).
- Average invested capital per unit of time (for paid demos).
- Invested resources in a unit of time for either of these two types of collaborations (e.g. time investments).
- Average invested resources per unit of time for either of these two types of collaborations.
- Progress in accordance with a pre-agreed roadmap.
- Progress towards pre-defined goals.

Paid & Free Pilots
Outcome

For this type of collaboration and this phase of the collaboration funnel, it is advisable for the company to track the following result indicators:

- Percentage of completed pilots from the total initiated.
- Average cost of completing one demo, including both the Demand phase cost and the Live phase cost per unit of time.
- Collaboration specific outcome which will most likely vary from demo to demo but they should be mutually agreed upon at the beginning of each demo. (e.g. if the collaboration was geared towards lowering the onboarding of new clients on a certain corporate developed solution through the deployment of a startup owned technology, then the result indicator that needs to be tracked is onboarding time reduction; other examples might include cost savings, or new revenue).
- Average time to outcome.

Moving on to the next collaboration type: joint ventures.

Joint Ventures
Demand Phase

For this type of collaboration and this phase of the collaboration funnel, it is advisable for the company to track the following performance indicators:

- Number of requests received for joint ventures per unit of time.
- Number of requests sent for joint ventures per unit of time.
- Average cost of attracting one joint venture proposal per unit of time (this might include the travel budget of the startup collaboration team or certain event sponsorships).

For added granularity, a company might consider tracking this per joint venture type, such as new product development, market research, technology research etc.

Joint Ventures
Live Phase

For this type of collaboration and this phase of the collaboration funnel, it is advisable for the company to track the following performance indicators:

- Number of projects initiated per unit of time.
- Percentage of projects initiated from total received and sent per unit of time.
- If applicable (e.g. product development), progress of specific indicators similar to the ones for the internal teams we have discussed in the previous chapter.
- Invested capital per unit of time.
- Average invested capital per unit of time.
- Invested resources per unit of time (e.g. time investments).
- Average invested resources per unit of time.
- Progress in accordance with a pre-agreed roadmap of the joint venture.
- Progress towards pre-defined goals.

Joint Ventures
Outcome

For this type of collaboration and this phase of the collaboration funnel, it is advisable for the company to track the following result indicator:

- Average cost of completing one joint venture, including both the Demand phase cost and the Live phase cost, per unit of time.
- Collaboration specific outcomes which will most likely vary from joint venture to joint venture but they should be mutually agreed upon at the beginning of each demo (e.g. new revenue from products co-developed, dollars spent per insight obtained in the case of technology research etc.).
- Average time to outcome.

Moving on to the next collaboration type: venturing.

Joint Ventures

219

Venturing

Venturing Demand Phase

For this type of collaboration and this phase of the collaboration funnel, it is advisable for the company to track the following performance indicators:

- Number of requests received for venturing per unit of time.
- Number of requests sent for venturing per unit of time.
- Average cost of attracting one possible venture candidate per unit of time (this might include the travel budget of the startup collaboration team to certain hubs such as Berlin or San Francisco or certain event sponsorships).

Venturing Live Phase

For this type of collaboration and this phase of the collaboration funnel, it is advisable for the company to track the following performance indicators:

- Number of initiated investments per unit of time.
- Percentage of initiated investments from the total requests received and sent per unit of time.
- Total invested capital per unit of time.
- Average ticket size (investment) per unit of time.
- Average stake taken in ventures per unit of time.
- Progress in accordance with a pre-agreed roadmap of the joint venture.
- Progress towards pre-defined goals.

Venturing Outcome

For this type of collaboration and this phase of the collaboration funnel, it is advisable for the company to track the following result indicator:

- Average cost of taking a stake in a startup including both the Demand phase cost and the Live phase cost per unit of time.
- New revenue generated per unit of time as a result of investment made.
- New revenue to cost ratio (total cost of venturing incl. the internal costs such as salaries of the responsible people) per unit of time.
- Assets appreciation per unit of time.
- Assets appreciation to cost ratio (total cost of venturing incl. the internal costs such as salaries of the responsible people) per unit of time.
- Collaboration specific outcomes which will most likely vary from venture to venture but they should be mutually agreed upon at the beginning of each collaboration (e.g. market capitalization etc.).

Moving on to the next collaboration type: acquisitions.

Acquisitions
Demand Phase

For this type of collaboration and this phase of the collaboration funnel, it is advisable for the company to track the following performance indicators:

- Number of requests sent for acquisitions per unit of time.
- Average cost of scouting one possible acquisition candidate per unit of time (this might include costs associated with due diligence etc.),

Acquisitions
Live Phase

For this type of collaboration and this phase of the collaboration funnel, it is advisable for the company to track the following performance indicators:

- Number of initiated acquisitions per unit of time.
- Percentage of initiated acquisitions from the total sent per unit of time.
- Total invested capital per unit of time.
- Progress in accordance with a pre-agreed roadmap of the joint venture.
- Progress towards pre-defined goals.

Acquisitions
Outcome

For this type of collaboration and this phase of the collaboration funnel, it is advisable for the company to track the following result indicator:

- Average cost of acquiring a startup, including both the Demand phase cost and the Live phase, cost per unit of time.
- New revenue generated per unit of time as a result of acquisition made.
- New revenue to cost ratio (total cost of acquisition incl. the internal costs such as salaries of the responsible people) per unit of time.
- Assets appreciation per unit of time.
- Assets appreciation to cost ratio (total cost of acquisition incl. the internal costs such as salaries of the responsible people) per unit of time.
- Collaboration specific outcomes which will most likely vary from acquisition to acquisition but they should be agreed upon when the acquisition is made. (e.g. market capitalization etc.).

Acquisition

221

A word of advice: time bound cohorts are important. What do we mean by that? We use "per unit of time" behind most indicators. We've done that because we believe in self-benchmarking, meaning you are going to compare the performance of a certain activity from one quarter to the next or compare quarter one of the current year with quarter one of the previous year. Time bound cohorts (and self-benchmarking) will give you the ability to understand if your company's collaboration arm is getting better over time or is struggling.

We advise you to create your own set of indicators specific to your own context as we don't think it is possible for us to create something that will work in every company or will offer the needed granularity. We only hope that the above has offered you a leg up in your quest of creating something that speaks to the specific needs of your company.

Measuring the collaboration funnel(s) will add much needed clarity and transparency to the collaboration effort. This in turn will help to create a positive attitude across the business towards collaboration initiatives.

How to measure individual investments
Given the fact that in most collaborations the startups are fairly mature and that they have an existing validated offer in the market, measuring individual initiatives will focus more on the impact they are having (financial or otherwise) rather than measuring their progress as is the case with internal investments. One of the best ways to measure that impact accurately is with a financial modeling method called Monte Carlo.[101]

If Monte Carlo reminds you of gambling, there's a good reason for that, being codenamed after the Monte Carlo casino in Monaco. Born of statistical sampling methods which stretch back, as far as we can trace, to the Comte de Buffon in 1777, it wasn't until the mid 1940s that it was officially named while being used on top-secret nuclear weapons projects in the United States.

It wasn't used for financial forecasts for decades. It took a Harvard Business Review article in 1979[102] to popularize Monte Carlo in the world of corporate finance. It has since been widely used to analyze the potential future return of investments ranging from stock market options to startups.

The problem that Monte Carlo was designed to solve simply asks; how can we accurately predict the future state of something uncertain? If we all had access to a crystal ball, the answer would also be simple. Unfortunately, no such crystal ball exists. As a result, the only way for us to be accurate about a future uncertain event is to express it as a distinct range with a probability of the future event occurring within that range.

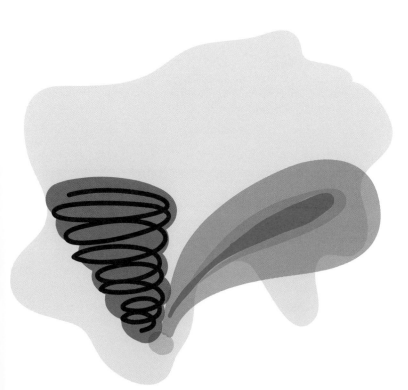

What if you don't use Monte Carlo? Well, think about the last time you created or read a business case. For those in corporate Venture Capital, think about the last time you read a pitch. For anyone who doesn't fall into one of those categories, we are sure you'll be able to play along regardless. We are willing to bet that your business case or pitch had a spreadsheet calculation that forecasted revenue and/or profit at least 5 years into the future. We are also willing to bet that it expressed that revenue or profit in 5 years as a single number with a plus or minus range on it, for example, year 5 profit at $150,000 +/- 50%.

On closer inspection, that prediction appears to offer a guarantee. It states, with certainty, that year 5 profit will be between $75,000 and $225,000. In interpreting the range, we tend to consider, or even state, that the number between the high and low bounds of the range as the most likely outcome.

What we're talking about here is not which day of the week Christmas Day will fall on next year. Instead, we are asking questions about much less predictable events such as the chance the next hurricane in the Gulf of Mexico will hit New Orleans five days after it has been officially identified.

Expressing the outcome in terms a Monte Carlo simulation might produce, we may discover that there is a 40% chance that a hurricane will make landfall anywhere between 100 kilometers east and 65 kilometers west of New Orleans five days after it was identified in the Gulf of Mexico. In short, the Monte Carlo simulation turns uncertainty into a measurable result that can be acted upon.

How safe is that range and how likely is it for the predicted middle number to occur? Let's consider these questions separately.

The range is computed using a single percentage that is intended to represent the maximum uncertainty of the outcome. That level of uncertainty is a critical input because we use the top and bottom of the range it produces as the worst and best case outcomes. Thinking about your last business case or investor pitch, how much effort and analysis did you put into deciding your +/- percentage? If you're like most, the percentage was either mandated or you guessed. That calls into question the value of the range in deciding the best and worst case.

Now let's examine the middle number of the range. Does it really represent the most likely occurrence? That depends on how the number was derived. If you, again, are like most, you would have taken educated guesses at the most likely outcome of each of the variables in the formula you are trying to calculate at some point in the future. These guesses may even have been derived from a pro-forma financial statement. This combination of educated guesses then accumulates into the outcome of your formula. The result is an educated guess derived from a number of other educated guesses. Is this accumulation of educated guesses all that accurate? Not really. There is a risk associated with each guess that is not accurately reflected. Some guesses will be more accurate. Some will be less so.

This raises another weakness of the +/- range approach common to most business cases; we have no way of asking how likely it is for the outcome to fall into any other range besides the absolute best and worst case. What if we want to know the range that is 75% likely to occur? We cannot answer this question. If you are tempted to answer by using a +/- of 75%, that will only return the absolute best and worst case in a range that is guaranteed to be between 2 numbers that are 150% apart from one another.

Great. Now we know the method we've been using for years is flawed. What can we do to make it better? Monte Carlo, of course!

Monte Carlo is a method that uses statistics and computational brute force to produce a range of outcomes and an associated probability that the actual outcome falls within that range, like the hurricane example above. Unlike the single best guess formula above, Monte Carlo asks for a maximum and a minimum for each variable in the formula you are forecasting at some point in the future. It then randomly selects a number in the max to min range of every variable and computes the value of the formula. Then, it takes thousands of those randomly selected variables within their ranges, computing the formula each time.

For example, say that the formula you are looking to forecast has only 2 variables: "profit = x + y." Let's say that "x" ranges from 1 to 3 and "y" from 1 to 2. If, for ease of explanation, our Monte Carlo simulation only selects whole, non-decimal numbers, it would calculate the possible outcomes as:

Profit = 1 + 1 = 2
Profit = 1 + 2 = 3
Profit = 1 + 3 = 4
Profit = 2 + 1 = 3
Profit = 2 + 2 = 4
Profit = 2 + 3 = 5

Therefore the range of possible outcomes for profit is $2 to $5. Because we asked for the absolute max and min of each variable, the probability that we express for the true value to be contained in this range is 100%. In other words, we have forecast that there is a 100% chance that profit will be between $2 and $5.

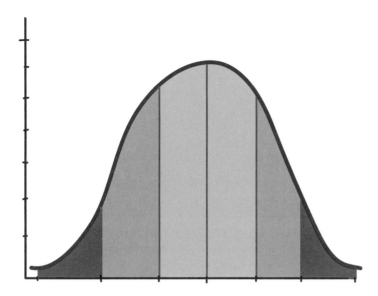

Most scenarios are not as simple. In the case of a profit formula, each variable has much more variation. That variation can be modeled using a probability distribution called the normal distribution. It's the bell curve that we all fell victim to in college at some point. We can use the normal distribution for every variable because of something called the Central Limit Theorem.[103] An explanation of why that is true is within the scope of a statistics textbook; feel free to look it up if you want to explore further.

As long as we have some data for each variable (technically, a sample size of 30 or more data points), the Central Limit Theorem applies and we can use Monte Carlo with the normal distribution. Note that if a variable in your formula is obviously not normally distributed, the appropriate distribution should be used. For example, if a variable can only be true or false, the binomial distribution should be used. If you are in doubt at all, use the normal distribution.

Monte Carlo then uses the ranges provided for each uncertain variable and the normal distribution to select a random number in each range to compute thousands of different scenarios for a formula. Because each variable was selected with the normal distribution, the output looks like the bell curve described above.

We can then slice and dice that curve into ranges with associated probabilities, as described above. In doing so we transform raw numbers into statistical probabilities which will give us a real understanding of the likelihood of future outcomes.

Now that the technicalities are out of the way, phew!, let's explore what Monte Carlo can do that a typical pro-forma business case cannot.

The main power of a Monte Carlo analysis is in its ability to slice and dice ranges of outcomes with associated probabilities. Using the profit in year 5 of a startup's business model as an example, we could answer any number of questions, including:
- What profit range is 99% likely to occur?
- How likely is it that profit will be between $200,000 and $600,000?
- How likely is it that profit will be above zero?

225

Returning to the ranges for each uncertain variable in your formula, there is an interesting side effect to explore. Say we have one variable that has a fairly tight range where the best case is 50% higher than the worst case, and another variable that has a best case that is 500% higher than the worst case.

Which variable could use more analysis and more data? The one with the wider range, of course. Using Monte Carlo analysis enables us to reveal the parameters that require more data and experimentation. It provides another view on where the riskiest assumptions are in a business model. It also allows for simple, and very robust, what-if analysis across all variables in a formula at the same time. Contrast that with the ability to alter only 2 variables at a time in a traditional financial sensitivity analysis.

Another exciting possibility provided by the discrete ranges of each variable in a formula is the ability to calibrate our estimation of those ranges. Humans are not particularly good at estimating future uncertain events. We typically estimate ranges that are too narrow as we chronically assume we know more than we do.

This systematic overconfidence is especially dangerous when we attempt to estimate with precision the likely outcomes of a business case. Research has not only shown this tendency for overconfidence[104] but also that better estimation is possible through calibration.[105]

What kind of calibration? Let's try it ourselves. Imagine the Eiffel Tower. What range, from absolute tallest to absolute shortest, is 100% certain to contain the true height of the Eiffel Tower in meters? Try it now.

Thinking about the problem in 2 parts can be helpful. In other words, what height is impossible for the Eiffel Tower to be taller than? Could you make that height shorter and have it remain impossible for the Eiffel Tower to be taller than it? If so, reduce the height and ask that question again until you can't reduce

the maximum height further. Repeat that process in reverse with the minimum height (i.e. what height is impossible for the Eiffel Tower to be shorter than?) and you have as accurate a range as you can get. If you tried that on your own, you can find the actual height of the Eiffel Tower below to see if your range was accurate.

We can perform the same hack when it comes to Monte Carlo ranges for a business model formula. What we should NOT do to construct ranges is guess what each variable is likely to be and add a +/- buffer to it to absorb error. While this feels safe, the initial guess anchors the range we derive artificially. By splitting the range into the 2 discrete questions of max and min, we avoid the many human biases that creep into our decision-making when we try to guess a point value accurately. This creates a more accurate range for Monte Carlo to act on. Then when we run Monte Carlo, it smoothes any errors in our ranges by, as explained above, running thousands of permutations and combinations of values in the ranges for each uncertain variable in a formula. This frees us from needing to be precisely accurate with a point estimate, which is not after all what we humans are good at.

Let's return to our original need for a method like Monte Carlo in measuring the impact of an individual investment. Just like a pro-forma business case, we need to know the formula for the impact we are trying to understand. That formula can typically be derived directly from the startup's business model and their sales funnel. Let's take a new bank credit card as an example. Say that we are deciding if we should launch the card in a particular national market. We will only launch if the uptake is likely to be 5,000 credit cards in a month. What do we know about the sales funnel for a credit card? Say we know that:

- People will see our ads for the credit card and decide if they want to visit the information webpage about it.
- Of those people, some will request more information about the card.
- Of those people, some will submit an application for the card.
- Some of those people will like the card so much that they will apply for another credit card from the same bank and might even recommend others to visit the website for the credit card.

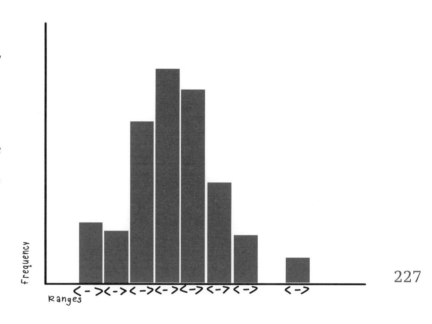

What we've just described is a standard funnel that is described by something coined by Venture Capitalist Dave McClure called Pirate Metrics[106] and which we looked at in more detail in Chapter 4.

We can now take the elements of our funnel and express them in a mathematical formula for profit. Once we establish ranges for each uncertain variable in our formula, we can apply Monte Carlo and get an output that looks something like this.

No matter how you slice and dice this, it is the picture of accuracy for your formula.

As you can see, this way of approaching estimations has clear benefits over traditional methods. Furthermore, this approach is very much connected to a product's development roadmap. Using Monte Carlo to create estimations helps product teams prioritize investments in different parts of their business model based on different potential outcomes. It can also help determine the fail conditions of an experiment by starting from a desired outcome.

You will recall that in Chapter 5, we proposed the simpler PERT technique when looking at the value-to-cost ratio of a product idea. PERT is a great way to estimate investments at an early stage when teams need to focus more on moving the product forward than making the most accurate predictions. However, when a team crosses a certain maturity threshold, Monte Carlo becomes the superior forecasting tool.

Validate before you acquire

In this chapter we have examined four principal startup collaboration types, seen how to measure the success of the venturing unit, and discovered how we can more accurately estimate the likelihood of entering into a successful venture.

But for some corporations looking to jump start innovation, one option is more tempting than the others: acquisition.

It's a tempting option and one which is certainly practiced across sectors and industries. For example, PwC predicted that 2016 would be the "year of merger mania" in healthcare.[107] And it was, with more than 30 acquisitions in the US alone.[108]

The problem with M&A as a prime way of generating innovation-driven growth generally starts after the acquisition papers are signed and reality kicks in. A Harvard Business Review report puts the failure rate of acquisitions close to 90%.[109] To put this number into perspective; it is worse (or at least comparable) to the failure rate of venture backed startups, 75%.[110]

Many reasons have been put forward as to why the failure rate of acquisitions is so significant; including cultural misfit, ambiguous strategy, and failed due diligence. But they all have the same outcome: the acquisition fails to meet its forecasted returns.

Some time ago, a healthcare corporation asked us to assist a team to re-examine the business model for one of their products which had been acquired from an external source.

Four years after the acquisition, the numbers were not only flat but nowhere near the expected growth target. So much so that even without depreciation at current growth rates it would have taken more than five hundred years to break even (not a joke, actual numbers).

Using the Business Model Canvas we started to examine the business model and the assumptions on which it was based.

It was soon obvious that there were more assumptions than knowledge in the treatment's business model.

So what needed to happen for the treatment to meet its projected financial return? We started experimenting on all the assumptions hindering the treatment from being successful.

Experiment after experiment, the cold reality unveiled before us. The assumptions, upon which the financial success of the product was based, were invalid. Given certain company and industry constraints, it soon became obvious that the acquisition shouldn't have happened in the first place. The writing on the wall couldn't have been clearer.

The only option was to move to examine damage control options including discontinuing the product, stopping further investments, or reducing operational costs.

It took an emotional toll, seeing a passionate team getting disillusioned with the prospect of the product they worked on for so long never meeting its goals. But this got us thinking. Isn't there another, better way of doing due diligence? How can we escape the ludicrous financial return forecast trap?
Perhaps it is time for a new M&A process which focuses on a

more accurate cost/benefit map. That process would look to:
1. Do financial due diligence first.
2. Map the business model of the business about to be acquired.
3. Understand the number of invalidated assumptions in the business model.
4. Create a financial return & profitability forecast in order to understand the impact assumptions have on the outcomes, or surface other assumptions.
5. Write all the assumptions upon which the financial return & profitability forecast is based. Join them with the business model to understand their business model implications.
6. Experiment on the assumption.
7. Decide whether or not the acquisition still makes sense.

We are not saying that the current M&A processes, utilized by corporations worldwide, are 100% faulty and they should be scrapped, but we believe they can be improved. As it relies heavily on experimenting know-how, we are not suggesting the above proposed process to be better (or faster) either. But incorporation of hypothesis-driven-entrepreneurship in M&A might yield superior bottom-line results by challenging head-on, fictitious-return predictions.

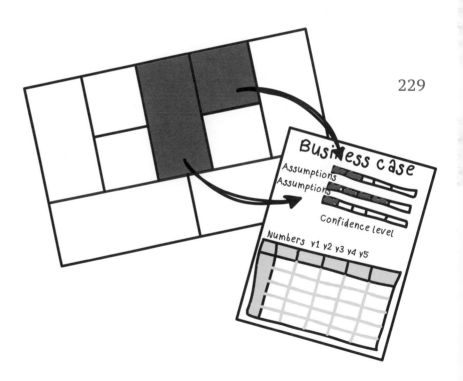

Most importantly, we are not advocating that M&As should be sidelined in favor of other startup corporate collaboration options. But, as with everything else in life, there is a time and a place for each option.

Writing in the HBR in 2016, Eddie Yoon and Steve Hughes talked about the way in which every enterprise, large and small, has its share of missionaries and mercenaries. They commented that: "For successful collaboration between a startup and established company, correctly match-making like mindsets is critical." But they also highlighted the benefits of mission-oriented collaborations which focus on something other than pure financial suc-

cess in order to deliver mutual benefit and a successful project.

In this chapter we've examined the benefits and risks of corporate startup collaborations. We've shown that by asking the right questions and running the right analysis organizations can greatly increase their chance of success.

An ending word of advice. It might look like collaborations with startups live far from the core of a company. And with that view, one is rightfully entitled to be concerned about these partnerships not being connected to the company's overall goals. However, there is a tool that can help with the alignment, the Innovation Thesis. No startup collaboration should be started before its alignment with the company's Innovation Thesis is checked.

Worksheet - Startup Collaboration Maturity

Before deciding to start collaborating with startups, consider testing the maturity level of your company regarding startup collaborations. This will give you an idea of what elements to improve, as well as helping to estimate the chances of success of a collaboration.

The startup collaboration maturity assessment Dan put together when working with companies pursuing open innovation comprises eleven multiple-choice questions. Each question has four answer prompts. Select from these the ones that most closely reflect your company's reality. For each question; answer one is 1 point, answer two is 2 points, answer three is 3 points and answer four is 4 points. In the end, add up your score and see where your company lands on the spectrum. Also, be aware of the questions where you scored the poorest; these are your company's main collaboration maturity blockers.

Answer the following questions:

1 **We have a clear innovation strategy that's helping us scout the startups we want to collaborate with.**
   1. We don't have an innovation strategy.
   2. We have an innovation strategy, but we don't use it when we look for startups to collaborate with.
   3. We sometimes check the innovation strategy when we look for startups to collaborate with.
   4. We constantly check our startup collaborations against our company's innovation strategy.

2 **Startup collaborations are an integral part of our growth strategy.**
   1. Startup collaborations are seen with much skepticism by the majority of our employees and leaders.
   2. Startup collaborations are just a "nice to have thing" for our company; we mainly do it for marketing purposes.
   3. We look at startup collaborations only for specific topics, and we deploy this vehicle only in certain contexts.
   4. Startup collaborations are an essential vehicle for our company's growth, taken very seriously by our company's employees and leaders.

3 **We have very clear and pragmatic goals for our startup collaborations.**
   1. We mainly do startup collaboration because it's "cool" and everyone else in the industry is doing it.
   2. We have some goals for our startup collaborations, but they are neither clear nor pragmatic.
   3. We have goals for our startup collaborations, but we don't use them in decision-making or evaluation.
   4. The goals for our startup collaborations are clear, pragmatic, and constantly used to evaluate the activity.

4 **We have a clear and transparent checklist that we use before entering any startup collaboration.**
   1. We don't have a checklist – the selection is made based on gut feel.
   2. We have a checklist to evaluate startup collaboration, but we rarely use it as it's not that good/useful.
   3. We sometimes use our checklist but not for every deal as the checklist is not developed.
   4. We have a checklist, and we constantly evaluate every deal against it.

5 The legal department is involved early in the startup collaboration process, preventing issues from appearing later.
   1. We don't run our startup collaborations deal by the legal department beyond just sending contracts.
   2. We sometimes involve the legal department but only in selected collaborations.
   3. We involve the legal department in all of our collaboration deals, but we don't get influenced by their advice that much.
   4. We always involve legal, early in the deals and follow their advice.

6 The final decision for a deal for a startup collaboration rests with the individual business unit that would benefit the most from the collaboration.
   1. No; the final decision for every collaboration rests with our C-level.
   2. Not really; the final decisions for every collaboration are taken by a specifically proposed group in our company.
   3. The final decision for every collaboration sometimes involves the individual business unit that would benefit the most from the collaboration.
   4. Yes; the final decision for a deal for a startup collaboration rests with the individual business unit that would benefit the most from the collaboration.

7 Our tech infrastructure is set up to make collaboration and integration of 3rd party solutions easy.
   1. Our tech infrastructure is something from the stone-age; no chance to run anything there.
   2. As old as our tech infrastructure is, we do our best to run 3rd party solutions on it, but this is not easy, requiring much work from the IT department.
   3. We have decent tech infrastructure, but the IT department still needs to be involved extensively in every integration.
   4. Our tech infrastructure is state of the art, making integration with 3rd party solutions easy. On top of that, it's also very well documented, making the involvement from the IT department minimal.

8 We have a specific budget for startup collaborations on top of the internal innovation budget.
   1. We don't have a specific budget for these activities. Money is usually taken from other budgets such as marketing, IT development, or even internal innovation.
   2. We have a specific budget for startup collaborations, but it's not adequate for our ambitions, so often we take money from other budgets.
   3. Our internal innovation and startup collaboration budgets are one and the same, but they are distinct from other budgets in the company, like the ones for marketing or IT.
   4. Our startup collaboration budget is separate from the other budgets, and it's always adequate for what we plan on doing every year.

9 We have a very robust and analytical process to assess the degree of risk/uncertainty of startup collaborations.

1. We don't care about risk and uncertainty. This will be solved once the collaboration starts.
2. We have a process of assessing risk, but it's not analytical and it's based primarily on the talent of our employees to find the right startups to work with.
3. We have a fact-based process of assessing risk and uncertainty, but we don't use that often, preferring not to be slowed down by it.
4. We have a very clear analytical process to assess the degree of risk/uncertainty, and we use this with absolutely every collaboration

10 We offer specific training for the employees in our company responsible for startup collaborations:

1. We have a very inclusive approach to selecting people responsible for startup collaborations; everyone is accepted, and they learn this skill on the job.
2. The training we offer our employees responsible for startup collaborations is hardly sufficient for them to do their job well; they learn more on the job following the training.
3. We offer specific training for our employees responsible for startup collaborations, but we only do it once when we on-board them; the rest is going to be developed through experience.
4. We offer specific training for the employees in our company responsible for startup collaborations, and we make sure their skills are up to date every year.

11 We have clear documentation about what it takes to collaborate with our corporation, including specific payment terms, brand usage, access to customers, data privacy, etc.

1. Documentation?!? What documentation?!? We don't have time for that.
2. We have documentation, but we rarely send it to the startups ahead of the collaboration; we prefer to sign the deal first.
3. We have a sort of documentation, but it's not that up to date.
4. Our documentation is best-in-class, and we are very transparent about these things with the startups way ahead of signing any deal.

Scale:
<22 novice collaborator
22-35 competent collaborator
>35 expert collaborator

The scope of your maturity level determines how easy it will be to successfully collaborate with startups. If you are a novice collaborator, be aware of the pitfalls and weak spots. Determine your priorities and focus on what is needed right now to start collaborating. Even if you are more mature as a company, it makes sense to use this test to keep iterating and improving on your company's ability to collaborate with startups.

Download the worksheet here

234

There are 4 typical models of corporate startup collaboration:

- Paid or Free pilots.
- Joint Ventures such as new product development, market research or technology research.
- Venturing (buying a stake in a startup).
- Acquisitions.

Understanding how these types vary will help you understand what indicators you need to put in place to measure their success.

To understand and improve the performance of startup collaborations, corporations need to look beyond just the final results of the collaborations.

Before initiating any startup collaboration, corporations should check the alignment of that collaboration with the innovation strategy.

Conversations on Innovation

David Rasson

Center of Expertise Lead Innovation, ING Belgium & The Netherlands ING

David has been with ING for more than two decades. During this time he has worn many hats in sales, finance, operations, IT and in recent years innovation. His primary objective these days is to make the bank an innovation-enabled one. And to achieve this goal, David is working to partner the European headquartered bank with startups around the world.

Innovation Accounting: ING is known around the world for innovation - at least in the banking sector it's a reference name. So, why is ING interested in partnering with startups? Is this a way of admitting the bank doesn't have the "internal power" to do the more "radical forms" of innovation?

David Rasson: On the contrary; we have very smart and creative people internally too. But we look at working with startups to complement our internal capabilities. And at the end of the day I think that all companies should have very clear ideas of things they want to build themselves and things they would like to partner with others on. It's not realistic to think that you can build everything perfectly yourself; no one can.

In the company we have identified a number of value spaces, as we like to call them, where we want to put our disruptive bets on. Like, for example, housing or financial health. And in these value spaces we look to either build disruptive solutions ourselves or partner with others that can help us win.

You see, at the beginning of the FinTech hype, it was a competition between the incumbents and startups; or at least that's how it was perceived by both sides. Today, I think, we collectively understand as an industry, that it's not a matter of competing, but a matter of collaborating.

IA: What forms of partnerships do you normally use?

DR: On top of our internal innovation efforts where we try to build our own FinTech solutions, like Yolt for example, we also invest in startups through ING Ventures. But we also have an M&A arm where we acquire startups. And lastly we partner with startups that help us solve some problems we have identified, be it internal problems or problems our customers have.

IA: How do you measure the success of these activities?

DR: We've been working with startups for more than 6 years now and this was a learning journey for us as well. We learned how to collaborate more effectively and how to measure our success better.

As you can imagine we have different measures of success for every single type of partnership. And within each type we tend to treat everything as much case by case as possible. This offers us the granularity we need to understand success and failure better.

But at the end of the day what we want to do is to deliver impact. And impact can consist of different things. If we talk about customer facing solutions, we look at customer facing indicators like the number of customers using the solution, numbers of paying customers if that's the case, churn and even cross sell.

For example: when it comes to our partnerships we look at the number of successful Proof of Concepts (POCs) that go into commercial production from the total number of partnerships we have initiated in a partnership batch. In simple words we look at how many FinTech startups get implemented in various departments in ING. We do this with a "local for global" mindset, meaning that we aim at generating impact in one business unit with a mindset to scale towards other business units or geographies afterwards. Meaning that further down the line we analyze how many of these POCs get scaled across our geographies.

What's interesting to mention here is that we never aim for a 100% implementation rate. If we were to say we want all the selected startups to find a home in ING it might prompt us to not take enough risk. It might make us scout startups which are sure bets; basically investing in incremental innovations not the disruptive ones. That's why we never aim for 100%. On the contrary if we ever get to 100% implementation that's a red flag for us. That's telling us that we weren't ambitious enough in the selection process. In general we set our ambition at about 50% implementation rate. But again this is not a benchmark or "line in the sand" for us; this is more of an ambition or vision. Otherwise if we were to be strict about it we might run the risk of triggering the wrong behavior both internally and with the startups we work with.

Another indicator we look at constantly is time. How long is it taking us to implement a solution from a third party vendor? And time is very interesting as it's not just impacted by how fast the startup is moving or how well the startup's technology integrates with our infrastructure; but it's also heavily influenced by our support processes, for example procurement, risk, legal, compliance, finance, and in general, I would say by our culture.

Banks in general are not known for speed. As an industry we have a reputation for lengthy partnership and acquisition cycles, up to 24 months in some cases. But in our defense we are a regulated industry where fines for not being compliant are usually in the higher 8 digit figures. I'm not saying we are happy with lengthy cycles or that we aren't doing anything that's in our power to shorten them, I'm just saying that startups should manage their expectations if they want to work with banks. In ING for example we aim at 12 month cycles from the moment we decide to work with a startup to the moment the solution is live with our clients and all the contracts and agreements are signed.

If we talk about internal facing ideas it's not always that straightforward to come up with indicators; especially when we try to solve problems around cybersecurity or data management, for example. But at the very least, in addition to keeping an eye on the time it takes to partner, we look at defining what success looks like, the uncertainties that will prevent us from being successful and then look at experiments' result data and see if there is a connection between these and our idea of success.

IA: Any advice for the corporations that want to work with startups? How about a piece of advice for the startups themselves?

DR: For the incumbents I would say: try to see the world from the startups' perspective too, don't be dictatorial. You need them as much as they need you. Adopt an honest partnership mindset where you are clear on the things you can do, the ones you can't and the things you are expecting from the partnership. Be fair with yourself and be fair with the startups. This will go a long way.

And remember to always try to get better from one year to the next; use data.

My advice for the startups would be that they need to focus on their business goals, don't expect the bank to do business development for you or expect the bank to help you navigate the world. At the same time, don't accept to do free work if you already have a proven solution with traction in a certain market.

Treating people like assets.

Measuring Innovation HR Capabilities

Are innovators born or made? Were you born challenging the status quo and looking for new ways or are your curiosity and need to explore reflections of the environment you were raised in or the education you received?

Well the answer, as with so much in life, is it depends. There is evidence that creativity, which is a known attribute of innovators, is in part due to heredity. For example, several gene studies, although small, highlight two neurotransmitter systems contributing to creativity, and these pathways can differ in individuals.[111] However, studies of twins, for example, reveal that only about 20% of creativity is heritable,[111] opening up the way for innovation to be learnt or improved alongside other skills.

Think of it like this: if you want a career as a top-flight basketball player, it helps to be tall. However, without the right skills you are only going to be, at best, an average player at your local basketball court. No chance for you to make it to the NBA.

Innovation ability, like speed, endurance, height, longevity and other human traits, is not evenly distributed. When you think about it, we humans are so varied, why should innovation ability be

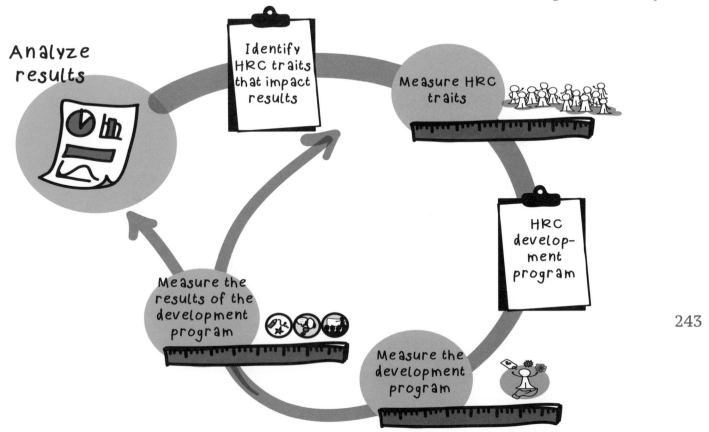

any different? And, like other human abilities, the innovation skills which we have won't be identical to other individuals. More importantly, those innovation skills will need to be honed if we are to make the most of them.

If that's the case, if innovators are part made, part born, how can you tell if you have the right mix of innovators within your company? And how can you tell if you are developing the right innovation skills for the organization's end goals?

Measuring human resource innovation capability is more complex than measuring the innovation process. This is primarily because, on top of measuring result indicators and the processes the company has in place to develop the capability, you also need to measure traits (characteristics).

Understanding the innovation capabilities in your company will, on one hand, inform the needs for capability development and, on the other hand, may offer some clues with respect to the likely results of the innovation ecosystem.

A large-scale study found that "innovation talent is statistically predictive of business results."[112] So much so that the same study concluded that: "Innovation talent is highly correlated with positive business results. Innovators have significantly higher innovation scores than the general population. Within the population of innovators, top scorers are associated with a larger number of positive business results than bottom scorers."

Further research done by McKinsey & Co. compared innovation proficiency for 183 companies against economic-profit performance.[113] Their analysis showed a strong, positive correlation between innovation performance and financial performance. So being able to predict your workforce's capacity to innovate is very valuable indeed.

Take for example a company whose teams find it difficult to come up with relevant experiments to test their ideas. That lack of experimentation means that teams will not only take longer to reach the sustain phase, many ideas won't even get that far. As a consequence, the Cost of Innovation goes up whilst the benefits go down. Early identification of that struggle with experimentation could prompt HR to intervene with appropriate training for individuals or teams.

Moreover, once you know a person's specific innovation abilities, you can better match them to projects and pair them up with complementary teammates.

In practical terms, you should start by looking at your company's innovation ecosystem and understand its results. Starting from a "what is the problem we have?" type of question can help you better understand the capability traits you would need to develop.

Say, for example, you look at the portfolio distribution of your company and see you primarily have CORE ideas in both the portfolio and the funnel. If the problem you're trying to solve becomes "we should future-proof our company; and to do that we need more radical new business models" your people need to be educated and encouraged to come up with "beyond the CORE" ideas.

Or, in case you see that the ATS indicator is outside your expectation or exponentially higher than that of your competitors, you can look at how to educate teams to move faster and Venture Board members to take faster decisions.

Obviously, there are multiple factors affecting an indicator but asking "what is the problem we have?" and going down the path of seeking to understand the HR capability traits impacting that particular indicator will set you on a path of continuous improvement.

From our experience, we've seen the following traits as being particularly important for breakthrough innovation work:
- Ability to learn.
- Curiosity.
- Humbleness (receive feedback).
- Ability to see the big picture (big picture thinking).
- Ability to collaborate effectively.
- Ability to inspire others.
- Open mindedness.

These traits, coupled with specific skills such as the ability to design and run effective business experiments, will increase the chances for success of the individual ventures.

Measuring and understanding human resource capability traits

Measuring traits

How do you measure capability? Well, there are many innovation capability assessments out there, one of which we have included at the end of this chapter. As with any other type of assessment, it is important to choose the one which best fits with your organizational goals. Some of the most notable options include: Innovator's DNA[114] based on the bestselling book with the same name by Jeff Dyer, the assessment offered by Trendhunter,[115] Foresight's assessment,[116] or the one used by Founder Institute in their startup selection process.[117]

245

Whichever assessment you choose, be it one of the above, the one we propose at the end of this chapter, or any other - you can boost your chances of success by:

- *Using the assessment on the right population:* Depending on your goals, you might want to consider deploying the assessment company-wide. On the other hand, you may initially want to concentrate on a narrow group such as employees of a certain business unit or a certain hierarchical level. This decision is going to be up to you; but you need to give careful consideration to your goals before making the call.

In general, a well-designed and deployed innovation capability assessment will help you better understand what kind of innovation talent you have in your company. It will also provide more clarity around what kind of people you need to hire to complement the people you already have.

The more granular the assessment, the more insights you are going to get with respect to the precise training needs in the period to come. For example, you might learn about a particular skill a certain group of employees is missing or the training needs of a particular business unit.

So once you have assessed a good swath of your workforce, you should ask yourself a big picture question: do we have the right mix of talents for the goals of our innovation strategy?

Measuring human resource capability development

Measure HR Development

- *Using the assessment to compliment empirical data.* Innovators may not fit into the traditional employee mold. Innovation assessments may well therefore highlight individuals who may have previously been overlooked, perhaps shining the spotlight on those who have a good holistic viewpoint or who like to take risks.

- *Making sure the assessment is easy to understand.* If the questions are not clear, the results you'll be getting will most likely fail to reflect the reality.

- *Sharing innovation assessment results with the teams.* If employees are comfortable sharing their assessment results with each other, it can be of great value to the team. The more we can understand and empathize with others, the more we leverage our different abilities for greater results.

- *Using assessment data to inform team design and project assignments.* A strong innovation team should align with the project mission and vision.

In a study of more than 3,100 U.S. workplaces, the National Center on the Educational Quality of the Workforce (EQW) found that on average, a 10 percent increase in workforce education level led to an 8.6 percent gain in total productivity. But a 10 percent increase in the value of equipment increased productivity by just 3.4 percent.[118]

If you need to improve your human resource capability, in all probability you are eyeing training programs. Capability development activities come in all shapes and sizes. From simple one day workshops to extensive programs stretching over months and from peer-to-peer sessions to communities of practice.

Regardless of the type of program you want to deploy in your company, you probably want to get some numbers. These will serve as leading indicators for the efficacy of the training program and, ultimately, the outcomes of the innovation ecosystem. Some indicators that we would recommend you strongly consider are:

Number of training modules per unit of time (usually per year). It is useful to examine this indicator on a topic by topic basis and correlate the topics you are offering with the results from the assessment. If, for example, you have seen in the assessment that employees are struggling with generating radical new ideas, it might make sense to look at the number of ideation training modules you are offering them in a year.

Number of hours spent in capability development programs by the workforce. This can also be computed as a percentage of the total available work time. And it might be worthwhile looking at this a bit more granularly, through the lens of topics. Specifically, reviewing how much time is being invested in up-skilling people on topic A vs. B.

In case your programs are voluntary, you can look at the number of people that have applied for the training as a percentage of the target population. A low conversion in this case might mean one of several things. The training may simply not have been properly marketed to your people. On the other hand, your target population may already have the knowledge they require in that area or just aren't interested in furthering those particular skills. Independent of the reason, we would encourage you to compare the numbers between different capability development initiatives in order to spot patterns and potential areas for improvement.

In the case of mandatory training, you can look at how many people you have trained in a unit of time as a percentage of the target population or how many people you have trained as a percentage of the target population.

Another good indicator for voluntary programs is the Attendance Rate. This might indicate how engaged your people are with the program or it might offer you some clues with respect to the quality of the facilitators. In any case, a low attendance rate will have repercussions; not least, your employees' future ability to innovate. This in turn might impact the overall outcomes of the innovation ecosystem.

The Drop Out Rate, like the attendance rate above, is a good indicator to have in mind when trying to understand the success of your capability development program and ultimately predict the impact it will have on outcomes. In case you are offering remote, on-line training, you can expect a drop-out rate of 93% to 40% according to a recent study.[119] So if your program delivers a completion rate over 60% (meaning that out of 100 participants starting, more than 60 complete the training) you can pat yourself on the back.

For the programs which include various assignments for the attendees to complete, you can analyze the Assignment Completion Rate.

Once the capability development program is finished, you can ask the participants to submit a *Net Promoter Score* valuation of the program. This score will give you some insights into the things you need to improve on for the next program.

If you are hoping to implement community best practices in your company or a peer-to-peer circle for people to get further

247

coaching after a formal training, you can look at measuring the *number of participants* in these events as well as their *frequency*.

Since capability development programs are going to require a certain investment from the company side, you might consider looking at how much was spent on human capability development in a unit of time (most likely yearly). Furthermore you can compute the annual human resource capability development cost as a percentage of sales. And in some cases, we have seen companies adding this number to the total Cost of Innovation.

In the case of organizations that have democratized training, giving their employees an annual budget they can use for personal development, you can look at the average percentage of personal development budget being used.

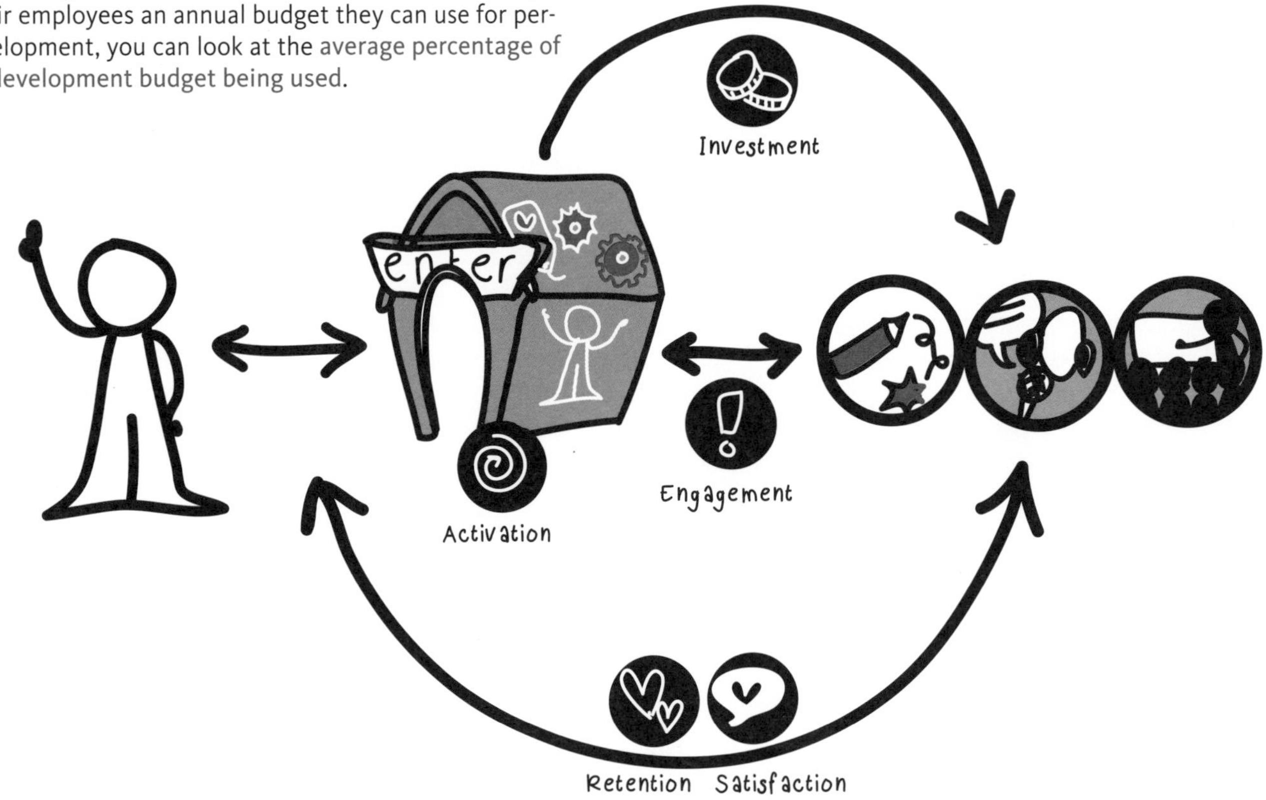

Investment

Activation

Engagement

Retention   Satisfaction

Activation

- Number of training modules per unit of time.
- Number of hours spent in capability development programs.
- Number of people that have applied for the training as a percentage of the target population (for voluntary programs).
- Number of people you have trained in a unit of time as a percentage of the target population or how many people you have trained as a percentage of the target population. (for mandatory programs).

Retention

- Attendance Rate (or how many people have attended to date as a percentage of the target population in the case of voluntary programs).
- Drop Out Rate.
- Assignment Completion Rate.

Satisfaction

- Net Promoter Score.

Engagement

- Number of participants in community run capability development programs.
- Frequency of community run capability development programs.

Investment

- Annual human resource capability development investment.
- Average percentage of personal development budget being used.

249

Surface intangible assets
3

The numbers from the indicators above can offer you some hints with respect to the result you can expect from your investment in capability development.

But before talking about measuring the results of capability development, it is worth noting that a one-size-fits-all approach to employee development isn't necessarily a good idea as people and skills are inherently diverse. Exceptional leaders don't leave it up to the HR department to create career development programs for their team members. Rather, they personalize coaching, support, and teaching opportunities based on day to day interactions. Furthermore, exceptional leaders don't just wait on company-wide programs offered by the HR department; they understand the nuances of how people grow week by week and month by month and adjust their actions accordingly.[120] Doing so will mitigate the findings of a 2016 study showing that only 39% of millennials strongly agree that they learned something new on the job in the past 30 days.[121]

Measuring the results of human resource capability development

Measure result of activities

As fun as workforce development activities may be, all investments made in capability development need to result in attitude and skill transformations that will ultimately move the company forward.

In traditional accounting terms, the go-to result indicator for the workforce's performance is Workforce Productivity. Workforce productivity is the amount of goods and services that a group of workers produce in a given amount of time.[122]

Not surprisingly, as straightforward as this productivity indicator sounds, it is tricky to deploy it in the context of innovation.

Take for example a team that, despite its best efforts, was forced to "kill" their idea. However, in the process of experimenting and validating the idea they have gathered some interesting insights that they will use when starting a new idea. How can productivity be measured since they haven't shipped one single unit of the initial product and they haven't made one single dollar of new revenue? On the contrary they just burned some cash.

In another example, picture a team that has validated a problem in a very tempting market. However, for reasons outside of their control, the team wasn't able to secure any internal support to continue past this point and they were forced to shelve the idea. What would the workforce productivity indicator show?

Therefore, when it comes to innovation, we need to adapt the way we look at productivity. Given that innovation work entails a great deal of uncertainty, we need to look at productivity through the lens of validated learnings and decisions taken.

  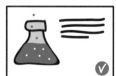

In our opinion, workforce productivity, in breakthrough innovation, can be defined as the amount of validated learning generated and consequent decisions taken by a group of people in the shortest amount of time possible.

Furthermore, the capability indicators need to be adapted for every hierarchical level. This is because the effectiveness of an innovation team looks different from the effectiveness of a Venture Board, for example.

Innovation team

252

Some result indicators for innovation HR capability at **innovation team level** might include:

- Number of ideas aligned with the Innovation Thesis generated/submitted by the employees in a unit of time. This particular indicator looks at the ability of the employees to come up with new growth ideas that are in line with the direction the company wants to take. Depending on the granularity you need, you can look at the number of ideas generated relative to the portfolio distribution (core ideas, adjacent ideas and transformational ideas). From our experience, we can tell you that, in the absence of a clear call for ideas, a clear innovation challenge, or a clear Innovation Thesis, most of the new ideas that will be generated bottom-up will be core and adjacent in nature.
- Experiment Efficacy showing how many of a team's experiments resulted in learnings.
- Number of unassisted experiments designed. (knowledgeability)
- Decisions taken or suggested, independent of management or Venture Board inputs.

You won't be surprised to see that these capability indicators are connected with the indicators we examined in Chapter 4. Specifically: Learning Velocity, holistic confidence in the venture, cost and time spent in stage. Following the abstraction principle, these will in turn impact other indicators downstream.

At Venture Board level you can consider the following HR capability result indicators:

- Decision Speed. This indicator looks at how long it takes a Venture Board to reach a decision with respect to a venture; whether that decision is stop, pivot or persevere. Take a look back to Chapter 5 if you need to refresh your understanding in this area.
- As much as we would encourage any Venture Board meeting to end with a decision, we know that sometimes that's not the case. Therefore, it makes sense to track the time it takes the Venture Board to make decisions with respect to a venture.
- Connected to the indicator above, you can look at the number of Venture Board meetings resulting in a decision being taken. This is particularly interesting if you want to understand if the Venture Board is functioning as a governing body. If there are no decisions being taken or only a small percentage of meetings end with a decision, then the Venture Board is not fully acting as a governance body.
- Quality of the decision. Just taking decisions, and taking them fast, is not enough. These decisions need to ultimately have an impact on the company's growth. Therefore, every now and then it is good to look back at the quality of the decisions by the Venture Board. In this retrospective analysis, the easiest thing to analyze is whether or not investment decisions (go) have led to successful ventures being developed. If the contrary is true, you might consider doubling down on Venture Board training or investigate the root cause of the issue. Keeping track of the "hit rate" can help you improve over time as you build more knowledge and ability in the Venture Board members. It may also be important here to analyze the decision making process itself; helping the Venture Board members to learn to ask the right questions in order to base their decisions more on the data from validated learnings rather than from gut feeling.

Venture board

253

As above, these capability result indicators mirror the funnel indicators we reviewed in Chapter 5, specifically: number of ideas stopped per stage, number of ideas progressed per stage, and average time spent in stage. And these ones, again following the abstraction principle, will in turn impact indicators from the layer above them.

Executive team

254

When it comes to **the executive team** of the company the HR capability result indicators you can consider are:

- Number of times the executive team is engaging with the Innovation Thesis per year. This shows if the leaders of the company are actually championing innovation as a vehicle for delivering on the company's growth goals.
- Time spent on innovation. Following on from the above indicator, the time executives allocate to innovation can also signal how high innovation sits on the strategic agenda and how much leaders understand the importance of innovation. Many top thinkers such as Rita McGrath and Mark Johnson propose looking at the time spent on innovation by executives to understand if a particular company is taking innovation seriously. In an HBR Podcast Interview, Mark actually suggested that executives should spend about 10 to 20% of their time on innovation; and in particular on creating and following up on innovation strategy.[123] This particular indicator is even more interesting to track over time, following a training program.
- Decision speed on budget allocation. This indicator shows how long it takes executives to align on budget allocation for innovation. This indicator correlates with how high innovation sits on the executive agenda and how important it is believed to be for the future of the company.

CHAPTER 8
Measuring Innovation HR Capabilities

Conclusions

The innovation HR capability measuring system needs to be in-sync with your company's expectations from innovation and the workforce. Therefore, the measuring systems are most likely going to vary from company to company as they are tailored to specific needs. However, when creating your company's system we would advise you to have a couple of things in mind.

First of all, in order to create a robust HR capability measuring system, you need to stop confusing effort with outcomes. Maybe you remember how on the series "Seinfeld," George Costanza would leave his car parked at the office on purpose, so that his boss would think he was working long hours. That's an attempt to take advantage of what psychologists call input bias, the tendency to use the signs of effort to judge outcomes. When actually the two may have little to do with each other.

In her research at Harvard Business School, and her book "*Sidetracked*," Francesca Gino studied how difficult it is to accurately measure employees' performance and what you do about it. In one study, researchers showed people a short presentation and then asked them to rate its quality. Some were told the presenter spent eight hours preparing. Others were told they spent just 30 minutes. Not surprisingly, people who thought the speech took eight hours to prepare gave it higher ratings.[124]

Secondly, make sure your capability measuring system is measuring something that matters - something that will result in impact later down the line. In an experiment, graduate students were asked to count either the number of papers they completed or the number of total pages. Even though both groups did the same amount of work the people counting pages gave themselves a higher productivity rating.[125]

Lastly, remember to always zoom-out and look at the whole picture. Francesca Gino once worked with a retailer that tried to motivate employees with specific sales targets tied to monthly bonuses. Right away, performance improved. But a few months later, the company realized that employees were buying extra merchandise themselves in the last week of every month to hit their target, then returning it the next week. Once the retail managers looked at monthly and weekly data, it was obvious what was going on. So before you judge how productive your people are, ask if the data in front of you tells the whole story. And do not assume the employee with his car in the parking lot the longest is the one delivering the best results.

255

Worksheet - Assess your company's innovation HR capability.

The following assessment will help to demonstrate an aptitude for innovation. Don't forget that a good innovation team will include a mix of innovation capabilities; so not everyone on the team needs to score high on this scale for the team to deliver results.

Also, no matter how innovative a person may appear today, they can still continuously boost and refresh their skills. Think of capability development like you think of cleaning your house; you need to do it constantly, not only when you first buy the house.

Now try to rank the following statements in the most truthful manner.

Download the
Worksheet here

Scale:
10p - 20p - better suited for exploitation of an existing validated idea.
21p - 32p - somewhat of an innovator that can also do exploitation work. Ideally suited for incremental innovation.
33p - 40p - strong breakthrough innovation ability.

	Strongly Disagree (1p)	Somewhat Disagree (2p)	Somewhat Agree (3p)	Strongly Agree (4p)
I prefer moving fast and working on the details later.				
I see failure as part of the learning journey.				
I think that detailed plans can hinder the development of new ideas.				
My biggest strength is coming up with new ideas or thinking of new solutions.				
I typically approach a challenge with an open mind and a flexible mindset, accepting any possible outcome.				
I welcome feedback and use it to improve.				
I sell my ideas effectively and work hard at enrolling and converting others to my vision.				
For me, experimenting is the most exciting part of innovation.				
How do you feel about the following mantra: "it's better to beg for forgiveness than to ask for permission."				
If in my company a process is mandatory but it has no impact on work that I'm doing I will ignore it and move on.				

Innovation is a skill that can be taught, although some people are more inclined to be innovators than others.

Human resource capability traits need to be understood first before capability development programs are designed and deployed.

Investments in innovation human resource capability development impact directly the innovation ecosystem and can thus be measured in the innovation ecosystem outcomes.

Conversations on Innovation

Christian Lindener

Christian Lindener is a serial entrepreneur turned corporate innovator. At the time of the interview, after spending several years in the telecommunication industry as part of Telefonica's Wayra accelerator, Christian was heading up the Airbus Incubators & Accelerators. As an intrapreneur, he experienced both open as well as closed innovation. Having had primarily leadership roles in innovation, Christian knows better than most what it feels like to hire for mindset and develop skills.

Innovation Accounting: Many large companies nowadays are trying to upskill their labor force on innovation. We've seen anything from one-day workshops to months-long intrapreneurship programs being used to teach employees the skills and tools needed to innovate. But then again, in all honesty, there isn't that much radical/ breakthrough innovation coming out of corporations. Why is that?

Christian Lindener: I think that the problem starts at measurements. Large companies usually get their first step wrong, which is gap analysis.

I think the first thing companies need to do is to assess their starting point. Basically, companies need to understand what skills people already have and what skills are missing or not fully developed yet before starting any capability development initiative.

Many skills from the core business are useful in innovation too. However, many more need to be developed, as running the core business is much different from starting something up. Some companies, for example, have a core business where things need to work 100% of the time, all the time; there is no room for error when people's lives are on the line. But in innovation things are a bit different; at least at the start of the journey you make a lot of mistakes and you learn, but these mistakes need to be intelligent mistakes, mistakes from which you actually get better and don't cause irremediable damage.

What I've learned in my career is that it is not just one skill set you need to develop and you are done. There's a lot of things people can and should learn, a lot of methodologies, a lot of tools. So I always suggest looking at the entire landscape and understanding every aspect of skills and mindset development before going ahead and engaging in workshops or training programs.

Also if you don't understand the gap it is very difficult to measure how effective you are in bridging that gap. Essentially, measure the impact of the money you spent on training people.

Also, a thing I learned is that you constantly need to measure people's skills. This is not something you do once at the beginning and you are done. The needed skills, especially in innovation, evolve, adapt and change as quickly as the market does. So skills you need today might not be the skills that you need tomorrow. So you have to constantly adapt the training programs you are offering otherwise you run the risk of your people being skilled in dated methodologies, tools and even technologies.

Also, you should never decouple the skills from the impact. People should only be upskilled in the things that they will be able to apply and that will ultimately drive impact for the company.

IA: What is the risk of not measuring anything around capability development efforts and just doing upskilling?

CL: The most obvious one would be that you spend money and you don't know what you got in return for the money spent or how this investment is moving the needle on your performance. I'm not talking about justifying the investment to the CFO, I'm talking about connecting effort with impact.

If companies weren't to measure anything they wouldn't know how to improve the training offered to their employees. And I am not talking about doing more entertaining training programs, I'm talking about doing programs that will allow our people to be more effective in their work. So you always have to measure how your people are performing, are they moving faster, are they taking decisions faster, are they able to lower the cost of innovation, are they coming up with bolder ideas, are they performing in a team; these are some of the things I'd encourage everyone to look at. And from here, you'd know how to improve your capability development offering.

IA: What are some of the things you've seen work when it comes to capability development programs?

CL: Entrepreneurship or innovation is about experience, is about doing. Too many programs are set up and designed around teaching a skill or methodology but too few are focused on teaching the mindset or giving people the real experience of what it means to start something up.

Making corporate people more entrepreneurial should never be the goal. This is per se, something that is not possible in my opinion. Most people pursue careers in corporations because they want the security, the clear career path, the predictability of the work. So making these people change 180 degrees and have them give away the corporate car and the parking spot is very close to impossible.

Capability development programs should focus on giving employees the experience of starting something up and show the company how many people are actually good at this. Separate the people that want to do the core business from the people that are a bit more risk tolerant and take their energy from moving things from 0 to 1. I'm not saying that innovation training programs should be reserved only for a handful of employees, I'm saying that you need to be honest with your employees when it comes to what's expected of them. And the only way I've seen companies being able to do it is by giving them an experiential learning experience. For example, you can do that by lowering the initial investment in an idea. It's not really experiential when you give someone in the company 700,000 euros to start something up when startups usually get moving with a fraction of that, say 10 or 20,000 euros.

It's not enough if you give people a bunch of books to read and then you put them in a training program where you teach them how to perform a certain task or use a certain canvas. This only gives them a false sense of knowledge. Entrepreneurship is about doing and as long as the capability programs don't focus on the doing aspect people will think that they know how to do things but in fact, the only thing they know is how to fill in a template. This is why you need to place a lot of emphasis on giving people the real experience of what it means to be in a startup. You want, as much as possible, to remove the safety nets a large company offers.

Ultimately it all comes down to
who you are, and who you can be.

Chapter 9
Measuring Innovation Culture

This chapter wouldn't have been possible without the contribution of our friend and colleague Cris Beswick

In the field of corporate innovation, one of the terms you are most likely to hear is "a culture of innovation." It's at the center of the conversation when the market success of companies like Netflix, Gore or Zappos is discussed. On the other side of the coin, it also comes up when people try to understand why a company has been unable to grow beyond its legacy core or has been slow to capitalize on trends.

That's why a culture of innovation sounds so appealing: it seems to be a cure for everything, the Holy Grail of innovation. Which leader wouldn't want to enable a strong innovation culture in their organization? Yet in our opinion, this important topic still remains way too vague, obscured by layers of "fairy dust," fallacies, naive imitation and "snake oil" salesmen offering to enable a complete culture change in just one offsite retreat.

Innovation culture
So what exactly is a culture of innovation?

Any culture is a set of common values, beliefs, habits, attitudes and behaviors that bind a group of people together. The culture acts as shorthand for how to conduct oneself in order to belong and enable the group to thrive.

Building a culture of innovation requires an organization to encourage and reward the values, beliefs, habits, attitudes and behaviors required for driving innovation. However, innovation is only one part of your company's cultural mix; melding with other desirable traits such as ethical behavior, diversity and inclusion, or transparency to deliver a designed culture which is unique to your organization.

In our work we often describe culture to the leaders we work with using an easily relatable metaphor. We say that culture is like a cloud. You can see it exists, you can feel its effects; however, you can't touch it. But, similar to clouds, we have learned how to influence the culture to deliver desired results.

There are many benefits to a strong innovation culture. Companies with a strong innovation-focused culture tend to outperform those with a weak innovation culture.[126] In fact, the most innovative companies in the world enjoy a significant "market cap premium" meaning their shares are worth a lot more per dollar of revenue than their less innovative peers.

And then there's the research done by Dr. James R. Gregory who looked at the correlation between intangible assets, including innovation culture, and the Cash Flow Multiple. The reason the Cash Flow Multiple was chosen was that Dr Gregory considers it to be more accurate than other financial indicators.

The Cash Flow Multiple is calculated by simply dividing the stock price per share by cash flow per share, providing a value that reflects both cash flow and market capitalization. The outcome of the research revealed that financial benefits are enjoyed by companies with strong intangible assets, including an embedded and recognized culture of innovation.[127]

267

But can it be measured?

So how do you measure culture? Well, you can't; or at least not directly.

In a conversation we had with Claire Howeson, Business Manager and Team Coach at the ecological cleaning products manufacturer Ecover, she mentioned that: "measuring innovation culture is where science meets art. There are plenty of things you can measure to get an objective view on. But there are also some, more holistic, things you will just get a sense of."

Remember what we told you earlier about the metaphor we use to describe innovation culture? Well, clouds can't be measured either. When meteorologists talk about measuring clouds they usually look at their attributes and the effects clouds have. For example, a popular indicator in meteorology is the okta. This unit of measurement describes the effect clouds have in terms of sky cover. Sky conditions are estimated in terms of how many eighths of the sky are covered in cloud, ranging from 0 oktas (completely clear sky) through to 8 oktas (completely overcast).[128]

Similarly, you can recognize if a company has an embedded culture of innovation by looking at its attributes and the effects those attributes have on the workings and results of the company. For example, one measurable attribute could be workforce behavior and the link to engagement. Employees in organizations with a strong innovation culture tend to feel free to challenge the status quo and to experiment. They are also more likely to be resilient to setbacks and, more importantly, change. Thus, a strong innovation culture tends to produce higher levels of employee engagement.

Finally, you can recognize if a company has an embedded culture of innovation by looking at results. A company with a strong and embedded innovation culture is one that regularly generates new solutions, launching them in the market, and creating positive financial results or societal value. A BCG study found that companies pursuing transformation and focusing on culture as part of the transformation were 5x more likely to achieve breakthrough performance than companies that neglected culture.[129]

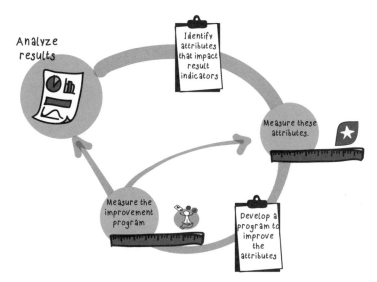

In practical terms, if you want to measure your culture of innovation you need to look at your company's result indicators first and see how many of these are directly impacted by culture. Then draw up a list of cultural attributes that impact these results before measuring the presence of these attributes in your company. This process is indeed very similar to the way human resource capability is measured, which we discussed at length in the previous chapter.

Let's take ideation as a simple example. If your company has a certain portfolio distribution ambition and you notice that, in spite of your best communication and training efforts, the only ideas that are allowed in the funnel are incremental improvements, it might be that you have a cultural challenge on your hands. A culture of conformity and sticking to the beaten path will never accept radical new ideas.

But measuring attributes is easier said than done as there are hundreds if not thousands of attributes you can think of or measure. So first you need to gain clarity around which attributes are important for your company. This clarity is rooted in the purpose innovation serves in your company.

For organizations that consider breakthrough innovation as a tool for growth, we would encourage the measurement of the following attributes:[130]

- Tolerance to failure
- Diversity (cognitive, background, gender and, above all, opinion)
- The practice and encouragement of continuous improvement
- Ethics (honesty, integrity, promise-keeping & trustworthiness, fairness, concern for others, respect for others, law-abiding, accountability[131])
- Frictionless collaboration
- Adaptability
- Empathy
- Psychological safety
- How much do people see innovation as being part of their day-to-day job; in particular for people that don't have innovation written on their business cards.

At the end of the chapter, we have prepared a short survey which your people can take in order to understand your company's innovation culture and how well it is embedded in your company. This is in no way the only survey you can use to assess the innovation culture of your company; there are countless surveys and cultural assessment tools you can pick from. But when making the decision to use one tool over another, you need to consider how you will use the survey and what actions are likely to be required depending on the results. We would also urge you to retake the survey on a regular basis to measure changes within the organization's cultural outlook and identify further actions which may be required.

Once you have a good idea of the current attributes the culture in your company has and the attributes which are lacking, you can start work on improving things.

Measuring innovation culture development

269

If the analysis of attributes gives you a current perspective of the innovation culture in your company, the measurements for cultural development activities paint a picture of what the culture might look like in the future. In other words, the indicators for the innovation culture development activities are to some extent leading indicators for the things to come.

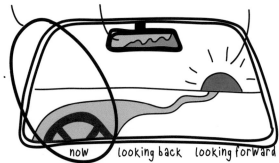

Measurement of the cultural attributes

Measuring the impact of the innovation culture on the company's results

Measures of the innovation culture development work

now   looking back   looking forward

270

Innovation culture development activities come in all shapes and sizes but the ones we have seen being used most frequently take the form of development workshops. Some indicators you can use to track the process of cultural development are:

The number of training modules offered per unit of time (usually per year). It is useful to examine this indicator on a topic by topic basis and correlate the topics you are offering with the results from the attributes assessment. If you've seen that people complain about a lack of tolerance to new ideas, then any training programs should probably place more emphasis on the topic of diversity and tolerance or of attitude to risk. Or if your company is experiencing a high number of allegations or complaints related to ethical behavior, you can look at how many ethics-related training sessions have been conducted in a certain time frame.

The number of hours spent in innovation cultural development programs by the workforce. This can also be computed as a percentage of the total available work time. And it might be worthwhile looking at this a bit more granularly, through the lens of topics. Specifically, reviewing how much time is being invested in developing attribute A vs. attribute B.

In case your programs are voluntary, you can look at the number of people that have applied for the training as a percentage of the target population. A low conversion rate in this case might mean one of several things. The training may simply not have been properly marketed to your people. On the other hand, your target population may consider the topic of the training to be not that relevant to them; in which case you may need to step up your communication game! Independent of the reason, we would encourage you to compare the numbers between different innovation culture development initiatives in order to spot patterns.

Another good indicator for voluntary cultural development programs is the Attendance Rate. This might indicate how engaged your people are with the program or it might offer you some clues with respect to the quality of the course content, feedback and/or facilitators.

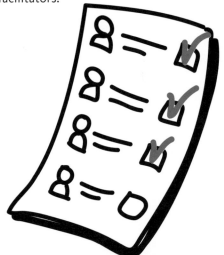

The Drop Out Rate, like the Attendance Rate above, is a good indicator to have in mind when trying to understand the success of your innovation culture development program and ultimately predict the impact it will have on outcomes. Again, for more clarity you can compute and compare this topic by topic. For example, ethics training drop-out rate vs. diversity training.

In the case of mandatory training, you can look at how many people have attended to date as a percentage of the target population and see how long it will take you to achieve critical mass for a certain topic or in a certain department.

For the programs which include various assignments for the attendees to complete you can also analyze the Assignment Completion rate. An example of such an assignment can be Pulse Check. For Pulse Check the program's attendees need to perform a series of interviews to understand certain innovation culture issues and the efficacy of the measures put in place to mitigate them. An assignment completion rate for Pulse Check can look at the number of employees performing these interviews or the number of interviews performed.

Once the innovation culture development program is finished, you can ask the participants to submit a Net Promoter Score evaluation of the program. This score will give you some insights into the things you need to improve ready for the next cohort or program. But don't go pat yourself on the back if the Net Promoter Scores are high. Net Promoter Score is a good tool to gauge satisfaction but is widely known to have some issues.

Since cultural development programs are going to require a certain investment from the company, you might consider looking at how much was spent on cultural development in a unit of time (most likely yearly). Furthermore, you can compute the annual cultural development cost as a percentage of sales.

Now let's talk about the elephant in the room. We can't talk about innovation culture development without talking about the importance of process changes that need to happen in parallel with culture development.

There is a raging debate on the topic of culture following process or vice versa. Although we don't think we can give a definite answer to this question, we only want to emphasize that, like capability development, when you engage in cultural development you need to consider all layers of the organization and the complementary parts of the work system (goals, roles, processes, values, communication practices, attitudes and assumptions).

Take, for example, a large municipality that considers collaboration and teamwork as core parts of its culture.[132] This particular municipality has made it mandatory by law that any execution or change to the execution of the commission's directive must be reviewed, discussed or voted on in a public forum. Because the municipality's leaders want to present a united front to the public, every potential change is therefore first subjected to an internal review process. This results in multiple reviews before anything can be presented to the public.

271

Every reviewer has their own presentation style and perceptions of what is important. The reviewer's expectation is that their feedback will be incorporated into the document and the presentation. The authors of the document often find themselves in a position of having to change the modifications quickly and also have little time to prepare for the public meeting.

Essentially, what might have been a simple proposal becomes enmeshed in internal politics and personal one-upmanship as the draft document is sent out for review, modified, re-modified and changed again, often leaving the original authors with the mammoth task of managing conflicting inputs. "Designed by committee" is not a favorable term for good reason.

Do you think our examples above reflect a collaborative culture? Does collaboration mean, "do what I say because I have a bigger title than you"?!?

We will let you answer the question of culture following process, or vice versa. In any case, if you see no change of performance after your investment in cultural development, it might be worth looking at process change before labeling the cultural development investment a failure.

Activation

- The number of training modules per unit of time.
- The number of hours spent in innovation cultural development.
- The number of people that have applied for the training as a percentage of the target population (for voluntary programs).
- The number of people you have trained in a unit of time as a percentage of the target population or how many people you have trained as a percentage of the target population. (for mandatory programs).

Retention

- Attendance Rate. (or how many people have attended to date as a percentage of the target population in the case of voluntary programs).
- Drop Out Rate.

Satisfaction

- Net Promoter Score.

Engagement

- Number of participants in community run capability development programs.
- Frequency of community run capability development programs.

Investment

- Annual human resource capability development investment.
- The average percentage of personal development budget being used.

273

Surface intangible assets

Conclusions

If you feel like you are having a deja-vu moment right now and you have read this chapter before, you are not far from the truth. There are many similarities between cultural development and skills development, at least from the perspective of measuring. But there are differences as well. Probably the most noteworthy difference between the two is that cultural development outcomes are more difficult to measure than capability development outcomes. Therefore, for culture, you are better off measuring attributes and analyzing the delta in attributes before and after the development activity. Obviously, this will not be enough and you will also have to corroborate the attributes measurements with the ecosystem's results for an accurate picture.

You should always consider all the other ways of working across your company when looking to measure and/or improve culture. Poor performance after an investment in cultural development doesn't always mean a failure of the development program. It might also mean that processes, values, or incentives are not aligned with the desired culture.

274

Worksheet - Assess your company's innovation culture

The following assessment was designed to give you an idea about the attributes of your company's innovation culture and the degree to which the culture is embedded in your company. This survey was developed in partnership with Cris Beswick and is based on his extensive experience of building cultures of innovation in companies around the world.

When distributing the survey to people in your company, make sure you distribute it both vertically and horizontally in the organization, as a culture of innovation is not just reserved for the people that have "innovation" in their title or people that are in a certain hierarchical position.

Download the worksheet here

Scale:
10p - 20p - your company doesn't yet have a developed culture of innovation.
21p - 32p - your company has pockets of innovation culture but it's not yet embedded.
33p - 40p - your company has a strong innovation culture.

As with most assessments, it's worth taking a look at how individual questions were answered, not only at the end result. Furthermore, if you want a higher resolution picture of your company's innovation culture you might consider running some interviews alongside the assessment.

	Strongly Disagree (1p)	Somewhat Disagree (2p)	Somewhat Agree (3p)	Strongly Agree (4p)
Our organization and employees have constantly displayed the willingness to change and adapt.				
All employees are given the opportunity to take their own new ideas forward.				
Contributing to innovation is seen as a part of every-one's job.				
In our company, failure is seen as part of innovation and people failing are not sanctioned.				
Diversity of opinion and perspective is sought from across the organization and beyond.				
It's easy to collaborate with others in our company.				
Everyone in our company understands the role inno-vation plays in growth and survivability of the company.				
Taking calculated risk is en-couraged in our company.				
Challenging/questioning the status quo is a behav-ior that's promoted in our company.				
New ideas regarding any part of our business are openly received and con-sidered.				

Innovation culture is part of the overall culture of the company.

Culture in itself can't be measured: you can measure the attributes of the culture through the impact they have on the results.

You can also measure your efforts in improving the culture of your company.

Conversations on Innovation

Paul Cobban

Chief Data & Transformation Officer at DBS Bank

Since 2009, Paul has been leading the transformation of DBS Bank. In this period, the Singapore headquartered bank has been recognized as a leading financial institution by many entities including Euromoney, The Banker, and Global Finance. The bank's transformation journey was acknowledged by Harvard Business Review as one of the top 10 transformations of the decade alongside Netflix, Amazon, and Microsoft.

Innovation Accounting: DBS Bank is known around the world for its transformation. A big part of the transformation had to do with changing the culture. Tell us more about how you have approached cultural change and how you were measuring the cultural change.

Paul Cobban: In general, you can't talk about transformation without talking about culture. Transformation means changing behaviors and a culture is a set of behaviors.

Of course, measuring progress of any transformation is somewhat challenging, and even more so when you talk about measuring the shift in culture. To measure our progress towards a culture of innovation, we had to be very specific about how we define innovation. At DBS, we settled on something very simple that everyone could understand and get behind. Innovation for us is defined as something different that creates value.

Therefore, a culture of innovation is a set of behaviors that encourage the development of something different that creates value. At DBS we agreed that we were going to look at five behaviors that are fundamental for innovation: being agile, being a learning organization, being customer obsessed, being data driven, and experimenting and taking risks.

And then we started measuring these behaviors. For some, it was easier to do than for others. For agile, for example, we looked if teams were following agile techniques and rituals. With experimenting, on the other hand, we took a different approach. We set ourselves a target to see if we were able to achieve it. Concretely, we set ourselves to run 1,000 experiments per year.

But generally speaking, for all five behaviors, we were identifying what was preventing us from making that behavior happen. It could have been a process, a certain cultural trait of the workforce or even a certain artifact that people were using.

Then we came up with experiments to see if we could overcome that blocker and obtain the desired behavior. If one of the experiments resulted in a positive outcome, that particular thing we did became our new way of operating and we had to scale that across the entire company.

IA: From experience, we know that organizational culture is very much intertwined with the "culture of the place." For example, Scandinavian companies are very consensus driven – which is connected to the culture of the countries. How did you manage this in the Southeast Asian context?

PC: I think that a strong corporate culture in many ways trumps the social culture. Not completely, but to say it another way, if you've got a weak corporate culture, then you're more or less at the mercy of all the social culture.

We designed our transformation around rituals and giving people ownership of them. We have for example a ritual called "Wreckoon." This ritual gives people permission to voice or have a contrary view. By establishing and labelling the ritual, you're giving people a safe space and the psychological safety to operate. The fun involving this ritual and the high energy it brings to creative brainstorming and broader discussion is contextualized for the Asian culture that is hierarchical and somewhat reserved. It offers the safety to share honest opinions.

So, when scaling our transformation in our more than 29,000 people company, we made sure that everything we were implementing was contextualized to work with the social culture of the employees. While at the same time, never losing sight of the behaviors we wanted to see being adopted.

IA: As a Chief Data & Transformation Officer, you've had many things to overcome to bring about change. What are some lessons you can share with our readership?

PC: If you want to change yourself or others, you will have to learn to feel comfortable being uncomfortable. And you have to be comfortable with the criticism you'll receive.

When we introduced one of our meeting rituals, MOJO, I was accused of introducing kindergarten management. MOJO stands for the two key roles that need to present in every meeting. "MO" is the Meeting Owner tasked with stating the purpose of the meeting, summarizing the meeting at the end of it and thirdly, probably most importantly in our social culture context, giving equal share of voice to everyone participating. "JO" on the other hand is the Joyful Observer, spending 30 seconds at the end of the meeting summarizing how well "MO" did those three things he was supposed to do. A little side note – now we have a digital "JO" in the form of an app. At the end of the meeting, there's a very simple app people bring up on their phones and they rate the meeting owner on five dimensions. At the end of each month, each person who's been an "MO" at least once during the month will get a report and we'll tell them how well they did on those five dimensions. It tells them how they're trending over time and also how they compare to the rest of the company.

Well, some people felt almost offended that I was spoon feeding them on how to run a meeting. But somehow, little by little, everybody adopted it. And in time, even the people who described it as kindergarten management and may not have gone through the formal ritual themselves, saw the benefits.

In essence, you need to tell yourself, "If I'm not feeling uncomfortable, maybe I'm not doing something different and breaking the old habits."

Another thing I learnt on this transformation journey about people not wanting change, is a myth. People really want change. That's why they go on holiday or they change jobs. What's preventing people from changing, however, is fear. So, it's a leader's job to remove the fear from the transformation or change process. That's the only way people will get behind a new behavior or a new way of working.

It's not about us versus them,
it's about winning together.

CHAPTER 10

Innovation Accounting for CFOs and Shareholders

Who runs your company? Is it the board? Or is it "The Street?" It has long been believed that pressure from large shareholders leads companies to take myopic actions that are costly in the long term, and that insulating boards from such pressure serves the long-term interests of companies as well as their shareholders. This board insulation claim has been regularly invoked in a wide range of contexts to support existing or tighter limits on large shareholder rights and involvement, as well as to justify some companies' lack of innovation prowess.

However, Harvard Law professor Lucian Bedhuck's research proves otherwise;[10] investors are long term focused and they care about the future of the companies they invest in.

This means that companies have to be able to paint a picture of the future-proofing actions they are taking. True innovations often go unrecognized by the market in their early stages. Whether it is in the field of biotechnology, cloud computing or artificial intelligence, to take a few of today's

To measure the value created in the innovation process, New York University's professor Baruch Lev suggests tracking managers' strategies for transforming investments into strategic resources. That may be by preserving and protecting these resources from infringement and decay and deploying them individually by licensing patents (or more commonly in combination) in production and marketing. These actions are all aimed at creating value that enables companies to compete and maintain the supply of investment funds.

Every company should, however, find its own way of reporting its future-proofing activities. This will depend both on its internal and external environment.

For example, we have worked with a company that, by the way it is organized around members and their contribution, is structured as an investment company. For them it was fairly easy to report investments in internal ventures in a format which could be easily understood by the shareholders and the finance team.

287

Another example comes from a conference call Esther had with a CFO of an Asian white goods company. We learned that when accounting for the Cost of Innovation, this particular company took inspiration from the way oil and gas companies record the costs related to the search for minerals. Companies such as these record exploration costs which represent the investments made to discover mineral resources. And, separately, they record evaluation costs, which arise from validating the technical feasibility and commercial viability of the resources found. Labeling exploration and evaluation expenses separately enables the company and its investors to clearly identify which cost is related to the "search" and which relates to "execution." This expenditure rule is actually recognized under the European accounting principles in IFRS6.

innovation platforms, innovations often have long and flat adoption curves, as network effects and lack of understanding delay their embrace. A successful company like Amazon took a decade to become profitable, as e-commerce was only just beginning to take off. An ongoing dialogue with investors will help to show the potential of innovation efforts.[133]

The real challenge is to change the way we recognize not only R&D and innovation, but also the investments in strategic, intangible assets which companies are making in order to deliver ongoing value gained from the innovation process.

STOP   UP!

OP-EX   CAP-EX   EX-EX

Using this way of approaching costs related to innovation makes sense. Labeling the cost of searching for a new business model in such a way shows investors that this cost is connected to a high risk search, whereas operational cost or improvement costs are generally connected to lower risk activities.

The methods used by companies to paint the picture of the efficiency and efficacy of their innovation ecosystem will also partly depend on where the company is incorporated. For example, there is a significant difference in the accounting standards for R&D activities in Europe versus the US. Under the reporting requirements in the US (GAAP), R&D gets expensed and not capitalized. Under the European IFRS rules, research spending is treated as an expense each year, just as with GAAP. However,

development costs can be capitalized if the company can prove that the asset in development will become commercially viable. The benefit of the IFRS approach is that at least some R&D costs can be capitalized; turned into an asset on the company's balance sheet rather than of being incurred as an expense on the statement of Profit and Loss.[134]

The end result, as Professor Baruch Lev explained in an interview, is that, at least in the US, *"a company pursuing an innovation strategy based on acquisitions will appear more profitable and asset-rich than a similar enterprise developing its innovations internally."*

Showing that innovation works

The job of the Innovation Accounting system, therefore, is to show the investments the company is making in innovation and the outcomes arising from previous investments; thereby making visible the investment strategy and the way the company's innovation ecosystem works. Telling a "good future-proofing story" and demonstrating past successes helps companies to secure further investments and maintain an open dialogue with existing investors.

But the innovation accounting system's raw information might be unnecessary detail both for shareholders and even for some internal stakeholders like the controllers working the finance department. Companies therefore must have a way to display the information from the innovation accounting system in a shareholder-friendly way. Regardless of where your company is incorporated or what inputs you decide to take from other industries, it's important to have a template report that simplifies the information from the innovation accounting system and makes it digestible for less innovation focused people like the CFO, the finance team, or the shareholders.

Your report needs to speak to investors who are looking to understand the innovation-led growth potential of the company. It needs to bring clarity to finance people within the company, helping them to understand the impact of past investments in innovation. And it needs to speak to executives who are seeking clarity around the Efficiency of Innovation Investment. In other words, the report should simultaneously paint an accurate picture of the past and a somewhat "impressionist" picture of the future.

We therefore propose that companies consider deploying a template report made up of three columns.

The first column of the template report looks at the benefits the company got in this financial year from investments made in

the past 3 years*. Here, investors are going to find data about the revenue generated from past investments, profitability rates of past investments, impact of the collaboration and venturing deals the company had done, as well as the Efficiency of the Innovation Investment.

The second column of the template report looks at adding much needed clarity on this year's investments in innovation; making a clear distinction between internal and external innovation investment using both quantitative financial and quantitative non-financial data.

The last column of the template report paints a picture of the investments the company is making in upskilling the workforce and building a culture of innovation, again using both quantitative financial and quantitative non-financial data.

*If you wish you can adapt the template for your company and make the analysis over a 5 year period but we don't recommend you go beyond five years.

289

Outcome from investments made in the past 3 years

FINANCIAL
METRIC

Revenue from
products launched

New Product Vitality
Index for products launched

Efficiency of Innovation Investment from products launched

Innovation Profitability
Ratio for products launched

Revenue from acquisitions

Dividends from investments

Revenue from joint ventures

Revenue from pilots

Investments in internal innovation

	QUANTITATIVE FINANCIAL		QUANTITATIVE NON-FINANCIAL
Cost of Innovation		Number of ideas in pipeline	
R&D		Number of patents submitted for approval	

Investments in external innovation

	QUANTITATIVE FINANCIAL		QUANTITATIVE NON-FINANCIAL
Acquisitions		Number of acquisitions	
Investments		Number of investments	
Joint ventures		Number of joint ventures	
Pilots		Number of Pilots	

Investments in capability

QUANTITATIVE
FINANCIAL

Investments in
internal & external
trainings

QUANTITATIVE
NON-FINANCIAL

Number of
employees trained

Investments in culture

QUANTITATIVE
FINANCIAL

Investments in
innovation culture
development
programs

QUANTITATIVE
NON-FINANCIAL

Number of
employees trained

Surface intangible assets

3

Importantly, only a few of the items in this report are currently required to be reported in accounting based corporate financial statements. It's mostly new information and, as we have previously outlined, information which is critical for the assessment of an enterprise's ultimate objective: achieving growth through innovation.

Note also that, similar to accounting-based financial reports, the proposed template is made up of factual information; there are no managerial estimates, projections, guesses or assumptions. Furthermore, similar to the accounting-based annual financial reports, this template should be filled in at least once per year as part of reporting to the shareholders. As our good friend and Chartered Accountant, Hannah Keartland said: "this is not a one-time snapshot; this template should help companies build a picture over time giving them a deeper insight into the performance of the innovation ecosystem."

Let's be clear, we are not proposing yet another list of indicators. The report takes all the information provided by the indicators we spoke about earlier in the book and compresses them while at the same time putting them in a structure that makes it easy to follow.

The abstraction map is a useful tool to drive improvements in your internal innovation ecosystem. This template report builds on it, painting a picture of the performance of the entire ecosystem using aggregate data from the abstraction map, as well as other available sources in your company.

Again we want to highlight the fact-based nature of this template report. But, in case your company's finance team or investors demand it, you can also consider adding other bits of information from the innovation accounting system. Information such as the estimated aggregate risk adjusted value-to-cost-ratio of the innovation funnel and/or the portfolio distribution might make for a more colorful picture. Believe

it or not, finance people prefer pictures to tables of numbers. Furthermore, you would be pleasantly surprised to find out that some senior finance folks will actually be as concerned about portfolio balance and funnel performance as they are about the bottom line.

292

Conclusions

Whether you, as an innovator, like it or not, the interaction with the finance department is unavoidable. At the end of the day, your finance department is the one that's in charge of the portfolio of investments that the organization makes. It balances the risk vs. return of that portfolio, allocates the budget and interacts with external factors like the tax authorities or investors.

However, as you've seen in the previous chapters, and we are sure you've also experienced first-hand, financial accounting rules are not really fitted for measuring innovation. And being realistic, our Innovation Accounting proposals may only be accepted by the entire organization when the information is simplified and translated into a more accessible financial accounting language. We also have to be realistic in saying that we don't expect financial rules such as the American GAAP or European IFRS to change in our lifetimes in order to better accommodate innovation.

Therefore, compressing and simplifying the information provided by the innovation accounting system becomes an imperative if innovation is to be accepted as a viable growth option by your company and if innovation is not to be siloed in a far off lab.

Time for a warning. Too many times we have seen innovation minded people coming into meetings with their finance colleagues with an "us versus them" mindset. Yes you are right, maybe the finance people are not as familiar as you are with experimenting, yes they might be interested in Excel more than in the portfolio distribution. But in the absence of empathy, collaboration can't happen. So try seeing things from their perspective too; they are not ill intentioned and both of you are playing for the same team. Take your finance colleagues on a learning journey and build bridges not walls; you might be in for a surprise and you might just find your biggest innovation advocates sitting behind the spreadsheets.

Connecting Innovation Accounting to financial accounting will give everyone a trusted scoreboard that paints a complete picture, making it easier to know when your team is ahead. Most importantly, it will help to deliver a more open dialogue with investors. Who runs your company? Maybe it is time for an open partnership based on information and trust with everyone looking to innovate for change.

293

Conversations on Innovation

Prof. Baruch I. Lev

Professor of Accounting & Finance, New York University Stern School of Business

Professor Lev has been with NYU for more than twenty years. He was formerly with the University of Chicago, University of California, Berkeley (jointly at the business and law schools), and Tel Aviv University, where he had been the Dean of the business school. Lev has extensive experience in public accounting, finance and consulting, and served on various boards. Lev authored seven books, including the best seller "*End of Accounting,*" and has had more than 100 research papers published in leading academic journals.

Innovation Accounting: In innovation, failure is part of the game. But in an ideal case, teams fail smart, they learn and they get better for the future; building new products on top of the learnings from past failures. Is there a way to account for this and, if not, what would you say to financial controllers in large companies?

Prof. Baruch Lev: Let me answer by giving you an example. In pharmaceutical and biotech companies it's well known that even when a drug fails a test or a clinical trial and is being discontinued, the investment in this drug is usually not a total loss. Because the scientists learned a lot. They learned what not to do, they learned how to improve in the future. Overall it is not good news that the drug failed, but it's not a total loss. So this talk of learning from failure is really very important. Maybe the scientist that worked on the failed drug can write a research paper or a case study about what they tried. And this in turn, can strengthen the brand image of the company or it can be used for other marketing related activities.

There is the tendency to emphasize the successes, which of course is understandable, but we can't just completely ignore the failures. Unfortunately, today's accounting reporting methods aren't suited to record learnings but this should not prevent people from making experiments and it should not prevent finance people from encouraging experimenting...as long as it is done in a thoughtful manner.

IA: What about measuring the investments in upskilling people and, to a larger extent, the investments in developing culture?

PBL: What I found from my experience is that you have to look at productivity. Salaries in contrast are really justifiable expenses. Salaries are essentially payments for past services. The way leaders need to look at the costs of upskilling people that work in R&D and innovation, is not payment for past services, but investments aimed at generating future benefits. So if you can show, for example, that you moved the needle on the productivity of those people, you can have a conversation with the CFO on why that investment was needed.

I did something like this once for a company many years ago. It was a large European pharmaceutical company that had a continuous training program for mid-level executives. Hundreds of people were trained every year. The company was sending these people for three months, or sometimes even more, outside Europe and one and a half months inside Europe, to attend courses at universities and so on. This was a massive investment from the company. And I remember the CEO once coming to me and saying "Listen, Baruch. We feel good about it, but we need to show that this investment is really doing anything."

Since this was such an extensive program for such a large company, we had a beautiful data set. We had a good sample of people who went through this training and people who didn't go to this training. And we looked at measures of productivity, the productivity of the people in the departments that sent people to this program and the departments that haven't. And we came back to the CEO with some interesting differences that proved the investment was worthwhile.

So salaries and bonuses themselves are not investments. But training of employees is affecting the productivity of the workforce and this is an important investment. Therefore in an analysis, you have to show somewhere that these people that were trained are more productive than others. Otherwise, it's really a waste of time, and money.

IA: What would you say to finance people when it comes to measuring innovation and what would you say to the innovation folks? We are asking this because we have often seen in many companies, conversations that tend to have, unfortunately, a tone of "us versus them?"

PBL: Your observation is correct. I had a very similar experience in the context of intellectual property. Years ago I worked with a patent law firm. They needed to sit with the R&D people for several hours, sometimes several days, in order to really work out the mechanics of the inventions and file the correct documentation. But this created a major problem, after half an hour, the innovators would say: "Listen, I don't have any more time. I have to go to the laboratory and work. You figure it out. And that's it."

So one of the things that is difficult in the case of measuring innovation is to convince the people who work on innovation to devote time to being debriefed. They need to be patient, and report and measure the great things they do.

I don't want to generalize but innovators usually don't like reporting, they don't like to be quantified. They just want to get the needed resources and be left alone to spend them. So they need to understand that a condition for continuation of financing is to present the numbers that will justify the continuation of financing. Reporting and measuring is not done for reporting stake. Convincing CFOs or even the board to continue investing in innovation requires more than just a new patent or a new technology.

If you are the Head of Innovation and get a 3 year or even 5 year budget - which by the way, this should be the way to finance innovation, not just from one year to the next - people on the board really want to see, along the way, some kind of measures of success. Benchmarks that you are moving in the right direction. No sane person will tell you; "Take the money for five years. And then, in five years, we'll meet again and we'll talk about it." They would like to see every six months, at least, some kind of progress. Mild progress at least. Something like you got a couple of patents or you launched a product and you have several more in development. So, even if it's a long term horizon, you should be able to show along the way some measures of success.

I always give the example of bringing up kids. Your ultimate goal is that they graduate, let's say, university, maybe even medical school or engineering. So, you are going to give them a very long horizon, 20+ years. You're going to finance them over many years. But this doesn't mean that you ignore the grades that they get every three months or six months. You're going to sit with them and say, "Listen, you have to make more effort here, and more effort there." Even if it's clear that your horizon is a very long one.

So, if you are an innovator, even if you manage to get a long-term commitment from the board as you should get, you have to be able to show some quantifiable results along the way. Again, you need to be patient and work with the financial controllers along the way and report on the progress you are making every period.

At the same time finance people need to learn to speak the language of the innovators and try to understand them. They need to create a reporting process that is not too bureaucratic, blocking the innovators from doing their job. Otherwise you have nice looking reports but no innovation. The way reporting is done needs to be just right and both need to gain mutual trust and understanding.

Do! (or do not) There is no try.

CHAPTER 11
Starting
Tomorrow

Download the
Innovation accounting
playbook here.

We've come a long way since our first faltering steps started to examine why tradi-tional accounting may not on its own give a true and fair picture of an innovative orga-nization. Along the way we've looked at many aspects of measuring innovation. We've built an understanding of how you can delve beneath the surface to measure individ-ual teams or streams. We've helped you to understand how you can create a realistic business model portfolio map. We've also examined how you can measure culture. And we've seen how Innovation Accounting complements the existing accounting system in your company.

We've put together a playbook to help you put everything together. Here you will find the checklists, tasks, templates and tools you need in order to start implementing an innovation accounting system in your company.

In working through this book you've built your understanding of Innovation Accounting. This then is your roadmap to implementation success.

Start implementing
and developing
your own system

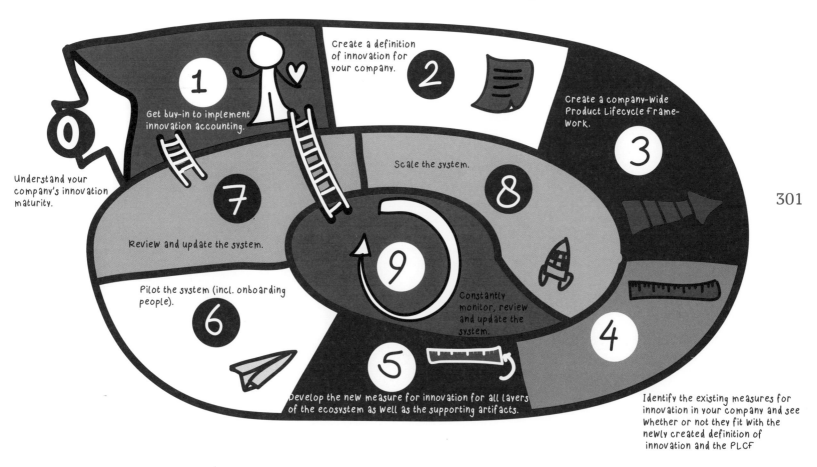

0 — Understand your company's innovation maturity.

1 — Get buy-in to implement innovation accounting.

2 — Create a definition of innovation for your company.

3 — Create a company-wide Product Lifecycle Framework.

4 — Identify the existing measures for innovation in your company and see whether or not they fit with the newly created definition of innovation and the PLCF

5 — Develop the new measure for innovation for all layers of the ecosystem as well as the supporting artifacts.

6 — Pilot the system (incl. onboarding people).

7 — Review and update the system.

8 — Scale the system.

9 — Constantly monitor, review and update the system.

AND FINALLY

You may have been tasked with developing an innovation accounting system or you may have taken the project on as one of your roles and responsibilities within your organization. Either way, this book has shared with you the tools and techniques you will need to succeed. You may not get your system perfectly aligned to your organizational ambitions right at the start. In fact we would be surprised if you did. But just as with innovation, the best way to learn and develop successes is to experiment.

Whenever it seems daunting, stop and take a breath. You don't have to do everything at once. In fact you shouldn't. Each step leads to the next and at every stage you will have a team around you to share the task. Always remember that Innovation Accounting is there to serve your organization, not the other way around. Whenever you find yourself questioning its worth, filling in endless forms or following endless processes then something has gone wrong.

But also remember that doing nothing is not an option, just as not innovating is not an option in today's fast-paced world. Having the right tools for the job doesn't just look towards plant and machinery. It also encompasses skilled people, and targeted systems and processes.

So take that first step on your Innovation Accounting journey. Learn, share, and experiment. The more you discover, the more you will appreciate just how powerful a tool your new innovation accounting system can be, not solely for your organization but also for its stakeholders, its customers and the wider society.

Dan Toma   Esther Gons

References

1. https://mashable.com/2011/10/17/gorilla-glass/?europe=true

2. https://www.pcmag.com/news/259303/why-is-gorilla-glass-so-strong#fbid=L9N-72Ja_0YJ

3. https://www.fastcompany.com/1665186/there-are-three-types-of-innovation-heres-how-to-manage-them

4. https://hbr.org/2017/06/the-4-types-of-innovation-and-the-problems-they-solve

5. www.digitaltonto.com/2016/how-smart-businesses-are-turning-academic-research-into-profits/

6. Larry Kelly, Ryan Pickel, Brian Quinn, Helen Walters, Ten Type of Innovation, 208

7. https://sloanreview.mit.edu/article/the-critical-difference-between-complex-and-complicated/

8. https://medium.com/sense-and-respond-press/digital-transformation-is-not-innovation-4a1d03feb4b2

9. https://thefutureshapers.com/digital-transformation-a-metrics-perspective/

10. The Myth that Insulating Boards Serves Long-Term Value, Columbia Law Review, Vol. 113, No. 6, pp. 1637-1694, October 2013

11. https://hbr.org/2017/10/why-ges-jeff-immelt-lost-his-job-disruption-and-activist-investors

12. https://www.innosight.com/insight/creative-destruction/

13. Baruch Lev, Feng Gu, The End of Accounting, 46-48

14. https://www.nytimes.com/2019/05/09/technology/uber-ipo-stock-price.html

15. https://www.sec.gov/Archives/edgar/data/1418091/000119312513390321/d564001ds1.htm

16. https://hbr.org/2018/06/why-we-need-to-update-financial-reporting-for-the-digital-era

17. https://hbr.org/2010/07/four-lessons-on-culture-and-cu

18. https://www.newyorker.com/tech/annals-of-technology/in-silicon-valley-now-its-almost-always-winner-takes-all

19. https://hbr.org/2018/02/why-financial-statements-dont-work-for-digital-companies

20. Jean E. Cunningham, The Value add Accountant, 27

21. Baruch Lev, Feng Gu, The End of Accounting, 120

22. Baruch Lev, Feng Gu, The End of Accounting, 125

23. https://ir.manutd.com/~/media/Files/M/Manutd-IR/Annual%20Reports/manchester-united-plc-20f-20141027.pdf

24. https://www.sportskeeda.com/football/are-top-level-football-players-employees-or-economic-assets-for-their-clubs

25. https://www.accountingtools.com/articles/straight-line-amortization.html

26. Jay Barney, Firm Resources and Sustained Competitive Advantage, 99-120

27. https://www.gartner.com/en/marketing/research/innovation-survey-2019

28. https://www.ft.com/content/cdfe-1b2c-5abf-11e4-b449-00144feab7de#axzz3l5ez9PAL

29. http://www.strategy-business.com/article/00295

30. http://www.strategy-business.com/article/00140

31. https://web.stanford.edu/dept/SUL/sites/mac/parc.html

32. https://www.newyorker.com/magazine/2011/05/16/creation-myth

33. http://www.thoughtworks.com/insights/blog/enterprise-needs-lean-product-development

34. https://hbr.org/2012/05/four-innovation-misconceptions

35. David Parmenter - Key Performance Indicators pg.5

36. David Parmenter, Key Performance Indicators (Third Edition), 43

37. David Parmenter, Key Performance Indicators (Third Edition), 42

38. David Parmenter, Key Performance Indicators (Third Edition), 45

39. https://www.ideou.com/blogs/inspiration/innovation-accounting-what-it-is-and-how-to-get-started

40. https://www.techopedia.com/definition/3736/abstraction

41. Baruch Lev, Feng Gu, The End of Accounting, 129

42. https://hbr.org/2016/07/kodaks-downfall-wasnt-about-technology

43. https://hbr.org/2016/03/how-much-is-trump-really-disrupting-politics-as-usual

44. https://warroom.armywarcollege.edu/articles/attack-drones-unmanned-aircraft-disruption-national-security-strategy/

45. https://www.newyorker.com/magazine/2014/06/23/the-disruption-machine

46. David Parmenter, Key Performance Indicators (Third Edition), Pg.112

47. https://www.movestheneedle.com/toolkit/

48. https://www.forbes.com/sites/under30network/2016/02/24/5-things-to-remember-before-founding-your-startup-this-year/#42029abf7fe3

49. http://theleanstartup.com/principles

50. https://www.smashingmagazine.com/2011/04/multivariate-testing-101-a-scientific-method-of-optimizing-design/

51. https://kromatic.com/blog/iteration-time-to-learn-not-time-to-build/

52. https://agilemanifesto.org/principles.html

53. https://www.pmi.org/learning/library/agile-problems-challenges-failures-5869

54. http://www.davidfrico.com/rico08a.pdf

55. https://arkenea.com/blog/agile-metrics/

56. https://www.plutora.com/blog/agile-metrics

57. https://www.sealights.io/software-development-metrics/10-powerful-agile-metrics-and-1-missing-metric/

58. https://www.intellectsoft.net/blog/agile-metrics/

59. https://blog.innovation-options.com/the-wom-prom-ratio-measuring-product-market-fit-48b0aebf324c

60. https://edessey.com/incubation-maturity-model/

61. Behrooz Omidvar-Tehrani; Sihem Amer-Yahia; Laks VS Lakshmanan. Cohort representation and exploration. Turin, Italy: IEEE Conference on Data Science and Advanced Analytics (DSAA) 2018.

62. Alistair Croll; Benjamin Yoskovitz. Lean Analytics: Use Data to Build a Better Start-up Faster. Sebastopol, CA: O'Reilly 2013

63. https://www.sethlevine.com/archives/2014/08/venture-outcomes-are-even-more-skewed-than-you-think.html

64. Johnson M.., & Suskewicz J. (2020). Leading From the Future

65. https://onlinelibrary.wiley.com/doi/full/10.1111/fima.12205

66. https://www.fastcompany.com/40515712/want-a-more-innovative-company-simple-hire-a-more-diverse-workforce

67. https://www.telefonica.com/documents/143545261/145069705/Intrapreneurship-10-lessons-from-the-trenches.pdf

68. https://www.inc.com/jessica-stillman/6-cognitive-biases-that-are-messing-up-your-decision-making.html

69. https://www.inc.com/jessica-stillman/why-mark-zuckerberg-is-a-terrible-role-model.html

70. https://neuroleadership.com/your-brain-at-work/seeds-model-biases-affect-decision-making/

71. https://www.pesec.no/improve-your-thinking-to-avert-bad-decisions/

72. https://www.pmi.org/learning/library/practical-risk-management-approach-8248

73. https://www.pmi.org/learning/library/risk-analysis-project-management-7070

74. For detailed explanations see Program evaluation research task, summary report phase 1 (AD-735) report by the Special Projects Office, Bureau of Naval Weapons, United States Department of the Navy.

75. https://kromatic.com/blog/the-rudder-fallacy-adopting-lean-startup/

76. https://www.weforum.org/agenda/2019/12/davos-manifesto-2020-the-universal-purpose-of-a-company-in-the-fourth-industrial-revolution/

77. https://www.mckinsey.com/business-functions/strategy-and-corporate-finance/our-insights/why-youve-got-to-put-your-portfolio-on-the-move?cid=other-eml-alt-mcq-mck&hlkid=8f56643d548b-4f0a970ee85766e3afe5&hctky=1495319&hdpid=21d88d24-5501-45e7-9eb5-22b17cbaba1d

78. https://www.mckinsey.com/business-functions/strategy-and-corporate-finance/our-insights/how-to-put-your-money-where-your-strategy-is

79. Benchmarking Innovation Impact 2020

80. Reset Your Innovation Priorities to Reflect the New Reality (2020) D.S. Duncan, A.Trotter, and B.Kümmerli

81. https://www.business-standard.com/article/opinion/new-product-vitality-index-117081801491_1.html

82. https://rebecca-schatz-on-innovation.blogspot.com/2012/10/3m-innovation-new-product-vitality-index.html

83. https://evannex.com/blogs/news/tesla-gains-massive-market-share-from-competitors

84. https://www.investopedia.com/ask/answers/020915/what-difference-between-capex-and-opex.asp

85. https://info.ivalua.com/uk-supplier-led-innovation

86. https://www.canalys.com/newsroom/worldwide-cloud-market-q320

87. https://www.theverge.com/2020/7/22/21334725/microsoft-q4-2020-earnings-azure-surface-xbox-gains-growth-profits-sales

88. https://hackernoon.com/is-azure-profitable-3531a14f6233

89. https://www.cnbc.com/2020/02/03/google-still-isnt-telling-us-about-youtube-and-cloud-profits.html

90. https://hbr.org/2013/05/why-the-lean-start-up-changes-everything

91. E. Ries (2011), The Lean Startup

92. https://kromatic.com/real-start-up-book/fake-door-smoke-test

93. https://techcrunch.com/2011/10/19/dropbox-minimal-viable-product/

94. https://www.wsj.com/articles/toys-r-us-bankruptcy-poses-challenge-for-toy-makers-1505832443

95. https://www.theunileverfoundry.com/highlights/hellmanns-quiqup-partnership-for-fresh-delivery.html

96. Mocker V., Bielli S., Haley C. (2015). Winning together: A guide to successful corporate-startup collaborations. London: Nesta

97. https://www.bsigroup.com/LocalFiles/en-GB/iso-44001/Resources/ISO-44001-Implementation-Guide.pdf

98. https://home.kpmg/us/en/home/media/press-releases/2019/09/new-survey-data-indicates-increased-confidence-and-investment-in-innovation-among-fortune-1000.html

99. http://www.infrastructure-intelligence.com/article/nov-2019/innovation-assured-environment

100. https://www.nasa.gov/directorates/heo/scan/engineering/technology/txt_accordion1.html

101. https://www.investopedia.com/terms/m/montecarlosimulation.asp

102. https://hbr.org/1979/09/risk-analysis-in-capital-investment

103. https://www.investopedia.com/terms/c/central_limit_theorem.asp

104. https://www.nytimes.com/2011/10/23/magazine/dont-blink-the-hazards-of-confidence.html

105. https://onlinelibrary.wiley.com/doi/10.1002/9781118983836.ch5

106. https://www.inc.com/walter-chen/aar-rr-dave-mcclure-s-pirate-metrics-and-the-only-five-numbers-that-matter.html

107. http://www.pwc.com/us/en/press-releases/2015/pwc-top-health-issues-2016-press-release.html

108. http://www.mobihealthnews.com/content/closer-look-30-mergers-and-acquisitions-2016

109. https://hbr.org/2011/03/the-big-idea-the-new-ma-playbook

110. https://www.inc.com/john-mcdermott/report-3-out-of-4-venture-backed-start-ups-fail.html

111. https://www.biorxiv.org/content/10.1101/700807v1.full

112. https://www.emerald.com/insight/content/doi/10.1108/IJIS-10-2018-0102/full/html

113. https://www.mckinsey.com/business-functions/strategy-and-corporate-finance/our-insights/the-innovation-commitment

114. https://innovatorsdna.com/innovation-assessment

115. https://www.trendhunter.com/innovation-assessment

116. https://aa.foursightonline.com/assessments/e4c6caf4b6eedc2281393a71176ac208

117. https://fi.co/dna

118. https://www.businessknowhow.com/manage/higherprod.htm

119. https://www.researchgate.net/publication/263348990_MOOCs_Completion_Rates_and_Possible_Methods_to_Improve_Retention_-_A_Literature_Review

120. https://hbr-org.cdn.ampproject.org/c/s/hbr.org/amp/2019/03/why-a-one-size-fits-all-approach-to-employee-development-doesnt-work

121. https://news.gallup.com/businessjournal/197234/millennials-job-hopping-inevitable.aspx?utm_source=alert&utm_medium=email&utm_content=morelink&utm_campaign=syndication

122. https://www.oecd.org/std/productivity-stats/40526851.pdf

123. https://hbr.org/podcast/2020/05/to-build-strategy-start-with-the-future

124. https://knowledge.wharton.upenn.edu/article/the-input-bias-how-managers-misuse-information-when-making-decisions/

125. https://hbr.org/video/2235472805001/measure-employee-productivity-accurately

126. https://www.strategy-business.com/article/11404

127. Making Intangibles Tangible: an emerging business issue, Journal of Brand Strategy 2020 vol.8, no.4

128. https://www.nationalgeographic.org/encyclopedia/cloud/

129. https://www.bcg.com/capabilities/digital-technology-data/digital-transformation/how-to-drive-digital-culture

130. https://www.staceybarr.com/measure-up/cant-measure-innovation-culture-quality/

131. https://www.southuniversity.edu/news-and-blogs/2017/07/ethical-principles-for-business-38725

132. https://www.linkedin.com/pulse/20141113051901-3078420-business-processes-impacts-in-shaping-organizational-culture/

133. https://www.weforum.org/agenda/2018/09/when-we-can-t-quite-put-our-finger-on-it-intangibles-and-finding-better-metrics-for-financing-technological-disruption/

134. https://corporatefinanceinstitute.com/resources/knowledge/accounting/capitalizing-rd-expenses/

307

Index

310

... and a very special 'thank you' goes to the people that helped us build the content of this book

Alexa Dembek
Allison Griffiths
Baruch I. Lev
Bruno Pešec
Christian Lindener
Clarissa Eva Leon

Claire Howeson
Cris Beswick
David Rasson
Francesco Mazzotta
John Patrin
Hannah Keartland

Paul Cobban
Peter LePiane
Sussana Jurado Apruzzes
Timan Rebel
Thomas Vogth-Eriksen
Tristan Kromer